To Mrs. Bet[...]

Thank you for everything.
I have enjoyed being
in your class for the
last two years.

Love,
Bela

BOOKS BY

NAN FAIRBROTHER

Men and Gardens (1956)

An English Year (1954)

THESE ARE

BORZOI BOOKS,

PUBLISHED IN NEW YORK BY

ALFRED A. KNOPF

MEN

AND

GARDENS

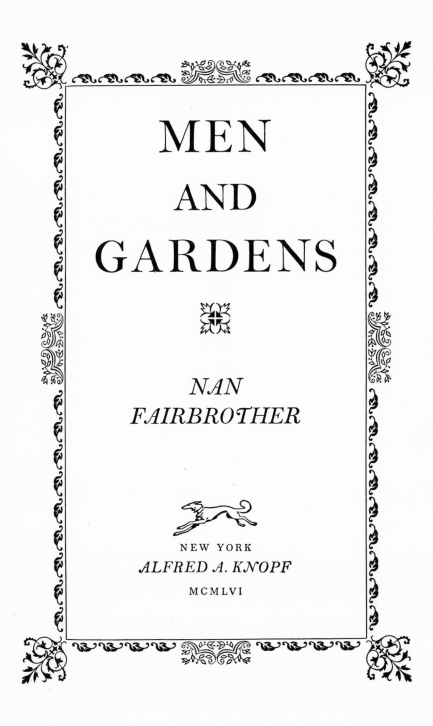

MEN
AND
GARDENS

NAN
FAIRBROTHER

NEW YORK
ALFRED A. KNOPF
MCMLVI

THIS IS A
BORZOI BOOK,
PUBLISHED BY
ALFRED A. KNOPF, INC.

L.C. catalog card number: 56–5786
© Nan Fairbrother, 1956

Published September 24, 1956
Second Printing, November 1956

THOSE THAT ATTEMPT THE PHILOSOPHER'S STONE,

FAILING OF THEIR END,

YET THEY DISCOVER MANY RARE THINGS

OF USE AND DELIGHT.

—John Woolridge

ACKNOWLEDGEMENTS

I SHOULD LIKE TO THANK *E. P. Dutton & Co., Inc., for permission to quote passages from the Everyman Library edition of the following books:* ANGLO-SAXON POETRY, *translated by Professor R. K. Gordon; Bede's* ECCLESIASTICAL HISTORY OF THE ENGLISH NATION, *translated by John Stevens;* GUDRUN, *translated by Margaret Armour;* AUCASSIN AND NICOLETTE *and* THE LAYS OF MARIE DE FRANCE, *translated by Eugene Mason;* THE TRAVELS OF MARCO POLO. *Also Penguin Books Ltd. for permission to quote from* THE CONFESSIONS OF JEAN JACQUES ROUSSEAU *translated by J. M. Cohen, and the Clarendon Press for a passage from* ANGLO SAXON POETRY, *translated by Gavin Bone.*

I SHOULD ALSO LIKE TO THANK the London Library, the British Museum, the Lindley Library, and Lady Barlow for allowing me to photograph books in their collections, and, above all, to thank the London Library for their unfailing help and patience with my almost complete inability ever to find the books I want. I can only say that I have never yet (as they tell me does happen) asked them to trace a book which I already had out myself.

N.F.

CONTENTS

. ix .

ILLUSTRATIONS

ILLUSTRATIONS

Kip's view of a country-house garden laid out in the seventeenth century.

Favourite flowers of the seventeenth century.

The first pineapple grown in England is presented to Charles II by his gardener.

Seventeenth-century London gardens round Saint James's Park.

A view of the seventeenth-century canal in Saint James's Park.

Topiary gardens (the best tree is in the hedge of the gardener's own cottage).

Inside an orangery.

The "new mode of gravel walks and grass plots, ornamental shades, fountains, and other Magnificent Ornaments."

The countryside converted to a landscape park. From Repton's Theory and Practice of Landscape Gardening.

The decline of the formal garden: Kensington Gardens in the early eighteenth century.

The transition from formal to landscape gardens at Chiswick House.

The landscape style perfected.

Follies in Kew Gardens. From Views of the Gardens and Buildings at Kew in Surry, *by William Chambers.*

Eighteenth-century flowers.

X-ray photograph of philadelphus. Radiograph by Herbert Flower, F.R.P.S.

Cross-section of a tulip bud.

The farmer's landscape: "Flatford Mill," by Constable.

Tea in the Garden "The Picnic," by Tissot.

CHAPTER ONE

WHY MEN HAVE GARDENED

THE CHINESE HAVE A WISE SAYING WHICH I
once found in a book of proverbs—"If you would be happy
for a week, take a wife: if you would be happy for a month, kill
your pig: but if you would be happy all your life, plant a
garden."

It is advice which reveals a high level of civilization with a
low standard of living, but when I was a romantic young woman
it seemed to me very shocking that the pleasures of eating should
be considered four times as satisfactory as the pleasures of love.
The Chinese, I felt, were wrong. But that was because I knew
nothing about the eating. I had never known hunger as famine,
but only as appetite between meals, and people who only know
domestic cats are not really reliable judges of tigers.

Yet even in my privileged ignorance of the hungry facts of
life, even in the most flowery days as a *jeune fille en fleur*, I never
doubted the more lasting pleasures of gardening. Certainly for
the time being there were more engrossing interests than planting
roses; for a certain stretch of youth and expectancy one shuts the
garden gate behind and goes off excited down the lane on other
errands. Roses in those flowery years have no roots in earth but
only in poetry; they are charms to wear in our hair.

Yet even the most eager and romantic settings-out were more

like going off on holiday than leaving home for good. I knew I should come happily back again in the end, and I latched the garden gate carefully before I left.

If you would be happy . . .

And who would not? For all men, Pascal says, "seek happiness, all without exception; however different the paths they follow, they all seek the same goal. . . . It is the only motive of all actions of all men whatsoever, even of those who are going to be hanged." But there are less perverse ways to happiness than the gallows, and many Englishmen have felt, like the Chinese, that "Whoever understands and loves a Garden may have Content if he will." Nor is the "joy of Husbandmen a flash and so away, but it is a setled and habituall joy . . . a cleare shining beautifull affection."

If you would be happy all your life . . .

"I have never had any other desire so strong, and so like to covetousness, as that one which I have had always, that I might be master at last of a small house and large garden." Poor Abraham Cowley, who knew so well what the Chinese meant, yet still lived, he tells us, "disappointed . . . of that felicity . . . in a hired house and garden . . . without that pleasantest work of human industry, the improvement of something which we call our own."

But why have men found happiness in gardens? Why, in such different lands and different ages, have so many paths led to this green and quiet enclosure for growing plants? Certainly the pleasures of mankind are limited, there is no great variety from Adam to us or from king to beggar, but even so it is easier to see why human beings should delight in eating or sleeping or making love, in power or gold or glory, than why they should be happy labouring to make one plant grow instead of another.

For the old Christian gardeners the answer was very simple. "If we believe the Scripture," says Sir William Temple, "we must allow that God Almighty esteemed the life of a man in a garden the happiest He could give him, or else He would not have placed Adam in that of Eden." "God Almighty first planted a garden": it is a fact they are all agreed on, but whether gardening can therefore be considered the first of the arts, there is some argument. For surgeons too have claimed their own art as the most ancient because of the "operation of taking the Rib from Adam wherewith the Woman was made." However this may be, our first parents were happy in their "sweet gard'ning labour" until they were driven from Eden, "and no doubt Adam was exceedingly grieved to part with it," says one gardener with warm fellow-feeling. Whether Adam and Eve gardened in the wilderness we do not know, and equally the "Advances Gard'ning made from Adam's Expulsion to the General Deluge, is dubious, there being little left of it." And no one, surely, could make a more cautious statement of a profounder ignorance.

For the seventeenth century, the expulsion from Eden fully explains man's love of gardens, just as the legend of the single creature divided once explained the love between men and women. We long to return to our first Paradise, and though "it is impossible for us, Adam's Posterity" ever to make a garden as fair as Eden, "yet doubtless, by Industry and Pains Taking in that lovely, honest, and delightful Recreation of Planting, we may gain some little glimmering of that lost Splendour, although with much difficulty."

> *All Bliss*
> *Consists in this,*
> *To do as Adam did.*

Traherne's lines are the opening theme of every other gardening book in the seventeenth century. Man is happy in a garden because God made him so, and to live in a garden is the nearest he can reach to Paradise on earth. But Paradise means garden in many other religions than the Christian, and we should like to know why not only humble folk, but "Kings, Princes, and the wisest Men of all Ages" have found their greatest content in a small enclosure of green hedges. "The unspeakable pleasure thoroughly to declare is past my skill: and I count it as if a man shoulde attempt to adde light to the Sunne with a candle, or number the starres." I dare say, but that gets us very little further, though it certainly inspires William Lawson to eloquence: "For it is not to be doubted: but as God hath given man things profitable: so hath He allowed him honest comfort, delight and recreation in all the works of his hands. Nay, all his labours under the Sunne without this are troubles, and vexation of minde: for what is greedy gaine without delight? but moyling, and turmoyling in slavery? But comfortable delight, with content, is the good of everything, and the patterne of heaven. And who can deny, but the principall end of an Orchard is the honest delight of one wearied with the worke of his lawfull calling? The very works in an Orchard and Garden, are better than the ease and rest of other labours."

We are delighted, yet still no more enlightened; but then he goes on to be more explicit. Gardening is the most excellent of all pleasures, he says, because it satisfies all our senses, "For whereas every other pleasure commonly fills some one of our sences, and that onely, with delight, this makes all our sences swimme in pleasure, and that with infinite varietie, ioyned with no lesse commoditie. What can your eye desire to see, your ears to hear, your mouth to take, or your nose to smell" that is not to be had in a garden?

Gardening, then, makes men happy, and it also, so the old writers assure us, makes them virtuous. "The aire and genious of gardens operat upon humane spirits towards virtue and sanctitie" —so Evelyn wrote to Sir Thomas Browne. "They doe bring to a liberall and gentlemanly minde," says Gerard, "the remembrance of honestie comliness and all kinds of virtues." This consciousness of virtue is quite clearly another source of contentment, and because all human happiness is precious, this too is to be treasured. But, like most pleasures, it needs a special kind of training before we can enjoy it: we must be brought up with a strict moral sense when we are young. And because I was brought up with no particular taboos about right and wrong, but only a vague general encouragement to common sense and kindness, Virtue and Vice have always seemed to me abstractions as unreal as the figures in morality plays. "You do whatever you like, but be sensible"—so I was always told by mild and reasonable voices as soon as I was old enough to choose, then left alone to learn by my own mistakes.

I dare say it is an excellent way to bring up young people as reasonable beings, but it has certain disadvantages later on. For one thing, we grow up without any Sense of Sin, and that is a pity. Not because we behave badly without guilt to nag us into virtue (for I have never noticed that the moralists behave either better or worse than the rest of us), but because a reasonable outlook robs us of some of the subtler forms of happiness. To me it seems just as strange that people should take a virtuous pleasure in being virtuous as that they should take a wicked pleasure in being wicked. But I can see that both are additional ways of being happy which I miss. I think if I were starting again, I should like to be threatened while young with some mild form of heaven and hell—not of course with really convincing threats, but just enough to make everyday life significant and exciting. I dare say it is one of the chief reasons why thoughtful adults turn to religion.

However, gardeners who believed that gardening was chosen by God himself to be man's greatest pleasure were comfortably convinced of their own virtue. "It is of great Consequence what sort of Entertainment and Exercise of the mind a man chooseth; for, according to that Choice, he either dignifies or dishonours his Nature. It is no small Felicity to a Man, when his Pleasure tends also to his Perfection: For most Men's Pleasures are such as debase their Natures," but virtuous pursuits raise human beings "to a very near Resemblance of the Angelick Order. . . . Natural Philosophy, Practical Mathematicks, and Gardening Operations" (we can see what the writer's own interests were) "lay a Foundation for a contemplative Genius, and produce a virtuous and useful old Age." How delighted he is with himself, and on he goes in a very ecstasy of virtue: "I little doubt, that if Angels were confined to these lower Regions, they would seek the Retirement and Pleasure of a Garden, as most agreeable to their heavenly Dispositions."

Grown-ups then, like children, enjoy being good; and gardening, so they all seem to have decided though they never really explain why, is a most virtuous occupation. "The End of this is Health, Peace, and Plenty, and the happy Prospect of Felicities more durable than any thing in these sublunary Regions." If we are to be moralists, I cannot see why growing flowers is a more virtuous way of spending time than taking opium, or any other selfish way of seeking happiness. But I can very well see that it is a more lasting pleasure, more socially acceptable, and certainly more healthy. Men seem always to have considered gardening as a moderate and healthy form of exercise, though few have been so explicit as the eighteenth-century clergyman who recommends his fellows to dig until they glow, but not until they sweat—"ad Ruborem though not ad Sudorem." And "if a man want an Appetite to his Victuals," a more homely writer tells us, "the smell of the Earth new turned up, by digging with a Spade will procure it, and if he be inclined to a Consumption it will recover him. Gentlewomen, if the ground be not too wet, may doe themselves much good by kneeling upon a Cushion and weeding. And thus both sexes might divert themselves from idlenesse, and evill Company, which often times prove the ruine of many ingenious people." Health and virtue, it seems, most happily united. And if such people consider garden labour beneath them (so he goes on, and we wonder what scorn he was smarting under), then they are wrong, "For we see that those fashions which sometimes seem ridiculous, if once taken up by the Gentry cease to be so."

Gardening will bring us long life, another gardener assures us, for "the spirits are still kept in a cheerfull temper and condition, and so work powerfully on the grosser parts of the body, conducing to Long-life." But without looking so far ahead, we might garden now for our digestion as many writers recommend, for the fruit and vegetables we grow ourselves will bring us health both in the eating ("a Table loaded with Flesh and Pudding cannot certainly be so wholesome") and in the growing, gardens "being places of divertisement after a sedentary repast, pleasant refreshments after a gross dyet, and such innocent exercises the best digestive to weak stomachs."

As for the Peace and Plenty which Switzer promises us from our gardens, they are, he says, "Select Places of Recess, where the Mind may privately exult and breathe out those Seraphick Thoughts and Strains, by which Man is known and distinguish'd as an Intelligent Being, and elevated above the common Level of Irrational Creatures." But the unfortunate prose style of the lesser eighteenth-century writers is not likely to convince us of anything, and from the many authors who tell us to retire to our gardens to recover from the *ennuis* of public life, I prefer William Lawson's heartfelt complaint: "Whither do the gods of the earth (great men) withdraw themselves from the troublesome affairs of their estate, being tired with the hearing and judging of litigious Controversies, choaken (as it were) with the close air of their sumptuous Buildings, their stomachs cloyed with variety of Banquets, their ears filled and over-burthened with tedious discoursings?" It is purely a rhetorical question, for we know the answer well enough by now: we are to slip away to our garden and close the gate fast behind us, for "This course of life about Orchards and Gardens is full of sweet rest, honest businesse, and modest pleasure. . . . It is far from covetousnesse, and even tied and married to all Offices of love and friendship. This is a quiet and pleasant life, worthy to be preferred before all honours and dignities."

Oddly enough, the garden books seldom seek to persuade us with the argument of Plenty. Our own vegetables are best, they say, fruit from our own trees will serve us all the winter, we may mingle Profit with Pleasure, but their chief interest in finances is a growing concern that our gardens shall not cost us too much in labour, an anxiety which increases with the steady increase in wages.

Yet gardeners have found some profit in their gardens besides much expense. As well as fruit and vegetables they have grown herbs for medicine, kept bees for honey, bred fish in their ponds for food on fast days or when meat was scarce, and women have made hair-dye from marigolds ("some use to make their heyre yelow with the floure of this herbe, not beinge content wyth the natural colour God hath given them"). Men—more practical perhaps, though it is difficult to know—have grown trees for timber, and I think it is Evelyn who tells us of the father who, as each of his daughters was born, planted for her a wood of trees which were felled and sold for her dowry when she came of age to marry.

But some of the possibilities of profit are much less convincing. Gardens are economical for training young farmers, so one writer urges, for "Experiments may be cheaply tried in a Garden before they are ventur'd at in the Field." Or they keep would-be emigrants from leaving England by providing much work on a small acreage—"employments here at home to keep them from stragling abroad." Nursery gardens are even more valuable, for they produce abundant food, which enables England "not only to ballance but undersell our Forreign Neighbours, to our great advantage and their detriment (which is almost equal to it)." We are no longer so frank about our foreign trade, though no doubt we are just as ruthless.

A tidy garden does not seem a very likely bait to tempt potential husbands, but a Tudor writer assures us that "Herein were the olde husbandes very careful, and used alwayes to judge that where they founde the Garden out of order, the wyfe of the house (for unto her belonged the charge thereof) was no good huswyfe." The value of gardens for "employing poor people" is constantly remembered: garden-making, says Sir William Temple, "will employ many hands, and circulate much money among the poorer sort and artisans." Even the very young might benefit, for collecting dung from fields and sheep-walks is a useful employment for "poor Parish children, of which there are too many." It seems a rather doubtful benefit of gardening, but Fairchild's way to improve the Mind and fill the Purse seems even more unlikely, and it would be a pity if gardeners had no more reliable incentive. "I have heard a learned Man say" (Fairchild himself feels the claim needs more convincing support than his own) "that where there was the greatest Opportunity of recreating the Spirits," (as in a garden) "the Mind was improved by that Opportunity: and that a Mind so improv'd found always the nearest Way to do Business, and fill the Purse."

Health, Wealth, and Happiness—they were the three gifts of the good fairy in the story, and they are three felicities which men have sought in gardens from the beginning. But gardeners have had other interests than health and wealth, although it may well be true, as Pascal insists so trenchantly, that no man has any other incentive than his own pleasure. Gardening, says one writer, is a "Kind of Creation," and it is a form of art which everyone, rightly or wrongly, considers to be within his talents. As with furnishing our houses, we all feel we can perfectly well lay out a garden, even though we should never presume to paint a picture or write a poem. The *Spectator* grandiloquently encourages us: "There is indeed something truly magnificent in this kind of Amusement: It gives a noble Air to several Parts of Nature: it fills the Earth with a Variety of beautiful Scenes, and has something in it like Creation." Yet fine gardens, so Bacon long ago warned us, are a rarer work of creation than fine buildings, and the gardens which we can consider as true works of art are rare indeed. But gardeners, although they may be humble by tradition, are quite confident enough to be undisturbed by the canons of fine art, which do not interest them. Gardening is a kind of creation which all will try, and if the garden created is seldom worth looking at as a deliberate design, that does not trouble our delight in the plants which are its living material. For man has a natural sympathy for the background of green life which surrounds him; all peoples have taken pleasure in trees and flowers, and the story of Eden was invented to explain a love of gardens as old as Adam.

The shapes we make for ourselves are geometrical, and the background of civilized life is more or less rectangular. Our rooms and houses are arrangements of cubes, our doors and windows, furniture and rugs, books and boxes—all their angles are right angles and all their sides are straight. Our streets and buildings are constructed of the same straight lines and flat planes, and if we use a curve, it is the exact and mathematical circle.

This geometrical setting of our urban lives has its own beauty. It can be spacious and orderly, an expression of reason in art, and

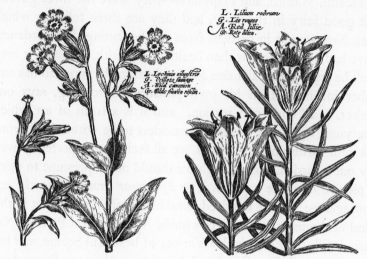

The shapes of vegetable life. Drawing by Crispin de Passe.

a fine building is intellectually satisfying in a new way which man has made for himself. But still we miss the shapes of growing things which we have lived with for a million years. We fill our rooms with flowers and plants, we set our cities with trees and green gardens, we use the shapes of vegetable life to humanize our geometric abstractions. For "God hath imprinted in the Hearts of most wise men such a Love to Plants in part as their Father Adam had in his state of Innocency."

So sailors, abroad on the empty wastes of the sea, must long for the teeming earth: upon those desolate levels must be haunted by the shapes of growing things, the shifting cover of leaves, the curved petals of flowers, the patterns of branches reaching up and out towards the light. Encircled like a hypnotized bird by the relentless horizontal ring of the sea, they must hunger for the horizons of the land, hilly and various and fringed with trees.

But I dare say sailors do not feel like that or they would stay on shore, and it was only because Coleridge was a land-lubber that his Ancient Mariner, weary of water water everywhere, thought longingly of woods in the leafy month of June.

Nor is it only that gardens are rich and various in their stuff of leaves and flowers. They change, too, from season to season. Spring and autumn are quite different compositions; summer and winter are separate ways of living. Even from day to day a garden changes while we watch, and gardening is a pleasure which custom does not stale. "Whatever else seems pleasant at first apprehension, at length becomes dull by too long acquaintance. But the pleasures of a Garden are every day renewed. A Garden is the only complete delight the world affords, ever complying with our various and mutable Minds."

The Chinese made gardens for different seasons and different times of the day—white flowers and lanterns for evening, coloured trees and ruins for autumn. They made, too, gardens which were evocations of favourite landscapes: sometimes the scene was copied in little, sometimes its atmosphere was evoked by suggestion—a dry watercourse of sand and stones to conjure up a distant river, a level stretch of sea-shore far inland. But the Chinese, and the Japanese in the same tradition, have a more delicate sensibility than ours. Their art seems to have a very particular genius for evocation—"Fallen leaves are piled against the doors," sighs a lover lamenting his dead mistress—and their most beautiful landscape paintings are stretches of suggestive space. Their gardens, too, must have depended on the inner understanding, and we should never know how to make, or even how to appreciate, a garden which suggested "the lonely precincts of a secluded mountain shrine with the red leaves of Autumn scattered about," or another which conjured up "the sweet solitude of a landscape in clouded moonlight, with a half-gloom between the trees." It is a long, enchanted way from our rose-beds and herbaceous borders and neatly mown lawns.

For the chief love of English gardeners has always been flowers: we have seldom thought of a garden as anything but a sheltered place for growing them to perfection. Roses and lilies, peonies and pansies—if flowers are gathered together in any place, then for Englishmen it is a garden. "Most men agree in taking Delight in a Garden well stocked with handsome and pleasant Flowers," and most of our gardening books are not books on how to make gardens at all, but on how to grow flowers. For it has seldom occurred to us that they are quite different things, as building a house is different from arranging the ornaments on the mantelpiece. So Englishmen have gardened to make a home for their flower favourites, for "what greater delight is there," asks Gerard in his herbal, "than to behold the earth apparelled with plants as with a robe of imbroidered worke set with orient pearles and garnished with great diversitie of rare and costly jewels?"

Not that we are alone in our flowery pleasures, for although it may be unprofitable to guess what Adam cherished in Eden, we know that the ancient Egyptians grew flowers to decorate their houses and gardens, to adorn their festivals and funerals. They grew roses, too, which they shipped to Rome, "a nation so refined and exquisite in all sorts of delicious luxury," though how they kept the flowers fresh on the long sea journey no one knows. At their banquets, so Sir Thomas Browne tells us, the Egyptians wore garlands of flowers which "had little birds upon them to peck their heads and brows, and so to keep them from sleeping at their festival compotations." Obviously formal dinners have always been just as dull, but whether Browne expects us to believe him we shall never know, for I often suspect that he is not as solemn as he sounds.

Many nations have kept gardens not only for pleasure, but to grow flowers for the adornment of festivals, both lay and religious; for to be an acceptable offering, said the Buddhists, the flowers must neither be bought nor gathered wild, but grown by one's own labour.

Nowadays it is only roses, I think, which we grow in gardens devoted to the particular beauties of a single flower, but the rose has not always been the queen of the garden. For centuries the carnation was valued beyond all other flowers; there have been gardens for tulips, for irises, for the lotus, and perfume gardens where only fragrant plants were grown. The particular treasure of Arab gardens was the date palm, which had as many uses, they said, as days of the year. And because they believed it was Allah's

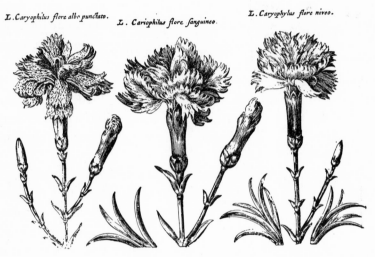

L. Caryophilus flore albo punctato.   *L. Cariophilus flore sanguineo.*   *L. Caryophylus flore niveo.*

For centuries the carnation was the favourite English flower.
Drawing by Crispin de Passe.

especial gift to the faithful, they considered it their religious duty to conquer all lands where it grew, which is a somewhat fairy-tale fashion of deciding one's frontiers on the map of the world.

Another use men have made of gardens everywhere is as se-cluded places for open-air living. In hot countries the formal gardens and courtyards are really unroofed extensions of the house. There were green theatres in the gardens at Versailles, and even in the chancy summers of England we have lived our life out-of-doors with astonishing persistence. "A house, tho' other-wise beautifull, yet if it hath no Garden belonging to it, is more like a Prison than a House." Yet to be useful in England our gardens must have not only "places of shade to skreen you from the scorching Sun Beams," but much more important, "Canopies to preserve you from the Rain, and boxes to seclude you from the too cold Breezes." In a climate quite unsuited to meals out of doors we have invented the picnic, driven, it seems, by some deep-seated urge to eat with no roof above our heads, even though afterwards we may go straight indoors to sit. For few English people, I have noticed, can see a veranda or a balcony or any convenient corner in a garden without immediately thinking how delightful it would be for meals. "In the heat of summer, what place is fitter for the table, than some sweet shady coole Arbour in the Garden?" Generations of English have agreed with Ralph Austen, and even the Victorians, though invalidishly nervous of the morning dews, encourage us "to take breakfast with the cheerful prospect of blooming parterres, redolent with odour and flowing with rainbow colours, pleasantly smiling before the parlour-window."

In the country we have a week-end house where the bedrooms open on to little balconies just large enough to stand at night and admire the garden by moonshine; just wide enough for stretching in the morning, and leaning on the rail to consider whether the mist which lies like milk on the meadows means that by noon the day will be gloriously hot. But these are not uses which ever occur to visitors. "How delightful," they say as they step out, for no one can resist stepping out on to a balcony. "If this were my bedroom, I should have my breakfast out here every morning." It is what they always say, smiling up happily at the ceiling of blue sky. And if it were their sitting-room, then it would be tea, I suppose, that they would eat on this awkward ledge scarcely wide enough to hold a chair. I sometimes wonder if the peculiarly English meals of tea and breakfast were not specially invented because they can be carried about and eaten in unsuitable places, and if that is why other nations have never felt the need of them, since they lack our strange urge for eating without a roof, but prefer their meals in comfort round the dining-room table.

But we cannot always be eating, and what could be pleasanter than to fall asleep in a garden, lulled "by hearing the slow motion of Boughes and Leaves, by soft and gentle aires, sometimes with a kind of singing or whistling noise, which will easily induce a sweet and pleasant sleep in summer time in some close coole Arbor, or shady seat"? Or if we stay awake, we can walk and talk with our friends, praising the Wondrous Works of God as the seventeenth century did, or discussing the lime in our soil as we do now, or considering the beauties of philosophy as Cicero did, and set aside a special portico for so lofty a subject. But what happened, I wonder, when the conversation degenerated to personal gossip, as conversations do? Who decided the exact point where the company must leave the philosophical portico and seek some humbler gossipy corner of the garden?

If gardens are good places for meeting welcome friends, they are just as good for avoiding unwelcome strangers, and gardeners in all ages have felt that to shut the garden gate is to shut out the whole world. "It is not the least part of the pleasures of a Garden, to walk and refresh yourself alone apart from company that sometimes may prove burthensome to you." The first thing we notice in pictures of early gardens is how secret they are, how walled-in and private; the Tudor gardens are scarcely more open, and even in the great pleasure-grounds of the Italian Renaissance there is still a little secret garden shut away from the public walks.

The summer-house, above all, should be hidden in some secluded corner, for "the more remote it is from your house, the more private will you be from the frequent disturbances of your Family or Acquaintance." The Chinese summer-houses—if we are to believe Sir William Chambers, and it is not at all clear that we are—were secluded for quite different reasons. They were "set aside for more secret and voluptuous enjoyments," hidden pavilions where the "fairest and most accomplished concubines would meet . . . to drink their tea, to converse, bathe, and swim . . . work, romp or divert the patron with music, singing, lascivious posture-dancing, and acting plays or pantomimes; at all which they generally are very expert." Or there were "Separate habitations, in which the ladies are privately visited by the patron, as often as he is disposed to see them, and be particular." If the patron were especially "disposed to be particular" and the day chanced to be hot, then he took his ladies to the Halls of the Moon, buildings "composed of a single vaulted room, made in the shape of a hemisphere; the concave of which is artfully painted in imitation of the nocturnal sky, and pierced with an infinite number of little windows, made to represent the moon and stars, being filled with hinged glass, that admits the light in the quantities necessary to spread over the whole interior fabric the pleasing gloom of a fine summer's night. In these Halls of the Moon the Chinese princes retire with their favourite women, whenever the heat and intense light of the summer's day becomes disagreeable to them, and here they feast, and give a loose to every sort of voluptuous pleasure."

The Chinese princes seem never to have known about the pleasure of being virtuous, or perhaps this was their particular form of virtue, for it all depends, of course, on one's point of view. But English gardeners are brought up differently, and their garden pleasures are very much staider.

> *Add to these Retired Leisure*
> *That in trim gardens takes his pleasure.*

Long before Milton, gardening was considered an ideal occupation for those who had retired from active life. All the books recommend it, but none more shrewdly than the country clergyman conscious of his unreliable temper and his doubtful success in the Town: "Happy surely they who find Satisfaction in those innocent Pleasures, instead of disturbing the World of their Neighbours, when they cannot be quiet themselves tho' no body hurts them. The Evening of Life is thus, to be sure, most wisely and agreeably spent. When the Decline of Nature tends to pevishness and a froward Weakness, and we cannot so firmly bear the Frowns of Fortune, the Ingratitude of a Friend, the Malice and Treachery of an Enemy, then to step aside, as it were, out of the World, a little before our Time, and give such a decent Turn to our Thoughts, as may hide the Weaknesses of human Nature, and at the same Time recreate our Minds with innocent and advantageous Pleasures, hath always been, and must always be, accounted Wisdom.

"It must be owned indeed that the Town hath its Pleasures as well as the Countrey . . . but how alluring soever the Pleasures of the Town may seem to us, whilst Health and Strength and the Gaieties of Youth last; yet considering the Difficulties and Dangers . . . which tend to mar all those Delights; we shall be inclined to declare in Favour of the innocent Simplicity of a Countrey-Life."

Thomas Fairchild was successful enough in the town, a prosperous eighteenth-century London gardener, but he, too, found that most men retire to the country. "The Books I have read, and the Conversation I have had with a great Number of the Trading Part of Mankind, inform me, that all the Care, Labour, and Industry of Men of Business tend to lead them in their latter Days into Quiet and Ease, as well as to provide Fortunes for their Families." And in this Quiet and Ease their main delight is gardening. Yet it is no use, says Fairchild, to imagine that we can turn at once from Affairs to Gardens: even in their city life men must learn "to delight themselves in Gardening, tho' they have never so little Room, and prepare their Understanding to enjoy the Country, when their Trade and Industry has given them Riches enough to retire from Business." Therefore the design of his book, he says, is "to instruct the Inhabitants of the City, how they may arrive at the Knowledge of managing and delighting in those Gardens, which their present Industry leads them to retire to, when their Business has given them sufficient Fortunes to leave off Trade."

Switzer, who has an unfortunate eighteenth-century style of writing in what he would call Seraphick Strains, tells us that in a garden we can prepare not only for retirement but for heaven. "The Soul is elevated to unlimited Heights above, and modell'd and prepar'd for the sweet Reception and happy Enjoyment of Felicities, the durablest as well as happiest that Omniscience has created." Other races have retired to gardens even more thoroughly, for the great Moghuls made gardens in their lifetime to be buried in at death. The Taj Mahal is a tomb garden, and so, I suppose, are our cemeteries. Nor, says Switzer, is there any more suitable place to die in, for in what more innocent Employ could "wise and intelligent Persons be found, when Death, that King of Terrors, shall close their Eyes, and they themselves be obliged to bid an eternal Farewel to these and all other sublunary Pleasures"?

Men have even sought immortality in their gardening, for it is "more beneficial to Posterity than any other Study or Employ whatsoever." "Trees and Vegetables have perpetuated some names longer and better than a pedigree of numerous offspring," and because they gave their names to flowers, great men have been remembered when their other fame is forgotten; and "Many of the ancients," says Sir Thomas Browne, "do poorly live in the single names of vegetables." Ladies especially, says Switzer, who is delightfully and absurdly fulsome about the Fair Sex, may make themselves everlastingly remembered by the simplest garden labour. "When Men are observ'd to busie themselves in this diverting and useful Employ, 'tis no more than what is from them expected; but when by the Fair and Delicate Sex, it has something in it that looks supernatural, something so much above the trifling Amusements of Ladies, that it is apt to fill the Minds of the Virtuous with Admiration . . . while these illustrious Heroins shine with unusual Splendor, and by their Actions perpetuate their Memories to the latest Date of Time."

Religion has planted many gardens, and not only the more or less useful ones which provided flowers. Frazer's *Golden Bough* pursues the sacredness of trees further back than any gardener need follow, and even the slightest of Latin scholars cannot help knowing that the Classical Ages treasured sacred groves. So did religions as different as the Egyptian, the Druidic, and the Chinese, for tree-worship seems a natural reverence in human beings. The followers of Zoroaster held a comfortable faith that gardeners went to heaven, and so, said the Buddhists, did their gardens, for "Herbs and trees, stones and rocks shall all enter into Nirvana." The Greeks made Adonis Gardens, pots of short-lived plants whose withering symbolized Adonis' death, but that can scarcely be why we now plant the elegant blue agapanthus in tubs for the summer. The Chinese considered that the cultured man must be skilled in seven arts, one of which was growing flowers. The Japanese made Tea Gardens of an exact perfection, where they met for the Tea Ceremony, an austere ritual which sought virtue in simplicity, through "the admiration of the beautiful in the sordid facts of everyday life." The Romans, so one writer tells us, set a religious value on myrtle for an even stranger reason: because "The sweet savour thereof when burn'd, became an atonement for the offence the Romans had committed in ravishing the Sabine Virgins. And the sacred branches were sufficient to purify them from so venial a sin. In memory of which offence and satisfaction the Romans erected a Temple dedicated to Venus Cloacina, the Goddess of such pleasures and Patroness of the innocent Myrtle."

But without considering any doubtful metaphysical virtues which gardening may have, there is a general feeling among the English writers that it is an excellent occupation for keeping idle hands out of mischief. "These Innocent Pleasures will both improve our Understanding and better our Morals. The Temptations to Vice are always taken off in Proportion to the Employments of those Minutes which are by many spent in Idleness." It was perhaps for the same reason that the Cistercians used gardening as a gentlemanly form of exercise, and it is certainly to keep idle tongues out of mischief that Laurence recommends flower-growing for ladies: "I flatter myself the Ladies would soon think that their vacant Hours in the Culture of the Flower-Garden, would be more innocently spent and with greater Satisfaction than the common Talk over a Tea-Table, where Envy and Detraction so commonly preside."

Humphrey Repton has an ingenious plan for using a garden to improve workhouse morals. The garden should be to the south

of the building, he says, and to the north a square yard surrounded by "bedrooms for the paupers." "The difference betwixt the cold darksome gloom of the north quadrangle, and the
warm cheerful appearance of the site towards the South may
easily be imagined; and suggest the idea of taking great advantages of the contrast.

"Let the back-yard be considered as a sort of punishment for
misbehaviour and refractory conduct, where, shut up between
four buildings nothing can be seen to enliven the prospect: while,
on the contrary, from the south terrace, cheered by the sun, the
view of the country will be delightful, since the immediate foreground consists of a garden." And he draws us a picture of the
South-side Virtuous enjoying the sun under the kindly gaze of
ladies in a neighbouring garden, who (being English) are taking
tea on the lawn. Nor does he forget the children, and "as the
reward of good conduct" he thinks they might be "supplied with
spades, and hoes, and tools, proportionate to their strength . . .
taught and exercised in the cultivation of the garden, and perhaps
drilled to become the future defenders of their country." We
wonder what task the poor little things were given for *bad* conduct. Yet Repton was a kindly man and lived from choice in a
cottage on a country street, for he loved "the cheerful village,
the high road, and that constant moving scene, which I would
not exchange for any of the lonely parks that I have improved
for others."

The Romans wrote out moral maxims in box-edging, a practice
Repton never suggests, and one unlikely to further either good
conduct or good gardening. They also encouraged gardens
among the peoples they subdued, for "it was always a Maxim of
Policy amongst them to amuse the People they conquored by
this means." For gardens are "naturally apt to fill the mind with
calmness and tranquility" and many writers feel them to be the
ideal place for working off bad temper. "What an influence they
have upon the passions of the mind, reducing a discomposed
fancy to a more sedate temper!" Or, as another says more
bluntly: "If my Dame be a little out of Humour, our Farmer

may find no less Diversion in his Garden than if he went a Mile or two to an Alehouse, and made the Breach wider."

"Adam had knowledge in simples," so one writer tells us, and certainly later men have made botanical gardens to study plants. They have made rock-gardens to satisfy their delight in small things—the "wee plants" which Farrer loved—and nostalgic gar-

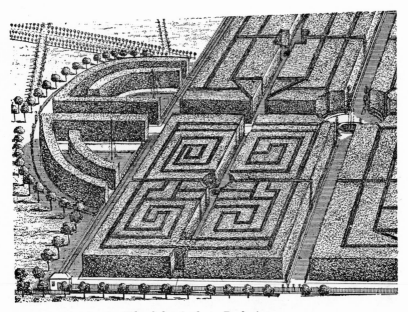

The labyrinth at Badminton.
A maze was similar but with low hedges.

dens to remind them of their native land because they were homesick. For it is not only the English who grow their western flowers in India; the Moghuls, too, were strangers from the Persian mountains, and made themselves reminiscent waterfalls in the flat gardens of the Indian plain. The Hanging Gardens of Babylon, so the story says, were built by Nebuchadnezzar to please his wife, a girl from the hills who sighed for home. They covered three acres of ground in the city, and were planted on sixteen-foot-wide terraces supported by arches whose four-foot-square pillars were hollow and full of soil so that trees could root through them.

Games have always had their place in gardens—mazes and labyrinths, archery and bowls, tennis and croquet—and gardeners have delighted in elaborate tricks and practical jokes. Surprise fountains have been popular at least since the Romans, for the younger Pliny had a trick bench which shot out water when it was sat upon. He also had a marble pool where supper was served

Playing paille-maille or pell-mell in Saint James's Park.

with dishes floating on the water. The Greeks made grottoes, though we think of them as an eighteenth-century folly; zoos and aviaries have always had their place in gardens; and topiary has been in and out of fashion ever since the Egyptians.

One of the more unlikely reasons for gardening is to have subjects of polite conversation at dinner, but "if one considers how difficult and dangerous a thing Conversation is now become," as one gardener complains, then it is not so unreasonable. Politics, he says, are dangerous, religion is unprofitable (he was a clergyman himself), and "to talk of the Weather is low mean and peasantly." Which is a nicety of etiquette I must try to remember when I next go out to dine. I will ignore both droughts and floods and talk instead of gardens, for without them "we who take delight in Flowers, should in some Measure be depriv'd of the benefit of human Conversation. How much Acquaintance doth their Rarity not afford to knowing Artists? How many pleasant Visits? How many friendly Conversations? And how many solid Reasonings? Certainly it is the sweetest Life of the World, and a very pleasant Entertainment to our Thoughts, to imploy them thus in the Contemplation of Flowers."

Even in the winter we can contrive our flowery Contemplation, for every gardener knows the pleasure of a pile of catalogues and a chair by the fire. But the old gardening books are an even rarer delight, and we soon grow fondly familiar with their vivid style and sunshiny preoccupations, their artful dedications, the long *s*'s and haphazard spelling, the smell, the parchment-coloured paper, the rubbed leather bindings ("they make a fine Sett in the Study"), and, above all, the careful ingenuous drawings of flowers and garden plans and Useful Inventions. To open one at the elaborate title page is as vivid a pleasure as opening a new garden gate. And so many different people live their lives between the two covers. There is the gardener, of course, with his earthy instructions for growing fine flowers, but there is the author, too, with his learned history of gardening since Adam. For though they are both the same person, they combine as uneasily as landscape pictures where the figures are painted by someone else because, as the children say, "I really *can't* draw people." Then there is the printer, who clearly regards the book as his own creation just as much as the writer's. It is not only the title page, with its astonishing variety of different types like a printer's advertisement, and the words alternately in red and black ink. It is not only the initials which begin each chapter, with their patterns of cherubs and birds and even of rabbits. But if we look closely at the decorations at the ends of chapters, they are not simply flowers, as we might suppose; there is a figure, too, and it is not Flora, not even Priapus, that shameless god of gardens, but the printer's own hero, Caxton, THE INVENTOR OF

The title page of a seventeenth-century garden book.

PRINTING. We can just make out the words on the laurel wreath which encircles his bust.

But of all the uses men have made of gardens, none is more original than that of the Old Man of the Mountains, an unscrupu-

lous rascal who planted a garden to recruit soldiers for his body-
guard. Marco Polo tells the story.

"In a beautiful valley enclosed between two lofty mountains,
he had formed a luxurious garden, stored with every delicious
fruit and every fragrant shrub that could be procured. Palaces of
various sizes and forms were erected in different parts of the
grounds, ornamented with works of gold, with paintings, and
with furniture of rich silks. By means of small conduits contrived
in these buildings, streams of wine, milk, honey, and some of pure
water, were seen to flow in every direction. The inhabitants of
these palaces were elegant and beautiful damsels, accomplished
in the arts of singing, playing upon all sorts of musical instru-
ments, dancing, and especially those of dalliance and amorous
allurement. Clothed in rich dresses they were seen continually
sporting and amusing themselves in the garden and pavilions, their
female guardians being confined within doors and never suffered
to appear. The object which the chief had in view in forming a
garden of this fascinating kind, was this: that Mahomet having
promised to those who should obey his will the enjoyments of
Paradise, where every species of sensual gratification should be
found, in the society of beautiful nymphs, he was desirous of its
being understood by his followers that he also was a prophet and
compeer of Mahomet, and had the power of admitting to Paradise such as he should choose to favour. . . . At his court this
chief entertained a number of youths, from the age of twelve to
twenty years, selected from the inhabitants of the surrounding
mountains, who showed a disposition for martial exercises, and
appeared to possess the quality of daring courage. To them he
was in the daily practice of discoursing on the subject of the
paradise announced by the prophet, and of his own power of
granting admission; and at certain times he caused opium to be
administered to ten or a dozen of the youths; and when half dead
with sleep he had them conveyed to the several apartments of the
palaces in the garden. Upon awakening from the state of leth-
argy, their senses were struck with all the delightful objects that

have been described, and each perceived himself surrounded by lovely damsels, singing, playing, and attracting his regards by the most fascinating caresses, serving him also with delicate viands and exquisite wines; until intoxicated with excess of enjoyment amidst actual rivulets of milk and wine, he believed himself assuredly in Paradise, and felt an unwillingness to relinquish its delights."

After four or five days the youths were again drugged and taken back to court, where they described, to the "eager curiosity and astonishment" of all hearers, the delicious garden they had left. They had been to Paradise, they said, through the favour of their chief. Yes, said the cunning old man, and so should everyone inherit Paradise who served his chief faithfully. Thus the Old Man of the Mountains recruited his famous band of Assassins, men so ruthless in killing that their name has passed even into our own Western language.

"A garden is an expression of Man in a state of Society." So one writer affirms, and it is a most interesting statement if only he had developed it, which he does not. But still we can make out for ourselves something of what he may have meant.

The irrigated gardens of hot countries are necessarily regular, but in England, where a fertile climate covers our land with green without any help from us, a gardener's task is not so much to grow the plants he wants, as to keep the unwanted plants from choking them. We weed far more than we water, and as it is no more difficult to weed an irregular garden than a regular one, and since we can turn any patch of land into a garden if we will, the gardens we make in England are not dictated by our climate, but are expressions of something in ourselves and the society we live in.

English gardens have been of three main kinds: the enclosed, the formal, and the landscape style. Within these three broad divisions there are many variations, but the three groups are none the less distinct, and they follow each other in the order given.

The enclosed style includes all gardens up to the seventeenth century, for though the space inside the enclosure may be laid out in all kinds of fashions, the main essential of a garden before the seventeenth century is that it should be strictly encircled by walls and fences, moats and hedges. Once inside the garden, you are shut in—or the world is shut out: they are two ways of looking at the same fact, depending, I suppose, on how one feels. But in any case there is no understanding between the world outside and the garden within; we could live all our lives in such enclosures and never have any conception of what lay beyond our walls.

The formal garden belongs to the Renaissance, and although it has a boundary, as all gardens must for practical reasons, the enclosure is only a convenience and no longer a barrier against outside chaos. For the great formal gardens do not ignore the world: they take it and dominate it. The foreground is moulded to a logical order of the mind, the distance is explored and regulated by confident vistas open to the horizon. The greatest of these gardens were created by Le Nôtre in seventeenth-century France, and were copied everywhere in the civilized world.

The landscape garden is an English style, and depends not on subduing the natural scene to a formal intellectual pattern, but on discreetly enhancing the original character of the landscape so that it shall seem even more typical yet still completely natural. This landscape gardening belongs to the eighteenth century, since when there has been no new style, but only different varieties of degeneration, and piecemeal revivals of older fashions such as herbaceous borders and wild gardens.

If we are going to consider the three kinds of gardens as three different expressions of man as a social creature, then we shall expect to find help in the books the gardeners wrote about their creations. And so we do, but the light they shed only falls obliquely. You can tell a man by the food he eats, so a Frenchman said. Yes. Or by the clothes he wears, or the books he reads, or the gardens he makes. But although *we* may recognize all his activities as so many different expressions of his personality, he will not, unless he is very self-conscious, recognize them himself. So that the garden books are quite unconscious that besides telling us how to turn our patch of earth into a garden, they are also expressing the way their age looks at the world, the state of their society. For if they insist on walls and hedges, if their chief instruction is how to shut off a garden from the world outside, then we may surely guess that their world is neither peaceful nor self-confident. We can think of the enclosed gardens as expressing men's fear of violence and longing for peace in a society where violence was common and peace unreliable, where the law was no great protection and every man must look after himself, where the struggle to survive kept men's thoughts at home and there was little time for curiosity about the far horizon.

In England the great formal garden has as little literature as it has few examples, for Versailles is French, not English. But of all styles of gardening this least needs words to explain it, since it states its own message with superb clarity. The spacious and orderly planning, the serene vistas into the open country—these proclaim with no need of books the assurance of a society confident in its power to dominate the surrounding world by its own intellectual force.

The landscape gardens are less superb and much less straightforward. If we had never known that such gardens existed but came on one by chance during a country walk, we might not even realize that it was in any way contrived, but think it at first glance only a stretch of unexpectedly fine country left happily alone. For gardening taste in eighteenth-century England had grown weary of man's intellectual dominance. Fashion now preferred Nature untouched by Man—or seemingly untouched, for the landscape parks are as carefully arranged as any seventeenth-century garden. But to suit a taste grown tired of order and formality and the Age of Reason, gardens must seem unsubdued by man's too-dominant logic, and within easy reach of London we must feel ourselves remote in some beautiful natural wilderness.

Gardens then, like other works of art, are part of the history of ideas, but a social historian might see too in the three stages of gardens the changing material background of England, from the poor cramped life of the Middle Ages, through the confident expansion of Renaissance exploration, to the high material comfort of the eighteenth century and the early Industrial Revolution, which drove men, since we are perverse creatures and never satisfied, to a self-conscious return to Nature and the Simple Life.

A gardener and his formal garden were master and slave, a precarious relationship since slaves revolt as soon as the master slackens his hold, and the gardens ran wild. But the eighteenth-century landscape parks were a mutual compromise between man and nature, and they have therefore lasted for two centuries with little attention except the grazing of cattle. Which is just as well, for we have created no fine gardens since, nor are we likely to unless we set aside our present preoccupation with the plants rather than the garden. Repton, at the end of the landscape style, believed that the next garden fashions would come from India: "We are on the eve of some great future change in both these arts" (gardening and architecture) "in consequence of our having lately become acquainted with scenery and buildings in the interior provinces of India. The beautiful designs . . . have produced a new source of beauty, of elegance and grace, which may justly vie with the best specimens of Grecian and Gothic architecture." What we were really on the eve of in the early nineteenth century was laurels and carpet-bedding, but no one could be expected to foresee the way ahead as so very depressing.

"Gardening, as an Art of Culture, since the commencement of the present century, has made rapid progress; but, as an Art of Taste, it has been comparatively stationary." So said a critic of the nineteenth century, and his charge is even truer of our own age. Modern architecture has looked to Corbusier, not to India; but modern gardening has not yet looked anywhere at all except to the cultivators of flowers: the "Gardenesque School," as the same critic slightingly calls it, which plans a garden simply for growing plants, a style "particularly adapted for laying out the grounds of small villas." But in time, no doubt, we too shall evolve a new way of gardening to suit our new way of building, and if any of our creations survive into the twenty-first century, then our descendants can amuse themselves too in interpreting the character of our age.

CHAPTER TWO

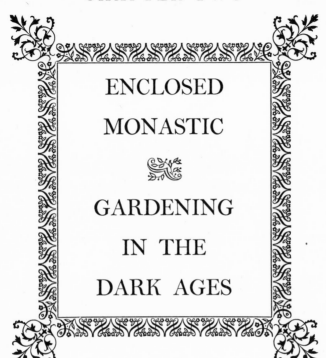

ENCLOSED

MONASTIC

GARDENING

IN THE

DARK AGES

W HAT GARDENS THE ROMANS FOUND WHEN
first they came to Britain, like the songs the Sirens
sang, it is now too late to guess at. The old Celtic legends are
haunted by dreams of a garden island peopled by gods, lying far
out in the western ocean, and this half-possible paradise has many
names: the Land of the Young, the Plain of Happiness, the Island
of Avalon where King Arthur went to heal his wounds. In the
early stories it is called Hy Breazil, and because the explorers
who sailed west and first reached South America thought they
had found at last this mythical flowery land, they gave the name
of Brazil to the country they had discovered.

There are longing descriptions of this garden island where no
one grows old and it is always summer:

> It is the most delightful country to be found,
> Of greatest repute under the sun;
> Trees drooping with fruit and blossom,
> And foliage growing on the tops of boughs.

A messenger sent to inspect this promised land comes back and
reports quite simply: "If all Ireland were mine, I would give it
up without regret to go and live in the place that I have seen."

In one of the most ethereally romantic of all legends, Gwydian
and Math, mysterious figures of strange magic, use their charms

and illusions to fashion a woman from flowers. "They took the blossoms of the oak, and the blossoms of the broom, and the blossoms of the meadowsweet, and produced from them a maiden, the fairest and most graceful that man ever saw." She is beautiful indeed, but proves most unreliable, though perhaps at that we should scarcely wonder, considering her background.

The Celts, then, must have loved flowers and gardens, but we shall probably never know whether the old inhabitants of Britain actually dug the solid muddy earth, and set real plants to grow on their rainy islands "beyond the limits of the then known earth," where the Roman soldiers of the first century, like the Roman missionaries five centuries later, were frightened to venture.

"The Isle of Albion is so-called from the white roses in which it abounds," but the Latin descriptions of the island are of marshes, forests, wild hills, "forlorn and swampy plains." Yet the soil "will yield all ordinary produce in plenty. It ripens slowly, but grows rapidly, the cause in each case being the same, the excessive moisture of soil and atmosphere." But there is no mention of gardening among the British, who were considered "unversed in plantation and other husbandry," and the inhabitants whom Cæsar found, lived on "milk and fleshmeat," caring nothing for vegetables. They preferred their tables loaded with meat and pudding.

Corn they certainly grew, for there is constant mention of crops and harvests in the Roman invasions, and we can still see the outlines of their little fields, ridged sometimes in terraces on the slopes of the hills. Woad, too, they may have cultivated, since it is not a wild flower in England, and since Cæsar tells us about their blue war-paint; indeed, it is one of the few scraps we all remember from our painstaking schoolday construing of the *Gallic War*. The priests, too, planted groves of trees for the worship of their gods, the sacred groves of the Druids which Tacitus mentions so disapprovingly, though whether they grew mistletoe, as we all imagine, he does not tell us.

As for the Romans themselves in Britain, Horace Walpole dismisses them as impossibly provincial. "A barbarous country, so remote from the seat of empire, and occupied by a few legions that very rarely decided any great events, is not very interesting, though one's own country." It may well be true, as he says, that "Roman remains in Britain . . . are upon a foot with what ideas we should get of Inigo Jones if somebody was to publish views of huts and houses that our officers run up at Senegal and Goree." Like Walpole, though I had not liked to say so, I also find our Roman remains sadly disappointing. After a beginning of hopeful interest we realize resignedly that we shall never come on anything to stir any imagination but the historic; that the only æsthetic pleasure we shall find is by turning our backs on the awful mosaics and considering the beauty of the site, for the Romans had a happy taste in sheltered hillsides facing south across lovely country.

Gardens are perishable creations, as every lazy gardener soon finds, and we can scarcely expect the archæologists to reconstruct them for us, but since the Romans built in Britain villas of considerable luxury, they must almost certainly have laid out round them the gardens they were used to in Italy—gardens, moreover, which would serve the double purpose of pleasing the conquerors and keeping the conquered innocently employed. Besides, these visiting Italians liked their diet varied with fruit and vegetables, which they introduced to England from the Mediterranean and called by the Latin names we still use in Anglicized forms: lettuce and radish, parsley and onions.

When the Romans left Britain in the fourth century "the foul hosts of the Picts and Scots land promptly from their coracles. . . . These two races differ in part in their manners, but they agree in their lust for blood. . . . As lambs by butchers, so are our piteous citizens rent by their foes, till their manner of sojourning might be compared to that of wild beasts." So says Gildas, a Welsh historian of the sixth century with a fine colourful taste for sensational horrors. Despairing of driving back their enemies without help, the British imprudently called in as mercenaries "those ferocious Saxons of unspeakable name, hateful to

God and men, bringing as it were wolves into the fold." Wolves who, finding the British to be poor soldiers and the land of Britain a pleasanter home than the one they had left, not surprisingly came over in force and invaded the country.

The northern tribes of the Dark Ages were energetically destructive, and with their advance the remains of Roman culture in Britain were swept away. Or so Gildas tells us—"The fire was spread from sea to sea. It destroyed the neighbouring cities and regions, and did not rest in its burning course until, having burnt up nearly the whole face of the island, it licked the Western Ocean with its red and cruel tongue. . . . All the colonies were levelled to the ground . . . all the inhabitants were slaughtered, with swords flashing and flames crackling on every side. Terrible it was to see, in the midst of the streets, tops of towers torn from their lofty fittings . . . fragments of bodies covered with clotted blood, so that they seemed as if squeezed together in some ghastly winepress. There was no burial for the dead, save in the ruins of their homes, or the bellies of beasts and birds." Even if we allow for Gildas's obvious love of bloodthirsty embellishments, it is quite clear that no one on either side had much time left for looking after the Roman gardens.

But the British were not crushed all at once. They rallied under the half-legendary Celtic King Arthur, and there was a time of comparative peace. But there is no mention of gardening in the Arthurian legend, though some of the stories have a flowery charm. There was the Bishop, for instance, who discovered the King and his knights in their retirement, and asked how he should convince people when they would not believe the wonder he had seen. He should clench his hand, said Arthur, and open it again, and as he unfurled his fingers a butterfly would flutter out. "What sort of a butterfly?" the children wanted to know, for boys of the twentieth century care more for reason than romance, but that is the wrong spirit for the Celtic stories, which often have this fanciful magic, borrowed by the Christians to make charming legends for their saints. There was Saint Scothinus, who walked across the sea as if it were dry land, but half-way over he met Saint Barra, who was sailing in a boat and was not unnaturally surprised that the sea should support a walker. Saint Scothinus explained that he only walked across the meadows. No, it was the sea, said Saint Barra and drew out a salmon to prove it. No, it was a meadow, insisted Saint Scothinus, gathering a handful of flowers, and so their argument seems to have ended.

After King Arthur the Saxon invaders were soon active again, and in a century of confused war the British were finally defeated. But this does not mean settled peace and time to garden. Gildas is dead now, and Bede takes up the story, yet even through the eyes of this gentle scholar the background looks savage enough. Certainly there is one halcyon period when "a woman with her new-born babe might walk throughout the island, from sea to sea, without receiving any harm," and the King, where he saw springs of water near the highways, "caused stakes to be fixed, with brass dishes hanging at them, for the conveniency of travellers." A little more encouragement and he might have planted public gardens round the springs, but we can feel Bede's doubt even as he tells the story. "It is reported," he qualifies, or "it is proverbially said," and in any case, this peace of municipal drinking-fountains was followed by such horrors that men could not bear to remember them and took out the dreadful year from the calendar: "It has been agreed by all who have written . . . to abolish the memory of those perfidious monarchs, and to assign that year to the reign of the following King." History is still a chronicle of war and murder and slavery and famine, and of the Plague, which first swept over Europe from Asia in the sixth century. It was an age of heroes, not of gardeners, and Milton, seeking a subject for the epic which was eventually to be *Paradise Lost*, considered, among other themes, thirty-three heroic stories from the history of Britain between the departure of the Romans and the coming of William the Conqueror. In the end he decided on "Adam Unparadized," as he calls it, because he felt the old stories were not entirely reliable history but partly myth, and a great epic must have for its subject the incontrovertible truth. It seems an odd reason now for choosing the legend of Adam and Eve.

In any case, the early Anglo-Saxons were not the stuff from which gardeners are made. Even before they invaded England they were never so happy as when they were at war. "They hate peace and can win honour more easily amid dangers. . . . They even think it feeble to win with sweat what can be won with blood," but it is only sweat which will win us our gardens. If we read the story of Beowulf hoping for anything but tales of heroes, we shall be as disappointed as Horace Walpole was with Chatterton's *Ossian*. "It tires me to death to read how many ways a warrior is like the moon, or the sun, or a rock, or a lion, or the ocean. Fingal is a brave collection of similes, and will serve all the boys at Eton and Westminster for these twenty years." It is only that *Beowulf* is the real thing, and is kept for the boys when they reach the university.

By now even the memory of Roman gardens has been lost, and their forgotten cities are mysterious ruins which stir the Anglo-Saxon invaders to wonder.

> *Curious is this stonework. The Fates destroyed it;*
> *The torn buildings falter: moulders the work of giants.*
> . . . . *Earth has the Lord-Builders;*
> *The dust holds them while a thousand*
> *Generations are ended. . . .*
> *Bright were the palaces, baths were set in the palaces;*
> [It is the ruins of Bath he is describing]
> *Till time when Fate the strong rescinded that.*
> *For then they shrank as pestilence came,*
> *Pest took their strong pride . . .*
> *And men . . . in a multitude fell down.*

It was not the Romans whom the Plague destroyed, it was the poet's own people who fell down in a multitude; but in any case, it is a gloomy subject well suited to the Anglo-Saxon spirit. For they are conscious always of death, and another elegiac poem describes what they felt to be the inevitable background of the lives of men: a dismal list of the various forms of violent death, where only one man "works out all his troubles when he is still a youth" and survives to live pleasantly in old age, though even then there is no hint that he spent his time in the trim gardens of retired leisure.

None the less, there is some evidence of gardening in a humble vegetable way among the Anglo-Saxons. They had orchards where they grew apples and pears, cherries and plums, for all these words occur in Anglo-Saxon forms; the very name *orchard* is an Anglo-Saxon word meaning an enclosure for plants. They grew some vegetables, too, particularly kale and the various sorts of onions or leeks (garlic being one), and these were grown in enclosed "yards" near the house. The Anglo-Saxon Riddles are rather tiresome puzzles in the Riddle-of-the-Sphinx style, but one about a rake was surely written by a genuine gardener: "I saw a creature in the cities of men, who feeds the cattle; it has many teeth; its beak is useful; it goes pointing downward; it plunders gently and returns home; . . . it leaves the fair herbs fixed by their roots, quietly standing in their station, gleaming brightly, blowing and growing."

They had herb-gardens, too, growing herbs both for medicine and to season the meat which was their chief food. There is a Nine Herbs Charm, a strange, jumbled mixture of pagan magic and Christian additions, telling how to make the nine herbs into a potion against a long list of infections, evil spirits, blisters, and poisons of all colours of the rainbow and points of the compass. This naturally gloomy race may also have grown flowers, either for pleasure or to provide honey for their bees, for names like *lily*, *rose*, and *poppy* are Latin words which were Anglicized in the new language. Certainly they kept bees, for they used the honey to make mead and as their only form of sugar. There is a charm which was to be chanted to a swarm of bees to keep them from flying too far before they settled, a nice balance of flattery and virtuous exhortation:

Alight, victorious women, descend to earth!
Never fly wild to the wood.
Be as mindful of my profit
As every man is of food and fatherland.

So important were their bees that men were kept to watch over them as a shepherd his flock, and the fine for stealing them in King Alfred's time was a hundred and twenty shillings. Just how serious this was we can tell from the fines for personal assault: "If anyone bind a churl who is innocent, he shall make compensation with 10 shillings: if he flog him, he shall pay 20 ss: if he dock his hair to insult him 10 ss: if he shave his head like a priest's, but bind him not 30 ss: if he cut off his beard 20 ss: if he bind him and then shave him like a priest 60 ss."

Besides making laws about bees and burning the traditional cakes, King Alfred was endlessly busy, as Asser tells us in his *Life*. He was clearly a most virtuous and active man, a model for all, and one of his more frivolous inventions was a clock of four candles burning six hours each. He also built what Asser calls "majestic and rich houses after his own new designs," but there is no mention that he laid out gardens round them, for Anglo-Saxon gardens were small and humble and useful, and not yet the preoccupation of kings, as they would be later on.

If we look at the Ordnance Survey map of England in the Dark Ages, we realize that the country had changed very little from the land the Romans described. Most of the chalk was clear, and the higher hill-tops, but the low-lying land was marsh and the rest forest: mile after mile of trees covering the "ill-filled mappes." Much of Surrey, Sussex, and Kent was covered by the Forest of Andred, an impenetrable tangle of hostile woodland which haunts the history of the time like a dark and mysterious threat. "The great wood which we call Andred . . . That wood is 120 miles long, or longer, from east to west, and 30 miles broad." In the forest were wolves and wild boars, its fringes sheltered outlaws and robbers, the Danes took cover there between their murderous attacks. "If a stranger travel through a wood off the path, and neither shout nor blow his horn, he may be assumed to be a thief, and as such either slain or put to ransom." It was clearly no place to loiter gathering primroses, nor to dig up roots of woodruff to take home and plant in shady corners of the garden. Are the neat villas of modern Surrey, I wonder, ever troubled by the old demons of the woods? Or does the dreadful Werewolf himself slink off across the tidy lawns, dismayed by our new magic of the same radio voice through every open window?—a spell more potent than his own eerie midnight howlings, for he could only frighten a few superstitious souls in the dark, but we have tamed the primeval forest to trim beds of standard rose-trees.

Against the savage background of the over-running of England by successive waves of invaders, and of the civil wars of rival tribes, Christianity spread slowly and fitfully, its doctrine of humility and gentleness astonishing these warlike races whose greatest pride was in pitiless courage. "It was a very difficult task," says Bede, "to incline the King's lofty mind to the humility of the way of salvation." Yet the new way did spread, first from the Irish Christians, who had never gone back to paganism when the Romans left, then from Rome itself through the new missionaries led by Augustine in the sixth century. A strange conversion it must have been, judging by the questions Augustine sends back to Rome asking advice of the Pope. May a man who has had an amorous dream, he asks, take Holy Communion? If the Anglo-Saxons had ever shown any sense of humour, we might suspect these sceptical pagan natives of thinking up unlikely questions for the pleasure of embarrassing the earnest missionary. But the questions were doubtless asked as seriously as they were answered by the Pope.

The problems were certainly awkward, and ferocious courage was a virtue of too obvious practical value for men to renounce it easily, yet the new religion spread steadily with its teaching of gentleness, and in Bede's history Christianity is a religion of humanity despite its unwholesome preoccupation with penances and chastity and the selfish saving of one's own soul. King Edwin's missionary sparrow was to become as famous as Lesbia's. "Such seemeth to me the life of men present here in earth . . . as if a sparrow, beaten with wind and weather, should chance to fly in at one door of the hall, and flitting there a little about, straightway fly out at another . . . the hall itself being then pleasant and warm with a soft fire burning amidst thereof, but all places and ways abroad troubled with tempest. . . . After the short space of this warm air, the poor bird returneth from Winter to Winter again. So the life of man appeareth here in earth . . . but what may or shall follow the same, or what hath gone before it, that surely we know not. Therefore if this new learning can inform us of any better surety, methinks it is worthy to be followed."

It is a sad, bewildered reason for changing one's gods, a settled sadness of the English spirit, which Christianity, for all its new promises, did little to comfort. Light-headed from hunger, drugged with constant prayer, the ascetic achieved at times the unlikely longed-for vision of troops of angels descending expressly from heaven to fetch his bright particular soul. But the promise of heaven was a feverish dream which faded on waking, and the honest Christian, like the honest pagan before him, realized that he knew nothing of death but the body's rotting:

> *Sharp and strong is my dying,*
> *I know not whither I must go;*
> *Foul and stinking is my rotting—*
> *On me Jesu, have you mercy.*

From Winter to Winter again—it is a sad refrain of English poetry, through the Middle Ages, and the early Tudor poets who write in language which needs no paraphrasing, until in Shakespeare it rises to a magnificent cry of despair from eloquent Renaissance man:

> *Ay, but to die, and go we know not where;*
> *To lie in cold obstruction, and to rot;*

Gardening in the Dark Ages

This sensible warm motion to become
A kneaded clod.

Like Bottom, the sparrow is wonderfully translated.

Yet despite this melancholy conviction, and against opposition more direct and bloodthirsty, the civilizing influence of Christianity spread steadily. The Danes came and slaughtered the monks of Lindisfarne, but were themselves converted; and Canute is a Christian king when he rows through the Fens past Ely and inspires the first English boating-song:

> *Merry sang the monks in Ely*
> *That Cnut Cyning rowed thereby.*

Scandinavia, the very home of the pagan invaders, was at last converted, and even the fierce Icelanders accepted Christ, though in a somewhat half-hearted way, insisting that if they had to be baptized in winter, then it must be in the hot springs, and still secretly praying to Thor before they set out on their perilous voyages. Indeed, the Christian teaching seems an incongruous doctrine for these astonishing merchant adventurers of the Dark Ages, who colonized Greenland and put out into the open sea of the North Atlantic, taking their bearings by the midnight sun and the change in colour of the water of the polar currents; who found that if you would reach Greenland you must "steer South of Iceland so that you have the birds and whales therefrom"; who watched for the "ice-blink," the reflection of the Greenland ice-cap above the horizon, knowing then that they would soon reach land.

Their attitude to this heroic sea-faring strikes us as surprisingly matter-of-fact. A father advises his son: "Always buy shares in good vessels or in none at all. Keep your ship attractive, for then capable men will join you." And when a party of sailors are driven off their course to reach America centuries before Columbus, making their way back to Scandinavia only with great hardship, they are criticized for not following up such a valuable discovery in a more businesslike way.

Yet even these practical heroes were taught to turn the other cheek, and they, too, listened meekly, though still perhaps unconvinced at heart, for the fierce old pagan songs could still stir men's spirits so that they forgot the new teaching, and hearing them, "Both sick and whole could think of nothing else. The beasts in the wood left off feeding, the worms in the grass, and the fishes that swim in the water, lay still to listen. . . . None wearied of his songs, or heeded the singing of the priests in the church. The bells rang less sweetly than they were wont."

The way to Saint David's Head in Pembrokeshire is along a strip of land reaching out into the Atlantic. As the road runs steadily westward the trees disappear in the bleak landscape and the stunted hedges change to turf walls, bright in spring with gorse and the pale waxy flowers of pennywort, and in summer sprinkled with tiny sheep's scabious like blue jewels, and the spikes of pennywort withered to great rusty nails between the stones. The cottages, without light or water still, huddle low against the wind: it is the only place I know where the houses shelter the trees instead of the trees making wind-breaks for the houses. For the whole land is dominated, even on the stillest summer day, by the merciless Atlantic gales.

It is not empty country. Since the people are poor and the holdings small, it is dotted with cottages, but they are each separate and remote in their struggle against poverty, set among the rounded Welsh hills, whose sweeping curves fold into each other like the interlacing patterns of Celtic art.

When at last we reach it along empty roads which seem to lead nowhere, the city of Saint David's is a village of humble houses, a conglomeration of the countryside enlivened with a quiet holiday air because of the summer visitors. And there, superbly incongruous in such a setting, from a hollow of the land which shelters it from the sea, rises the magnificent cathedral of Saint David.

We walked to it once along the coast, one day of violent storm with the wind screaming in from the sea and racing over the smooth crouched hills, a tangible and universal enemy. For even the rain here cannot fall as it does in sheltered places, steadily to earth, but is driven helpless in the tumultuous air, shattered against rocks and roofs and the walls of buildings, slanted, sharp as hailstones, blind against our faces. Every yard forward is a struggle, even to breathe is difficult, we are deaf in the gale which rushes past our ears and roars in the hollow of our mouth between our parted lips.

But once inside the cathedral, the storm is stilled to silence by the simple shutting of a door. Here the air is so calm that the flames of the candles reach upwards unmoving, so quiet that we can hear the echo of our softest footstep. And we have the strangest feeling that this enclosure of space is a different world, a treasure held in the hollow arching stones as we hold something precious in the hollow of our cupped hands. This volume of quiet air is a different element from the screaming wind outside; it is a special retentive medium rich with the beauty it has absorbed through hundreds of years: the music and the singing, the coloured light through stained-glass windows, the magnificent phrases of the Bible. Air which for so long has been moulded by the architecture of these stones holds ineradicable perspectives of order and serenity. All those centuries of beauty, we feel, are here in the stillness. The door is small and closes behind us, for this air is precious, and not to be scattered in the outside chaos of wind and rain and meaningless noise. The roof has held the singing voices; they have not been lost in the streaming gale but absorbed into the silence, as a book closed and put back on the shelf is not lost but only silent until we open it again and hear the same waiting voice. So we need only stand within the cathedral walls to feel ourselves part of its world of music and poetry and the intellectual beauty of arched and vaulted spaces, a grave quiet world where the gentle movements of man are significant and the background of his mind is peace.

Coming on it suddenly, we are overwhelmed by the difference, the impassable gulf between this church and the country we have come through. Here is the setting of a life of culture and ordered

leisure; men here were not struggling to drag a wretched pittance
from a grudging land, but building towers and palaces among
tall trees where the rooks caw as richly as they do in sheltered
inland parks. The constant singing must have floated like a
strange exotic perfume over the stony fields, and the peasants in
their poor huts could have had nothing in common with the
churchmen who lived here, men who knew English and Latin
and Greek, who could read and write, who understood music
and singing, who travelled and wrote letters and could create
from the stones of the wild shore this wonder of architecture.
Such a community must have been an aristocracy of culture, and
the surrounding countryside a barren sea dividing them from the
next island, the next great abbey.

I remember the same feeling from years ago, visiting the
ruined abbeys of Yorkshire on summer excursions of the school
art club—Fountains and Rievaulx and Kirkstall on the edge of
Leeds. They were outings which enlivened the summer terms,
for we were taken, boys and girls together, in large buses which
I, being old-fashioned, still like to call char-a-bancs. First we
were led round the ruins, whose beauties were eloquently
pointed out by a guide offering us far more information than
anyone could absorb on such sunshiny holiday afternoons. Then
we were left to find our own corner and sketch some chosen
vista through broken arches, all in the best eighteenth-century
tradition of picturesque ruins. But I would sit with idle pencil and
empty drawing-pad, and think how if I had lived in those grim
days, I too would have joined the Church, and accepted the
religion for the peace and culture of the life it sheltered. As many
did, for whatever reasons—kings and nobles besides quiet men
and scholars; and in these lordly ruins we feel, as we seldom do
in the defensive castles of the aristocracy, that here was the good
life, the delight in the civilized pursuits of man, the peaceful
routine of a gentle way of living.

Neither cathedrals nor castles belong to the true Dark Ages,
but they are evidence we can see for ourselves of the superior
culture of the Church in mediæval times, of a gulf between lay

and religious which in the history of the Dark Ages is still more obvious.

Even in its ostentatiously austere beginnings, the monastic life implies considerable luxury. It is a high standard of living which can afford to allow an able-bodied man to spend his whole life saving his own soul. And the fasting they so boast of is suspiciously like the artificial wildernesses of the eighteenth-century gardeners. If we are to fast, there must first be food to refrain from; the poor without food do not fast, but starve simply, and thereby, it seems, win no grace. It is the case of the Egyptian in the stories of the Desert Fathers, who before he became a monk was a herdsman sleeping in the fields and living wretchedly on bread and water. "Out of much tribulation and heavy toil," he admits, "I . . . did come to rest and refreshing in the monastic life, and what I had not, I now have."

In such a setting men could sit in peace, and as Bede's translator charmingly says, "entertain one another with the delights of the celestial life." There are constant references to the culture and education of the Church, and Bede found the monastery of Jarrow a sympathetic home. He kept the discipline and services, and "the rest of my time I was delighted to learn, to teach, or to write." It says a great deal for the monastic life that a man of Bede's gifts could work happily within it. For he is one of the true scholars, and inhabits an intellectual country far beyond the limitations of his age. Though he has his foibles, of course, including a quite astonishing credulity about miracles and a constant preoccupation with the right date for keeping Easter. For whether Easter should be kept according to the different calculations of the Celtic or the Roman Church seemed to Bede the most important of doctrines. It is almost a test of saints and sinners, and it is only because Bede is a mild and tolerant man that he can forgive the wrong date even in the most virtuous. "He was a good man, but . . ." and we know what is coming —he kept Easter on the wrong date. It is his hobby-horse, and at this remote distance of time and spirit seems to us an endearing enthusiasm. Yet we read him as a modern historian, and it is only when he says of some now legendary place "the ruins can still be seen" that we realize with a sudden check of surprise that his "still" is more than a thousand years ago.

As the monasteries grew richer, the life became even pleasanter —too pleasant perhaps, for certainly it roused the envy of the less fortunate. "The monks drink the best wines which God has established. They eat bread as white as hail; of all flesh do they eat also, so that their bellies are full and stuffed and they almost burst through the middle." No doubt envy makes an unreliable witness, but we know about the monastery which received a gift of wine from the French king and sold it because the quality was not good enough for fastidious Church palates.

Nor were the monks overburdened with work, for only about a third of the community of a monastery were monks; the rest were servants and lay brothers who did the manual labour; and every anchoress, so one authority advises, should have two maids to wait on her. Young women are urged to become nuns, not at all as a penance, but because the nun's quiet day is so much pleasanter than the life of the ordinary overworked housewife. But let the anchoress beware, he warns, of the vanity of admiring her "own white hands," the "too fair" hands of idleness (it is reassuring to find how much wicked vanity we are all now safe from).

In the Dark Ages, then, the good life was in the Church, and it is in its fruitful shelter that we must look for the arts, and for the gardens which men seem always to have made for their delight as soon as they have leisure. From the beginning the Roman Church encouraged gardening—"Hoe your ground, set out cabbages and convey water to them in conduits," said Saint Jerome. Cabbages seem unambitious perhaps, but still they make a beginning. Saint Benedict advises a garden for every foundation; the Cistercians in their lonely valleys had large gardens both within and without the walls; and the Carthusians, with their rule of solitude and silence, planned a separate plot for each cell. Everywhere gardening is actively encouraged, both for men and women, until the Abbess Héloïse complains in a letter to Abélard that it is unreasonable to expect nuns to do the hard work of a garden, that women are unsuited to such manual labour. It is rather sad to find that the passionate and romantic lovers have grown so domestic.

There were many reasons for the Church's interest in gardens: they provided suitably dignified work for the monks; grew

A medicinal herb. Drawing by Crispin de Passe.

fruit and vegetables, wine and cider, herbs for medicine, and flowers for the church; and quite certainly gardens were kept simply for the universal pleasure of gardening. Whatever the reasons, the Domesday survey shows clearly that there were large and flourishing gardens belonging to many of the monasteries, and very few others besides. For to survive in such wild times a garden had to be strictly enclosed, and the only wall which was strong enough to protect it was the fear of God. The gardens belonged to the monks, who were servants of God, and if anyone destroyed their gardens, then God would punish the offenders. It is strange that human beings can be coerced by abstract ideas into doing things they have no wish to do, but in an age of faith, religious dread was a rampart round a garden stronger than any man-made wall. It was the reason why even in those violent times church gardens could be planted in the open, as lay gardens could not for centuries to come. Of course, if the enemy did not happen to share the same religious ideas as the gardeners, then the abbeys and their gardens looked what they were, defenceless, and the Danes did not hesitate to murder the monks at Lindisfarne.

What a monastery garden was like we can see fairly clearly. The first ones were surrounded by cloisters, and the enclosed space divided by cross-paths meeting in the centre at a well. The beds between the paths were planted with trees and flowers "well-nursed well-watered and lovely." This entrance court, which was also a sanctuary, was not the only garden. There is a plan of an ideal monastery in Charlemagne's time which shows the various gardens there were likely to be. Besides the cloister garden there is the physic garden with separate beds of medicinal herbs, many of them flowers; there is a large kitchen garden with plots of vegetables not very different from our own (for the names are written on the plan); and the cemetery is laid out as a pleasure orchard, with ornamental and fruit trees formally arranged between the regular graves. Often, too, there were private gardens for the high officials, and the Sacristan had his flower garden, where he grew flowers to decorate both the church and the priests who worshipped in it. One such garden was called Le Joye, a simple proof of its keeper's affection, and Paradise was a common name.

The old church at Scarborough stands on the hill which divides the two bays. We used to spend summer holidays there when I was a child, and wandering about the old lanes behind the church, I once found a little wilderness of grass and wild flowers and scrabbling hens. It was surrounded by a crumbling wall which bore the street name of PARADISE printed out in large Roman letters on an authentic metal plate, and I remember still my delighted astonishment. It was as if authority had given official support to the fairy-tales, had blessed one's airiest fancies

From a painting of SILENE LINIFOLIA *in the Juliana Anicia Codex of Dioscorides' Herbal,* A.D. *512. "This being beaten when it is green with old swines grease, is good for the mad-dog-bitten and the throat-swollen, but being suffited it drives away serpents."*

as sober truth. And sitting on the wall, watching the heavenly hens as they scratched for grubs among the bindweed and nettles, I wondered who had found this humble corner enchanting enough to give it so celestial a name.

This floweriness of the early Church is especially attractive in the story of Saint Rhadegonde. As a girl in the sixth century, she was taken prisoner and brought up to be her captor's queen. But she left him and became a nun at Poitiers, where "she cultivated roses and other flowers that woven into garlands or scattered on the table to form a perfumed covering, ornamented the refectory." Bishop Fortunatus, a charming epicurean scholar, was her close friend. She would entertain him at flowery meals, send him small gifts of fruit and posies, and he would compose charming verses for her in Latin, sitting in a garden arbour surrounded by admiring nuns:

> *If it were the time of lilies,*
> *Or the fragrant crimson rose . . .*

If this seems a flowery extravagance of a gayer civilization than ours, and English monasteries seem to have grown mostly herbs for physic and vegetables for food, such gardens were not as dull as we might suppose. Not only are herbs often beautiful garden plants, like tansy or rosemary, or fennel with its white sheaths and yellow flowers and delicate green thread leaves, but the monks grew many plants as herbs which we think of only as flowers: peonies and gladioli, roses and lilies, which were a sovereign cure for poisons. Many flowers, too, they boiled with honey and ate as puddings, as we still decorate our party cakes with crystallized violets and rose-petals; it always seemed to me a kind of cannibalism.

Outside the monastery were the orchards where the monks grew a fine variety of fruit and nuts, though we cannot help suspecting that some of the trees in the accounts (for there are dates and pomegranates) were copied down hopefully from Charlemagne's list. Besides the half-legendary conqueror we all know, Charlemagne was an excellent gardener. He had a private garden where he tried new plants, and he sent out lists of trees to be grown on his various well-run estates. The exotics can never have been happy in Europe, but still there are many plants which the monks knew well—apples and pears, plums and cherries, hazels and almonds, peaches and figs and mulberries.

There were vineyards too, and fishponds, which certainly provided pleasure as well as food. "They sit upon the green margin of the huge basin, they see the little fishes playing under the water, and representing a military encounter by swimming to meet each other. This water" (though it is an anti-climax after the pretty fancy of the performing fishes) "serves the double duty of supporting the fish and watering the vegetables."

Lilium candidum, *the white lily.*

The monks' pleasure in their gardens was not always as straightforward as this ingenuous delight in fishponds. But if the more austere Christian teaching frowned on flowers as pagan frivolity, then the monks gave them symbolic meaning in the service of the Church. The white lily stood for Our Lady's chastity, they said, the red rose for the blood of the martyrs.

The four walls of the cloister garden symbolized contempt for oneself and the world, love of one's neighbour and of God. The grass always green was the greenness of a monk's virtues, a tree the ladder to the heavenly life, and so on. It is an easy enough game to play, but it seems a pity they could not read the seventeenth-century gardening books and be convinced once and for all that gardening is entirely virtuous.

In his cloister at Subiaco, Saint Benedict had a favourite garden of roses, whose thorns he took to tear his flesh when his thoughts were too preoccupied with wicked women—perhaps the band of naked dancers a jealous rival brought to perform in his cloister. We soon cease to be surprised at the saints exulting in perversions we should blush for—indeed, it is part of their charm that they have never heard of Freud—but, as a gardener, it is hard not to feel that Saint Benedict would have done better to come to his roses already satisfied, and settle down to enjoy them in a more straightforward fashion. It is rather sad to grow roses for their thorns.

But Walafred Strabo is a whole-hearted gardener. An abbot of the ninth century, he looked after his own little plot, and his verse account of the work to be done and the plants he grew is written by a gardener who wheeled his own barrow and transplanted his seedlings as lovingly as if they were children. First, he says, you must get a garden—any kind of garden. No matter whether the soil is light or heavy, the site on a hill or in a valley; as long as you work hard and are patient, harden your hands and dung your land well, you will succeed.

He has a little plot at his door, he tells us, and there in spring grows up a forest of nettles. So he takes mattock and rake and sets about the thick tangled roots twined as closely as a hurdle (for nettles, it seems, have changed their habits in the last thousand years even less than gardeners).

The nettles clear, he leaves the rough digging to sweeten in the wind and sun, then rakes it level, builds up the edges of the beds with boards, mulches it well with old manure, and sows his seeds.

Watered by the rain and dew, the little seedlings soon grow, and if there is a drought he draws up water from the well, not to sluice over them roughly but to scatter gently by hand. And if any corner of his garden is too hot or too shady, he moves his plants about until he finds a place to suit them.

Then he tells us what he grows, a list of herbs and vegetables and flowers, with a little poem in praise of each, as we might introduce our friends to strangers. He ends with the rose, but he has sung too long already, he says, to begin now on the praise

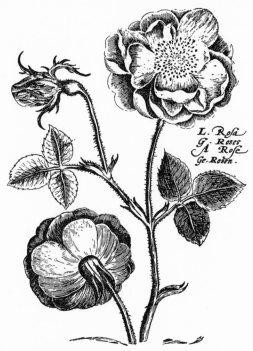

Drawing by Crispin de Passe.

of the rose and the lily, the rose for the blood of the martyrs, the lily for faith.

But we need not fear that Strabo will lead us off into the gloom of doubtful symbolism to justify his love of flowers. He is a true gardener, and his matted nettle-roots are more vivid than any pale symbolic lily. He begins his book with a charming dedication to a fellow abbot: that he should read it sitting in his garden beneath his fruit trees, in the shifting light and green shadows of a summer day. And we realize with sudden pleasure that the Dark Ages, which seemed so gloomy and unintimate and remote, were peopled, after all, with gardeners like ourselves.

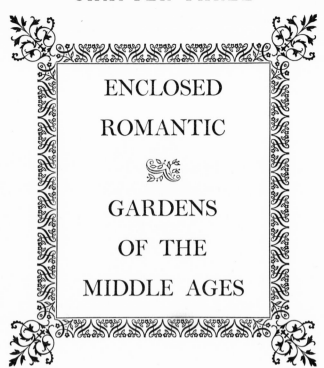

CHAPTER THREE

ENCLOSED

ROMANTIC

GARDENS

OF THE

MIDDLE AGES

ABOUT THE ACTUAL GARDENS OF THE MIDDLE Ages we know very little, but we know a great deal about the delight people took in them. They are places not for gardening, but for pleasure, for in the Middle Ages a garden is the natural setting for happiness. It is the atmosphere which matters, the enchanted delight, as if the garden walls were a magic barrier to shut out sorrow.

What we do know of mediæval gardens is not from gardeners, but from painters and poets and writers of romances. In picture after mediæval picture of the Virgin she sits in a garden among the leaves and singing birds, or on a turf seat sprinkled with flowers. In portraits, in views through windows, in scenes of saints' lives, there is often in the background a tiny garden enclosed in high white battlemented walls. All that palm beaches and Mediterranean moonlight are for modern popular romancers, their tiny enclosed gardens were for the Middle Ages. The hero first sees his lady among the flowers, which are no fairer than her face; it is in the garden they meet and promise to love forever; and if either of them is shut up by disapproving parents or jealous husband, the window of their tower is sure to overlook a garden where birds sing and flowers blow and it is always summer.

But they are not gardeners' gardens, these flowery enclosures of the Middle Ages, not plots of good black earth for digging; there is never any mention of weeds, and once inside the gate, our boots are never muddy, for these are the gardens of romance.

The first lay gardens we know about are very small. As England settled down under William the Conqueror, conditions slowly became peaceful enough for laymen to think of the quiet pleasures. But if their gardens no longer needed the fear of God to protect them, they certainly needed a wall, and at the beginning they are no more than small enclosures huddled against the castle, tiny plots of peaceful land won from the wilderness, close to shelter if danger threatens. The world outside is warded off by a high barrier, and to walk in the garden one must first have the key to unlock the heavy door.

These early garden plots are scarcely bigger than rooms, and as carefully shut in and protected. But at least they are open to the sky, and as for the view being hidden behind high walls, the Middle Ages had no wish to look out at the world; they knew too well that there were wolves in the forests (a twelfth-century writer gives instructions for taming them as dogs—a rather doubtful pleasure), there were stags and wild boars, and robbers more savage than either. Even the rule of the land was scarcely more gentle, when the King "shut the gates of mercy on mankind" and in a country newly conquered, crushed resistance without pity, laying waste rebel lands so ruthlessly that generations later whole regions were still described quite simply in the surveys as "vasta est."

But men longed for peace after the centuries of war, and in a harsh world a garden was a secret sweetness, doubly precious because of the violence outside. The early lay gardens are very simple, scarcely more than an enclosure of grass scattered with small flowers, the "flow'ry mede" of the poets and the tapestries and the foreground of mediæval pictures. There is often a raised seat of turf round the wall, sometimes a small fountain, and later on, as the gardens grew larger, leafy arbours and painted trellises, little clipped trees, and pots or beds of flowers—roses and lilies, peonies and irises, pinks and columbines, poppies and lavender, rosemary and golds, which now we call marigolds. These were grown with herbs and salads, and where usefulness ended and pleasure began, or whether they were ever separate at all, it is hard to know. For roses and lilies were still herbs against poisons; violets were a favourite relish for salads; and there are recipes for stewing primroses and cowslips and hawthorn blossom. Right up to the seventeenth century people would eat almost anything

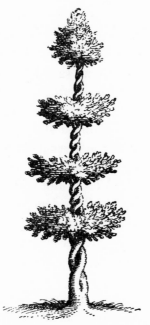

Mediæval-style topiary.

which grew in a garden, and Bacon tells a cautionary tale against eating monkshood, a flower "so poisonous that I have heard the eating only six or seven of the Blossoms in a salad, has killed a Gentleman in France." And if it killed a Frenchman, who, after all, can survive frogs and snails, what might it not do to the homely English?

Above all, in the Middle Ages, a garden was a private place, which the castle was not, with its communal rooms and enormous household, with servants everywhere, and freely wandering animals. Even in the bedroom there was a perch for hawks. So in the stories of the Middle Ages it is in the garden that the lovers meet (it seems, indeed, to be the chief function of their gardens) because only there can they be safe from interruption. Guigue-mar finds his queen in a garden "shut in by a wall of green mar-ble, very strong and high," where she walked "to be glad amongst the flowers." And in another favourite story of the Middle Ages, the hero Constant falls asleep under a tree, where the princess finds him "flushed as any rose," and falls promptly in love. "I found her in an arbour sweet, under a bough"—it could be the beginning of a dozen stories of gardeny romance. The *Roman de la Rose* is a long (and to us very tedious) tale of a quest through a symbolical garden, ending with the hero's winning of the rose and his lady's love. With its long descriptions of the magic garden it was popular all through the Middle Ages, and was retold by Chaucer in a version we seldom read now, a long verse romance which is dull and lifeless beside the timeless vitality of the *Canterbury Tales*. But it is typical of the garden romances which the Middle Ages loved, and they did not find the long flowery descriptions tedious.

As men felt safer, the gardens move out into the open and leave the castle's shadow. But they are still surrounded by walls or impenetrable hedges, still carefully shut in and protected. They may be larger, too, and divided into several enclosures, but still they are scarcely bigger than the ground plan of a house. And in all the pictures mediæval gardens have a curious pathos. It is such a tiny plot that men have claimed for their pleasure, such a humble unpretentious square they have set aside for happiness; they have asked so little and it is so precious, men and women alike crowd in so eagerly, till the surrounding walls are full of people, as if they were at a party and simply to be in the garden were delight enough. "The orchard" (for an orchard and a garden were the same thing) "was fair beyond content. Herbs grew there of every fashion, more than I am able to name. But at least I can tell you that so sweet was the savour of roses and other flowers and simples, that sick persons, borne within that garden in a litter, walked forth sound and well for having passed the night in so lovely a place."

For the English spirit of the Middle Ages was still conscious of the dark background of life—not only of violence and hunger and cold, nor of the Black Death which could kill so many that there were none left to bury the dead or gather the precious harvest for the winter, but they were conscious, too, of the darkness of man's ignorance and the uncertainty of salvation:

> *When I thinke thinges three*
> *I may never blithe be:*
> *One is that I must away,*
> *The other I know not which day.*
> *The third is my greatest care,*
> *I know not whither I must fare.*

It is a sad little verse which occurs over and over in the different versions of different dialects, one of many sad verses on the wretchedness of life and the certainty of death.

> *Wretched man why art thou proud,*
> *That art of earth y-maked?*
> *Hither broughtest thou no shroud,*
> *But poor thou came and naked.*

It is a despairing voice from the fourteenth century, haunted by the consciousness of man's mortality.

> *All we shall die, though us like ill.* . . .
>
> *Where is Paris and Heleyn?* . . .
>
> *Much sorrow I walk with.* . . .
>
> *When the turf is thy tower,*
> *And thy put* [grave] *is thy bower* . . .

It is the constant melancholy theme, for the mediæval Christians were as uncomforted by Christ as their pagan ancestors were by Thor and Odin. The Church might promise joy for the virtuous

in the next life, but the only life men knew was dark with hardship and injustice, and Paradise, for all the priests might promise,
was a reward rather to be hoped for than believed in with certainty, as they believed without question in the cold and hunger
which came with every winter.

Religion taught men to look at earthly life by the light of

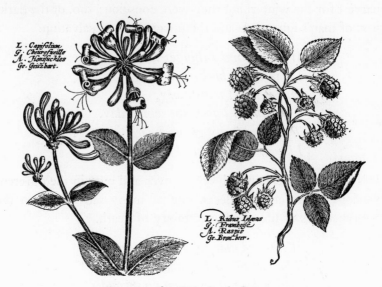

Drawing by Crispin de Passe.

eternity, but eternity is too dreadful a brilliance for mortal men
to live by. Seen in so inhuman a brightness, "the green garden
was become a little dry dust."

*"L'unique bien des hommes consiste donc à être divertis de
penser à leur condition"*—so Pascal said later on, and human
beings are mercifully frivolous. Eternity is no affair of ours, and
we shut it out by the frailest barriers of happy preoccupations.
So the gardens of the Middle Ages are a precious refuge from
besetting fears and doubts, a place where men can sit in the sunshine among the birds and flowers and be happy. And even the
flowers themselves have the oddest air of taking shelter within
the protecting walls, the wild flowers of the countryside grown
only to greater perfection—daisies and cowslips, foxgloves and

bluebells, campions and honeysuckle, forget-me-nots and thyme. They grow haphazard about the garden, not set in masses for effect, but singly like the fleurettes of the tapestries, as if they were individual creatures who had chosen for themselves this happy corner. Even the birds seek out this paradise, the magpies and finches and "little sweet nightingales" which crowd every hedge and branch, and hop about the ground between the flowers and the people.

Some of the pathos of these garden pictures comes perhaps from the limitations of mediæval art, for whether by intention or from lack of painter's skill, the people of mediæval pictures never smile. In the happiest settings they have an air of un-shakable sadness, as if life were incurably sorrowful despite its happy incidents. A Madonna sits in a garden bending over her child, who plays with a rose, and her head seems bowed, not from tenderness, but by the sorrows of the whole world. An angel leans his head upon his hand among the flowers, listening to his companion who plays upon a lute, and from the grief in his face we feel his heart must surely break. Botticelli's faces have this same quiet sadness, as if they remembered an old unhappiness which the eager joy of the coming Renaissance can never reach. It gives his Venus a strange mystery which haunts our memory long after we have forgotten the glowing beauties of later painters.

There is a theory that the weather of Europe is in long cycles of alternating warm and cold periods with roughly eighteen hundred years between peaks. The Dark Ages were a warm period, and in the Icelandic sagas the coast of Greenland was fertile, and the sailors made winter voyages in seas which now are icebound. It was the time of the ancient merchant adventurers and the discovery of America by the unbusinesslike heroes who sailed by the ice-blink. But as the peak of warm weather passed, the ice came south again and the climate grew harsher. The thirteenth and fourteenth centuries were cold, and to the miseries of a winter with scarcely food enough to last till the spring, with no light but rare candles, with no glass in the windows, with no knowledge to ward off the plague or the scurvy or the ague or the many other diseases which beset men, to all this was added the wretchedness of winters so cold that the seas froze and hungry wolves roamed over the ice from Norway to Denmark.

Small wonder, then, that the Middle Ages longed for the end

L. *Aquilegia*
G. *Aucholies*
A. *Columbine*
Ge. *Ackeley*.

Drawing by Crispin de Passe.

of winter, that if they shut their eyes and wished, it was always spring:

> *Bytuene Mershe ant Averil*
> *When spray biginneth to springe . . .*

Lyric after lyric begins in the same way.

> *Miri tim it is in Maie. . . .*

Gardens of the Middle Ages

Lenten ys come with love to toune. . . .

Up, son and mery wether,
Somer draweth nere. . . .

An index of first lines is a fanfare for the spring. It is as if they only came alive at the end of winter: "It was the time when meadow and copse are green: when orchards grow white with bloom and birds break into song as thickly as the bush to flower. It is the season when he who loves would win to his desire."

Reading their literature, we might think the whole year was a long ecstatic spring, so constantly do they delight in the new season, forgetting winter as a dark shadow in the background. And in their gardens it is the small flowers of the spring they love most dearly, primroses and violets and woodruff and periwinkle—"parwincke, joy of the ground."

This delight of the Middle Ages in flowers and gardens is a fragrance which they breathe over all their doings. They decked the streets of London with flowers and branches on saints' days and holidays, not only as we do with holly doubtfully at Christmas. Young ladies wore stockings embroidered with gladioli, and tenants paid a red rose yearly as a token rent instead of peppercorns. Their very wars were started in a rose garden, and end in the victory of a king who took for his badge the red and white roses united as a symbol of peace. And Henry III, in love with the Fair Rosamond, built at Woodstock, so they tell, a secret bower to hide her from his jealous wife. But James I of Scotland is the perfect hero of garden romance. Imprisoned in Windsor Castle, he looked out of his window, and as we could have told him he would from the stories, he saw a lovely girl walking in the garden. Very properly he fell in love at first sight, married her, and wrote his own book about it, the *Kingis Quair*. He describes the garden where she walked, and it is the very pattern of romance, "a garden fair, fast by the Towris wall," with "an arbour green" and shady alleys and thick screening hedges. "The sharpe grene sweet Juniper" is everywhere, and the song "now soft, now loud" of the "little sweet nightingale."

Even to their harsh religion, with its morbid delight in suffering and its threats of hell-fire, the Middle Ages bring a flowery charm. There are bills for flowers in the church accounts, "a dozen and a half rose garlands on St. Barnebe's day," woodruff garlands, rose garlands again and again, and holly and ivy for the church at Christmas. The priests in the churches wore crowns of flowers, and when a Bishop of Saint Paul's was installed, so Stow tells us, both he and the canons wore garlands of red roses. Even heaven is no cold abstract Utopia, but Paradise Garden, where Mary and Jesus delight in the birds and flowers; the Virgin is a garden lady and Christ the blossom she bears:

> *Of a rose a lovely rose*
> *And of a rose I syng a song.*

> *The rose ys called Mary hevyn quene*
> *Of her bosum a blossum sprong.*

"O fragrant rose," they call her, "O lilly chaste," "Lady flour of alle thing."

She walks with Joseph through a homely orchard which we delight in as much as they:

> *Joseph and Mary walked*
> *Thro' an orchard good,*
> *There was cherries and berries*
> *So red as any blood.*

> *Joseph and Mary walked*
> *Thro' an orchard green,*
> *There was berries and cherries*
> *As thick as might be seen.*

The mediæval Books of Hours and religious manuscripts are bordered with flowers, bright and gilded, painted with such care and love that they bloom still, fresh and lively on the centuries-old pages. Butterflies hover, caterpillars crawl, dragonflies shimmer among the coloured flowers which dwarf and encircle the sad little pictures of angels rejoicing with sorrowful faces. Christ on his cross is scarcely larger than a figure on a postage stamp, and if we gathered the Provence roses which twine so lavishly round the wide margins of his tiny picture, they would make a full sweet bunch to blot out all his miseries.

In one of the mediæval carols we still sing, Jesus comes to Mary in a garden.

> *He came al so still*
> *There his mother was,*
> *As dew in April*
> *That falleth on the grass.*
>
> *He came al so still*
> *To his mother's bour,*
> *As dew in April*
> *That falleth on the flour.*
>
> *He came al so still*
> *There his mother lay,*
> *As dew in April*
> *That falleth on the spray.*

It is a languid sweetness which has little to do with religion. We need only read "lady" instead of "mother" to change it to a perfect love-song, and Benjamin Britten's setting exactly catches the feeling of delicate preoccupied excitement. In the romances there is often the same curious mixture of religious and amorous. There is the story of the nun who turned prostitute while Mary took her place in the convent so that she should not be found out. There is the beautiful heroine of the Yonec story who was shut up by her jealous husband, and growing bored with her own company, prayed devoutly to God. She would like a young man to amuse her, she said. Other women had lovers who came secretly to keep them company, and she would like one, too. "May the Almighty God grant me my heart's desire." Her prayer was answered—for certainly she prayed from the heart— and a falcon flew in at the window, changed to the "fairest knight she had looked upon in all her life," and after a certain amount of somewhat unconvincing hesitation they "were happy together."

I dare say it is naïve of me to find this a rather unexpected manifestation of divine mercy. For the Middle Ages were the Ages of Faith—they told me so in my school history lessons, but I never knew that this was what they meant.

Indeed, to our age of conscientious virtue the whole code of chivalry looks rather dubious:

> *A dieu mon âme,*
> *Mon cœur aux dames,*
> *Ma vie au roi,*
> *L'honneur pour moi.*

If that is your rule of life, then it becomes a virtue "to love for the love of love," and for wives who are fair, adultery is a duty "for the love of lovely knights": "You are so lovely a knight, so sweet in speech and so courteous, that verily it is my lady's duty to set her love upon you."

In the thirteenth century the rules for this *Amour Courtois* were laid down in a code called *"Fleur d'Amour, ou Art d'aimer honnestement."* It is an aristocratic and courtly pastime sung by the troubadours to nobles and their ladies, people with little work to do and a great deal of very restricted leisure. There are not, after all, so many ways of passing the time if you are shut up in a castle for the winter without books or wireless, with no friends to call on, no town on one's doorstep with people and concerts and cinemas and theatres. They must manage as best they could, and the knights sat on cushions listening to tales of love, tethered by a silken thread to their chosen lady. It is a strange far-off picture, faintly lit by candlelight against the background of winter darkness.

> *Though love and all his pleasures are but toys,*
> *They shorten tedious nights.*

We feel they, too, would have sighed and quoted Campion if they had known he would write it three centuries later.

And in their summer gardens they made secret trysting-places for "clasp and kisses, many words and long silences," and the little boys, instead of Indians and Cowboys, played at knights jousting for their lady's favour, with plantain spikes for lances.

If the gardens of the Dark Ages belong to priests, the gardens of the Middle Ages belong just as surely to women. It is they

Drawing by Crispin de Passe.

who care for the flowers when their lords are away, fighting or hunting or off on Crusades. It is the woman who keeps the key of the garden door, who invites her *bel ami* in at her pleasure, who makes of the garden her private drawing-room. The small flowery fancies are women's fancies—the garlands and wreaths of flowers—and the figure who presides in the garden pictures is always a woman—Mary in Paradise Garden, or the strange lovely lady of the romances.

There have never been heroines, not even the dryads in their trees, more perfectly in harmony with their setting than the lady of mediæval romances in her garden. So delicious is her flowery enclosure, so hidden and intimate, that the leafy arbour becomes "a privy pleying place" and the very grass seems an invitation to love:

> On whiche men myght his lemman ley
> As on a fetherbed to pley.

And here, where it is always May, in this small secret room of a garden, waits the fascinating lady. "Her hair was golden, with little love-locks; her eyes blue and laughing; her face most dainty to see, with lips more vermeil than ever was rose or cherry in the time of summer heat; her breasts so firm that they showed beneath her vesture like two rounded nuts; so frail was she about the girdle that your two hands could have spanned her, and the daisies that she broke with her feet in passing showed altogether black against her instep and her flesh, so white was the fair young maiden."

She belongs so perfectly to her garden that it seems impossible to describe her without flowers. She is always delicately beautiful and very young, and the clothes she wears are more becoming than any women's clothes since. So successful they must have been that for centuries the basic fashion is almost the same, as if it had reached perfection and had no need to change.

Made of soft wool, her dress fits closely over her arms and shoulders, moulds her breasts and waist, then flows in swinging folds to her feet. We have gathered our full skirts since into a waistband, like a curtain; we have made them of stiff silks and shapeless taffetas, so that we have cut off our living bodies half-way and made of our skirts a lifeless shape much like a tea-cosy. But hers flowed out from the close bodice to the swaying hem in a sinuous smooth line like the petals of a lily, was made of softly hanging wool which swung as she moved, moulding the shape of her body beneath.

And as if to forestall all criticism of looking too Pre-Raphaelite, altogether too "greenery-yallery," she would bind up her long hair out of sight, and in the fifteenth century which is the best of all, would deck her head with extraordinary arrangements of formal and fantastic sophistication. No headdresses (for really one cannot call them hats) have ever been more extravagantly strange, with their sweeping curves of wings, their curious planes and angles, their horns and pointed spires and floating veils. (The horns in particular horrified good church-

L. *Delphinium*
G. *Pied d'alonette*
A. *Larkes Heele*
G. *Ritter sporen*

Drawing by Crispin de Passe.

men, who attacked them furiously and constantly forbade them, but such interest from high places naturally only made them more intriguingly fashionable.) Utterly impractical, audaciously exhibitionist, they are the perfect crowning foil for the simple dresses beneath. They are at their best in the first half of the fifteenth century in the paintings of the Flemish artists: Roger Van der Weyden, Campin, Petrus Christus, Dirk Bouts, Memling, David. In the pictures Saint Ursula and her eleven thousand virgins are martyred in the most becoming hats one could possibly imagine, and we cannot help feeling that an expedition, however virtuous, which set out in such *very* attractive clothes was bound to get into trouble sooner or later.

These headdresses are compositions of great abstract beauty, with their clear delicate lines and complicated surfaces of starched linen (sometimes in the pictures we can see the folds in the cloth like the folds in a matador's cloak). Yet their abstraction curiously enhances the faces which they frame. The sweep of eyebrows, the curve of a mouth, the slant of eyes—these are subtly emphasized and made significant by the airy wings, the wrapped coif. The faces of mediæval portraits owe much of their fascination to these outrageous follies of headdresses. But they fascinate us, too, because they never show emotion of any kind. They neither smile nor sigh, scorn nor tremble; we can make no contact with them as we can with faces which weep or laugh as we do. They look at us simply, grave and withdrawn in a world where we can never reach them nor even guess at what they might be thinking. There are pictures of saints who lie peacefully in green fields and gaze mildly into the cloudless blue sky. They seem quite unconscious that someone has cut a careful hole in their abdomen, and that their entrails are being wound out on a wheel as neatly as a sailor's rope. The martyrs are as unmoved as the audience who stand quietly by and watch.

We can see, in these great airy follies of hats sprouting from the heads of the fifteenth century, how poets could describe a woman as a graceful stem to carry the flower of her head. And these slender childlike women are of a beauty which haunted men's minds for hundreds of years, to reach its final expression in the grave young figures of Memling's triptychs. In this fifteenth-century religious painter the ideal woman of the Middle Ages finds her perfect portrayer. Her elusive beauty is caught surely and delicately before she changes, through the curious figures of Cranach and Mabuse, to the more conventional Venus of the Renaissance. She is straight and slender, her arms are still "the arms long and small" of the romances, as if they were made only for embraces; her long supple waist and small high breasts have the same curious unconscious sophistication.

Memling was a libertine, they say, which is perhaps why the women of his religious paintings are so unexpectedly seductive. Quiet and gentle they stand about his pictures; they lay their white hands together in prayer and gaze gravely at the Madonna. But it is a precarious innocence. If they only glanced sideways, if their faces showed only the faintest shadow of a conscious smile, they would be transformed at once from saints to sinners. They are the equivalent in paint of the Yonec heroine praying for a lover, of the amorous suggestiveness of "He came al so still." Composed to gentle meditation, their faces still have the provocative eyes, the full lower lip, the sleepy, almost sulky look of those whose thoughts are of love.

And if we set this lovely lady, not in a green meadow to worship Mary, but in a green garden to wait for her lover, she has the fascination of a depraved and innocent child. There she waits, in countless romances, sighing for love, trembling and pale with passion, her eyes dark flowers in the pallor of her face, twisting garlands of roses for her hair which hangs now loose and heavy, singing her *chansons de malmariée* in a soft siren voice, unlocking the garden door to draw in her lover.

She is a strange figure, this heroine of the romances, an invention of men's desires, shadowy and without personality, so that all the heroines are one, and we can no more remember them separate and distinct than we can the encounters of Spenser's *Faerie Queene*. She is made for love, "for love for love's sake," living for no other end, dissolving like a dream if we try to imagine her with any other occupation. She is the creation of the troubadours, a luxurious exotic for a sophisticated aristocracy, and Marie de France is her most famous singer. Marie's *Lays* are a retelling of the tales of Brittany, for the lady belongs to the Celtic stories with their doubtful morals and their preoccupation with love. The legends of the Anglo-Saxons are warlike and rowdy; they delight in fighting and hard drinking, and the beauty of women is simply a form of wealth to boast about. Their stories would never need Mr. Bowdler to edit them, as the Celtic stories so often would.

The Crusades of the twelfth century sent men travelling East as never before, and, returning home, the Crusaders brought back strange Eastern luxuries for their gardens: tents made of tapestry, pools for bathing, oleanders, pomegranates. They brought, too, Eastern romances of a curious languid sweetness, like the scent of hot-house flowers, and with heroines of the same exquisite family as the Celtic ladies. "It was in the time of summer heat, in the month of May, when the days are warm long and clear, and the nights coy and serene. Nicolette lay one night sleepless on her bed, and watched the moon shine brightly through the window, and listened to the nightingale plain in the garden." She climbs from her tower and escapes to the woods, where she builds a hut of leaves and flowers, and in this sweet shelter Aucassin finds her.

Floris and Blancheflour—their very names belong to the garden—is another Eastern story of two children whose loves seem to us somewhat precocious, for they began their preoccupation at seven, and by twelve were ready to die of passion. Blancheflour is sold as a slave to the Emir of Babylon (Thameral the English translator charmingly calls him) and is followed by Floris, who is carried into the harem hidden in a basket—not of washing, as we might expect in any other age, but a basket of flowers. There is a fairy-tale scene where Thameral chooses his wife in a garden, the fairest garden in all the world, where the merry birds sing, and about the garden goes a wall whose worst stone is of crystal. Beside a well stands the Tree of Love, always in bloom, and under this are brought the "maidenes clene" for the Emir's choice. The blossoms fall from the tree, and the maiden on whom the first flower falls is taken to be queen.

And if there any maiden is
That Thameral holds of much price,

Gardens of the Middle Ages

The flower shall on her be sent
Through art and through enchantement.

Of course.

But even to these flowery romances the English poet gives a
quiet melancholy. "Now be they bothe dead," he says quite simply at the end of his story, and brings us back from this fairy-tale
of love-sick children to his real world where people die and are
forgotten, so that suddenly the story fades to a faint and far-off
fancy against the dark background of eternity. Now be they
bothe dead.

Although he died in 1400, we think of Chaucer as the first of
the moderns for many reasons, and one of them is that he can
smile. Men have always laughed—as children laugh, even when
they are frightened—at farce or knockabout or misadventure.
And so they laugh in the Middle Ages. But they do not smile. We
smile from a balanced state, from security and self-confidence,
we smile affectionately at the ridiculous. And so does Chaucer.
He is the first great writer to rise above the crippling philosophy
of the Middle Ages, to feel confident enough for detachment, to
look round at his companions and find them delightful and ridiculous. For although he wrote the *Romaunt de la Rose*, and the
"Knight's Tale," which is a mediæval garden romance in the true
tradition, he wrote also the "Merchant's Tale" of May and January, which is a deliberate travesty of all flowery romanticism.
To elude her blind and jealous husband, the young lady meets
her lover in a pear tree. And as if this were not already an awkward enough rendezvous for passionate lovers, her husband re-
covers his sight at the most inconvenient moment possible. However, May is no dreamy mediæval heroine to swoon away in
trouble, but a quick-witted young woman perfectly able to turn
even so unpromising a situation to her own virtuous advantage.
Chaucer's Squyer is as exquisite a figure as Aucassin with his
yellow curls, but he is also ridiculous:

With lokkes crulle, as they were leyd in presse . . .

Embrouded was he, as it were a mede
Al ful of fresshe floures, whyte and rede.

So hote he lovede, that by nightertale
He sleep no more than dooth a nightingale.

Aucassin, for his sweet love, accepts the doom of hell, knowing he must suffer for his pleasure—"All the days of the world would his soul be in Hell for it." But Chaucer's Wife of Bath cares not a straw for such gloomy threats, although she might well have feared an even worse fate than poor faithful Aucassin, with her five husbands "withouten other companye." But she is triumphantly unrepentant. Christ, she says,

Spak to hem that wolde live parfitly;
And lordinges, by your leve, that am not I.

No indeed she is not.

Blessed be god that I have wedded fyve!
Welcome the sixte, whan that ever he shal.

And when men have once said boo to the goose of hell-fire, they are very near the end of the Middle Ages. They are ready to smile. Their gardens will no longer be a fortified retreat from a frightening world, but a place to play in, to amuse themselves like children. And when in the fanciful Tudor gardens they have played long enough to feel self-confident, then at last, for the first time, in the great gardens of the seventeenth century, they will look out over the garden wall.

CHAPTER FOUR

ENCLOSED

FANTASTIC

GARDENS OF

TUDOR

ENGLAND

W E MUST NEVER SAY TO OURSELVES THAT the Middle Ages ended in 1485, so Professor Trevelyan warns us. Well, I had never thought they did, nor at any other particular time for that matter, but since he suggests it, I do see what a very useful date it is, after all. The Wars of the Roses are over and England entering a period of peace under a strong monarchy, the world is suddenly exhilaratingly large and full of promise, the Renaissance has begun in Italy, the printing-press has been invented, and the English language has developed to a stage where we can still read it without difficulty.

Until now great men had felt safer if they lived in castles, or at least in houses which could be strongly defended, and their gardens with them. But when Leland travelled through England under Henry VIII, he found the castles everywhere empty and ruinous and their gardens vanished. For they were uncomfortable places to live in, cramped and cold and dark, and as the climate of peace became more settled, men began to build themselves pleasant manor houses whose only defence was against robbers, and to lay out gardens whose worst enemies were small boys stealing apples, as I dare say small boys always will. ("We was scrumping," they said, when I caught two smudgy culprits scrambling through the orchard hedge with their pockets bulging. "We was scrumping apples in your garden," they said with disarming candour, and I let them keep their apples in exchange for my new word.)

After the Dissolution the monasteries, too, were often converted to dwelling-houses, and new gardens laid out among the old orchards and fishponds. For the English seem born with a natural love of gardening, and the four million people of Tudor England gardened with the same enthusiasm that they gave to everything else. "Every Gentleman flieth into the country," said one observer, to hunt and hawk and plan his garden, and pleasure-grounds were laid out everywhere, even, so Stow tells us, in the middle of London. By the seventeenth century "there is scarce a cottage in most of the Southern parts of England, but has its proportionable garden, so great a delight do most of men take in it."

But what were these gardens like, which everyone delighted in, from cottager to king? The superb gardens of Renaissance Italy still survive for our admiration, but the gardens of Renaissance England can scarcely be called even country cousins of this splendour: they belong to quite a different family.

The English mind has seldom shared the great Classical conceptions. They do not suit us. When we do understand them, it is because we are Europeans and not because we are Englishmen. We seldom feel, even with our finest, even with Gothic architecture or with Shakespeare, that we are in the mainstream of European culture. We cannot trace the current backwards and forwards from Shakespeare, as we can from a much lesser European writer like Montaigne. As Milton says, Shakespeare warbles his "native wood-notes wild." He is "fancy's child." For we have had a power of vital and extravagant fantasy which has produced perhaps the greatest poetry in the world. And it is a strangely universal vitality which keeps alive for more than three centuries King Lear and Falstaff, Herrick's light fancies and Donne's intellectual conceits.

But in lesser minds this gift of poetic fantasy becomes merely curious and quaint. Uncontrolled by the fashions of Europe, the lesser productions of England are often merely odd. The strange clothes we designed for ourselves during the isolation of the Napoleonic Wars looked elaborately absurd set beside the French fashions when the wars were over, beside the authentic simple elegance of the Empire nightdresses. And Tudor architects, on the fringe of Europe, lavished their care on extravagantly fanciful chimneys, charmingly barbarous absurdities to build at the same time as the villas of Renaissance Italy. Henry VIII's Nonesuch Palace was well named, a fantastic top-heavy folly smothered with decoration. I can never more than half believe it existed, even though there are detailed pictures and it was Queen Elizabeth's favourite palace. It is like the Palace of Sheen, a name so remote and romantic that the solid bricks fade like a mirage in my mind, no more real than a painted gauze curtain, as elusive as the sheen on silk.

Nor were the insides of these mansions any less curious. Aubrey describes the strange house Bacon built at Verulam, with its awkward central chimney, its trick doors of mirror-glass, and its extraordinary decoration of pagan gods and local curiosities. Aubrey is the perfect person to describe it. "There was a very large picture: thus," he says. "In the middle on a Rock in the Sea stands King James in armour; on his right hand stands (but whether or no on a Rock I have forgott) King Henry IV of France in armour." We can only hope that poor King Henry did have his rocky pedestal, and we are not surprised that the whole place was "sold to two Carpenters for fower hundred poundes" and that they pulled it down "for the sale of the Materials."

The houses which have survived are almost equally fantastic and insular. Their planning is mostly haphazard, with no controlling logical conception; they are rich in curious incidental felicities, and, at its best, their decoration is wildly fanciful. At Audley End in Horace Walpole's time there was still a "Fish room, a spacious brave chamber, the ceiling and deep frieze adorned with sea monsters swimming. There are many grotesque friezes," and they, just as much as Shakespeare, are our native wood-notes wild. The delightful grotesque carvings at houses like Knole and Audley End owe very little to Europe, with their strange figures, clothed in leaves perhaps, or tailed like a mermaid, and topped by round English faces copied from the village cricket team or the bar parlour. They are a charming mixture of country bumpkin and poetic fantasy, of Bottom and the fairies.

The Tradescants were a family of explorers and collectors well known in the early seventeenth century. "That industrious searcher after rarities" one writer calls the father, and the rarities they "Preserved at South-Lambeth neer London" were the beginning of the Ashmolean Collection now at Oxford. But although they lived in the dawn of modern science, their curiosity was completely unscientific. They had no interest in classification or ordered knowledge, but collected their rarities from a simple childish delight in the quaint and curious; they were attracted by the fantastic as a jackdaw by bright scraps.

Divers sorts of Egges from Turkie: one given for a Dragons egge.

Easter Egges of the Patriarchs of Jerusalem.

Two feathers of the Phoenix tayle.

The claw of the bird Rock: who, as Authors report, is able to trusse an Elephant.

Penguin, which never flies for want of wings.

Dodar, it is not able to flie being so big.

Cat-a-mountaine.

Elephants head and tayle only.

Divers things cut on Plum-stones.

A Little Box with the 12 Apostles in it.

Jupiter Io and Mercury wrought in Tent-stitch.

A nest of fifty-two wooden cups turned within each other as thin as paper.

A Cherry-stone, upon one side S. Geo: and the Dragon perfectly cut: and on the other side eighty-eight Emperors faces.

Stories cut in paper by some of the Emperors.

*Flea chains of silver and gold, with three hundred links a
  piece and yet but an inch long.*
Old Parre's picture.

(I wonder how many of these treasures still survive in the
Ashmolean. I would like to see Old Parre's picture.)

Then follows a Variety of Rarities which, even by John Tradescant's catholic standards, are difficult to classify.

Instrument which the Indians found at Sun-rising.
*A piece of the Stone of Sarrigo-Castle where Hellen of
  Greece was born.*
A Brazen-ball to warme the Nunnes hands.
A glasse-horne for annointing kings.
*Blood that rained on the Isle of Wight, attested by Sir Jo:
  Oglander.*
Anne of Bullens silke knit-gloves.
Henry 8 hawking-glove, hawks-hood, dogs-collar.
A hat-band made of the sting-ray.
Black Indian girdles made of Wampam peek, the best sort.
Turkish tooth-brush.
An umbrella.
*A steel-glasse that shows a long face on one side and a broad
  on the other.*
*A copper-Letter-case an inch long, taken in the Isle of Ree
  with a Letter in it, which was swallowed by a Woman,
  and found.*

Although we should never suspect it from such a collection,
Tudor scholarship was already keenly aware of the intellectual
Renaissance of Europe. But the arts followed much more slowly,
for the intellect can travel fast along the paths of knowledge and
reason, but popular taste is a plant which must have time to grow
and develop. As our twentieth-century æsthetic has scarcely yet
caught up with the Industrial Revolution, so Tudor fashions in
the arts (as in gardens and popular museums) followed English
styles so vigorous that they flourished untroubled by foreign influences. Fashions from abroad were either ignored, or taken

confidently and transformed by our native traditions into "something rich and strange" and very different from the original.

The Renaissance style is still an alien in Tudor England, something rare and foreign, a curiosity brought home by travellers. Here and there we find it on tombs in country churches: a figure of the dead hero reclines on his coffin, beruffed and bearded and knickerbockered, his homely-looking head propped up awk-

Drawing by Crispin de Passe.

wardly on his elbow, and the whole thing painted, as likely as not, in bright fair-ground colours. And over this very Tudor figure is an elegant white arch decorated in delicate low-relief with the emblems of the Italian Renaissance, and flanked by classical pillars homesick for the sun. The style is no more at home yet than spring bulbs made to flower at Christmas, and we must wait for the proper season before it will grow and flourish.

So the gardens of Tudor England borrowed ideas from Italy, but like the country tombs, they speak Italian with an unmistakable and unrepentant English accent. Their atmosphere is all their own.

The villas of the Italian Renaissance were set in formal garden arrangements of great beauty. The grounds were designed as magnificent backgrounds for magnificent palaces, and man in such surroundings may talk with the gods if he wishes. But Tudor gardens are gardens which children would make for themselves to play in.

One of the charms of children, as of other young animals, is their irresponsible gaiety. They will always play with us. No matter how unlikely the time—wakened in the night perhaps, or crying and in trouble—they will always laugh if we persuade them. They have no feeling for the fitness of the occasion; they would never say, as we do: "This is no time for laughing," since for them it is always time. They carry no steadying burden of worry or responsibility, but are playful by a natural and unthinking effervescence of high spirits.

So, too, Tudor gardens are delightfully free of any suggestion that life is earnest. They are irresponsibly gay, and as Ophelia turned her sorrows "to favour and to prettiness," so they turn everything to fun. They delighted kings and commoners alike well into the seventeenth century, when European fashions at last broke through our deep hawthorn hedges, and the great gardens of England become European gardens.

> *The King was in the counting-house, counting out his*
> *   money,*
> *The Queen was in the parlour eating bread and honey,*
> *The maid was in the garden. . . .*

Behind the Tudor portraits there are gardens straight from nursery rhyme, where we half expect to see the Knave of Hearts running off with his mother's baking, leaping over the beds of flowers and silver bells and cockle-shells and pretty maids all in a row. They are gardens full of quaint fancies and naïve enthusiasms, of tricks and odd surprises, gay and charming and absurd. As for a controlling plan for the grounds as a whole, there was none. They were laid out, says Thomas Hill, according to the "spirit of the Gardener . . . lead by hops and skips, turnings and windings of his braine . . . by the pleasing of his eye according to his best fantasie." They cared nothing at all for the intellectual discipline of gardens which were designed as settings for fine architecture. For Tudor gardens were not intended as settings for anything at all but pleasure and the growing of flowers. In any case, they were too small to be a background for the house. The famous garden at Kenilworth was only one acre, and although some of the larger ones covered much more ground than this, it was only by an addition of various small gardens; there was no sense of space or planning. Their ideal garden was laid out so that, passing from one enclosure to the next, it was as if the visitor "had been magically transplanted into a new Garden." They liked their view, as Sir Henry Wotton says, "rather in a delightful confusion than with any plain distinction of the pieces."

Certainly the boundary was definite enough—there must be a firm fence or hedge for the "Verge and Girdle of your Garden" —but as for "the inward proportions and shapes of the Quarters Beds Bankes Mounts and such like," says Surflet, "they are to be divided by Alleys, Hedges, Borders, Rayles, Pillars and such like." And such like, and such like—you do not create the Boboli Gardens so. He is clearly bored by intellectual problems of layout and planning; each man, he says, must follow his own fancy, and the gardener's part is to help him follow it, no matter how wayward.

Even the monarchs of these gardens have, at this distance, the same fairy-tale quality of exuberant fantasy—Elizabeth with her orange wig and her learning, Gloriana of the cryptic virginity and the adoration of her poets; and Henry VIII with his six wives, so that I was always astonished, seeing pictures of him when I was a child, that his beard was not a bright and beautiful cornflower blue. But there are many surprises about Henry VIII.

"Bluff King Hal" they have called him, but he wrote charming verse: "Pastime with Good Company" we still sing, or at least listen to. And if that seems a subject so happily in character that it might almost do for his epitaph, he wrote on other, more unlikely themes: tender lyrics of the faithful heart.

> *As the holy grouth greene*
> *And never chaungyth hew,*
> *So I am, ever hath bene*
> *Unto my lady trew.*
>
> *Now unto my lady*
> *Promys to her I make,*
> *From all other only*
> *To her I me betake.*

I wonder which of his ladies he wrote it for.

Then he was a "pretty" figure, so an onlooker said, watching him play tennis at Hampton Court—"He is extremely fond of tennis, at which game it is the prettiest thing in the world to see him play, his fair skin glowing through a shirt of finest texture." I suppose he must once have been a fine young man, but portraits are not of the fine young men, they are of the famous, and the famous are mostly old, or at least middle-aged.

Henry VIII delighted in his gardens at Hampton Court, a pleasure-ground laid out by Wolsey but later seized and enlarged by the envious King, who became so fatherly-proud of his creation that when visitors arrived, even though it was "near night," he would take them round in the dusk to admire it. There were flower gardens lavishly planted with violets and primroses, gilly-flowers and mints, with sweet Williams at threepence per hundred and roses at fourpence. There was the Pond Garden, kept filled by "labourers ladyng of water out of ye Temmes to fyll the pondes in the night tymes," and still much the same now as it was when the King courted Ann Boleyn there. There was another garden, long since lost, which was full of brass sundials, twenty of them, each set on its own little mound, and costing four shillings and fourpence "the piece." And there was a Mount, so popular in Tudor gardens, a little artificial hill climbed by a path edged with hawthorn bushes which circled the slope "like turnings of cokil-shells." On the top there was a summer-house, and judging by the bills for glazing the windows, it must have been quite large enough for a family to live in.

A mount.

But Henry's chief delight was in his "beestes"—fantastic carved figures of animals painted and gilt, which sat on the tops of posts set everywhere about the gardens. Often they held banners, and it must all have been very cheerful and very ridiculous. In one small garden alone there were "11 harts, 13 lions, 16 greyhounds, 10 hinds, 17 dragons, 9 bulls, 13 antelopes, 15 griffins, 19 leberdes, 11 yallys, 9 rams and the lion on top of the mount."

Nor was that all, for the flower beds and paths were edged with railings, and these, like the barber's poles which the beasts sat on, were painted in vivid stripes of green and white, the royal colours. There are bills for painting them by the hundred yards, for there were railings everywhere.

Indeed, the Tudor gardens were as full of ornaments as they were of flowers. Besides an astonishing number of sundials, there were "columns and pyramids of wood," pilasters and obelisks and spheres and "white bears, all of stone upon their curious bases." In the garden of the Temple there were the twelve signs of the Zodiac set on posts, and at Whitehall, besides thirty-four heraldic beasts holding the royal arms, there was a "Parnassus Mount, on top of which was the Pegasus, a golden horse with wings, and divers statues, one of black marble representing the river Thames. It far surpasses the Parnassus Mount near Florence."

There was a great deal, too, of what the gardeners call "carpenters work"—trellises for edging the beds, and frames for training climbing plants over arbours, and the little nooks to sit in which they called "roosting-places." "RUSTIC SEATS AND PURGLERS" I once saw written on a notice at the gate of a country carpenter, and our pergolas are what the Tudor gardeners called galleries or covered ways. The summer-houses, too, were made by carpenters or even builders. "Banketting-houses" they called them, for they often held banquets there. At Whitehall there was a noble one with a roof painted like clouds, where Elizabeth received "certaine Ambassadors out of France." These summer-houses are a fine opportunity for interesting chimneys, so Bacon thinks, but Stow disapproves of such extravagant frivolities— "like Midsummer pageants," he says, "with towers and turrets and chimney-tops, not so much for use of profit as for show and pleasure, betraying the vanity of men's minds; much unlike to the disposition of the ancient citizens."

There were even houses in trees, as children build them, platforms which they climbed to with a ladder, and I wonder what Stow's ancient citizens would have said of the one Parkinson describes so admiringly: "I have seen a tall or great-bodied Lime tree, bare without boughes for eight foote high, and then the branches were spread round about so orderly, as if it were done by art, and brought to compasse that middle Arbour: And from those boughes the body was bare againe for eight or nine foote (wherein might be placed halfe an hundred men at the least), and then another rowe of branches to encompasse a third Arbour, with stayres, made for the purpose, to this and that underneath it: upon the boughes were laid boards to tread upon, which was the goodliest spectacle mine eyes ever beheld for one tree to carry." When the children were little, there was scarcely a tree in the garden without its few boards balanced rakishly across any likely-looking branches. It gave the garden a quite astonishing air of squalor. "Our tree-houses" the children used to call them, and, like John Parkinson, they would have appreciated the lime tree as connoisseurs admiring a veritable palace of tree architecture.

No one could help being fond of Parkinson, despite the dreadful Latin pun on his own name which he uses for the title of his book: *Paradisi in Sole Paradisus Terrestris*—Parkinson's Earthly Paradise. "A Garden of all sorts of pleasant flowers which our English ayre will permitt to be noursed up"—so he explains his title, and there is a frontispiece of the kindly bearded author holding a single flower as he might hold some precious treasure, a flower called sweet John, as we recognize from the illustrations later on, and we wonder whether he arranged the delicate and affectionate compliment himself. For he understands his own gentle nature and can praise it without offence. "Such men doe as it were send forth a pleasing savour of sweet instructions, not only to that time wherein they live and are fresh, but being drye, withered and dead, cease not in all after ages to doe as much or more."

The Tudor gardens, full as they were of ornaments, still had room for flowers and plants, though these were seldom left to grow naturally, but were trained into every kind of fanciful and amusing shape. Flowers were planted in patterns of "rampande lyons and dragons of marvaylous likenesse," bushes were cut into topiary figures of men and animals and geometric curiosities, and even hedges "made battlement-wise, in sundrie formes, according to invention, or carrying the proportions of Pyllasters, Flowers, shapes of Beasts, Birds, Creeping things, Shippes, Trees and such like."

Designs for Topiary.

Above all, the Tudor gardeners loved their knots—square beds laid out in symmetrical designs of interlacing hedges of box or lavender or thrift or other low shrubby plants. Of all the Tudor fancies, this seems most intimately their own, a kind of garden doodling, like the patterns children cut out from folded paper squares, like the fretwork designs on the walls and parapets of Tudor houses.

In these playful gardens there were parts laid out especially for play: bowling-alleys and tennis courts, archery butts and cockpits, and mazes, which they called labyrinths—"a delectable labyrinth," says one writer, and delighted to bewilder his friend therein "till he cannot recover himself without your help." There were pools for bathing and for fish, and if you made your Mount near the boundary of your garden, says Markham, you could fish over the hedge in your own moat: a delightful picture which somehow reminds us of Tristram Shandy's Uncle Toby.

They took, too, a particular delight in what they call "water surprises"—fountains spurting water in every unlikely and curious way, or suddenly drenching the unsuspecting audience; for this, they considered, was the most entrancing of practical jokes. At Whitehall there was a much-admired fountain worked by a gardener from a distance, and one of the few improvements Elizabeth made at Hampton Court was "a splendid high and massy fountain, with a water-work by which you can, if you like, make the water play upon the ladies and others who are standing by and give them a thorough wetting." If we can get used to such crudities in people who appreciated equally the most delicate lyric poetry, then we are less shocked by Shakespeare's dreadful clowns.

What we notice, reading about the Tudor gardens or looking at the illustrations, is how alive they are, how full not only of flowers and ornaments but of active human beings. They are best considered as an extension of the house, where people lived their lives in the open air as we never have done since. In the pictures they are doing all kinds of things which we have never since included in our garden scenes—playing cards, eating their dinner, paddling, making love, fishing, wandering in mazes, chasing each other, rolling on the ground, playing with monkeys, splashing each other with water from the ponds. Anything, in fact, but sitting still, which is what we do now. They held Revels in their gardens, Masques and Pageants, and Elizabeth received ambassadors in her garden at Whitehall, where I dare say her Latin was just as overwhelming among the gillyflowers and roses as anywhere else. We can understand the writer who describes the busy garden scene at Kenilworth: "the people, the fruit trees, the plants, the herbs, the flowers, the birds flittering, the fountain streaming, the fish swimming, all in such delectable variety, at one moment in one place."

Bacon in his essay "On Gardens" shows a feeling for space which is ahead of his time. Let the main plot, he says, "be not too busy or full of work"; but except for its size (and Bacon is very much a gardener on paper, where it is as easy to write 20 acres as 2), his garden proper is very little different from any other garden of his period. He describes a plan for a prince's pleasure-ground which he obviously considers is free from silly fancies; he despises knots and topiary work as fit only for children, but the decorations he suggests instead are even more fanciful and charm-ing. The main hedge, he says, is to be trained on "carpenter's work" into a series of arches, and above each arch a little turret to hold a cage of birds, and between them "some other little figure with broad plates of coloured glass for the sun to play upon." The bathing-pool, too, is to be "finely-paved and with images, and embellished with coloured glass."

At Hampton Court, in the old gardens which lie between the Orangery and the river, we can still feel what privilege has meant in England, how the English character has expressed itself when money and power were unlimited. The proud princes of Italy built proud palaces and gardens to match; the ceremonious court of France was perfectly expressed in the glories of Ver-sailles. But these have no real place in England. We are awkward at ceremony, embarrassed at display. The ambitious mansions of our eighteenth-century England are cold and theatrical and os-tentatious. For all their splendours, they have a curious air of the *nouveau riche:* we feel they were built, not as a fitting back-ground for a magnificent way of life, but only as a magnificent way of keeping up with the Joneses. As Dr. Johnson said of one

of them, "It would do excellently for a town-hall. The large
room with pillars would do for the Judges to sit in at the Assizes;
the circular room for a jury-chamber; and the rooms above" (the
bedrooms, which were skimped, as not being part of the fine
show to dazzle visitors) "the rooms above for prisoners."

Their owners, we cannot help suspecting, seldom used the
ceremonious front door, but strode cheerfully out at the back to
their dogs and horses in the stable yard, the only part of most of
these cold palaces with any atmosphere of life and affection.

The most famous shops of England have no imposing en-
trances, no fine windows, no lights or plate glass or thick carpets
or smart assistants. They are in back streets with only a modest
private-looking window, and nothing in it but a small plate
quietly announcing in old-fashioned type the name of a world-
famous tailor.

In England privilege is astonishingly discreet. Not a Lord
Mayor's coach driving through cheering crowds, but a closed
motor-car which slips through cleared streets almost unnoticed.
And the old gardens of Hampton Court are like the tailors' shops
and the closed car. Their privilege is in privacy and a complete
disregard of any impression they may make. As the pleasure-
grounds of a powerful king, they are a marvel of understatement.
But because they are an unforced and natural expression of something inherently English, they are still alive, even though they are
stripped now of their Tudor fancies of beasts and rails and sundials, unsuitably planted with the wrong trees and flowers, and
misnamed the Dutch Garden. They still have an authentic air, as
the seventeenth-century formal gardens have not—the great
parterre and the long canal which are only empty and desolate,
like the clothes we never wear because we do not feel at ease in
them, they do not suit us.

But these were the pleasure-grounds of princes. What of the
humbler gardens of ordinary people? For Stow talks constantly
of "fair garden plots" and "gardens of pleasure," and in Tudor
times more people were interested in gardening than ever before.
Reading the books of Instructions for Gentlemen, we realize that

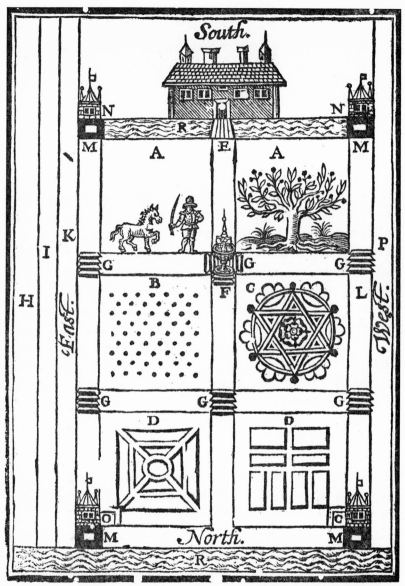

A Tudor plan for a garden. A. *All these squares must be set with Trees, the Garden and other Ornaments must stand in spaces betwixt the Trees, and in the borders and fences.* B. *Trees twenty yards asunder.* C. *Garden Knots.* D. *Kitching Garden.* E. *Bridge.* F. *Conduit.* G. *Staires.* H. *Walks set with great wood thick.* I. *Walks set with great wood round about your Orchard.* K. *The Out-fence.* L. *The Out-fence set with stone fruit.* M. *Mount. To force Earth for a Mount or such like, set it round with quick, and lay boughes of Trees strangely intermingled, the tops inward, with the Earth in the middle.* N. *Still house.* O. *Good standing for Bees, if you have an house.* P. *If the River run by your door, and under your Mount, it will be pleasant.*

there was no great difference between any of their gardens. The carved beasts and marble "inventions" of the wealthy were replaced in humbler gardens by clipped trees; instead of banketting-houses there were green arbours roofed with vines and walled with roses; but they are all unmistakably the gardens of Tudor England.

The first essential, as in mediæval gardens, was still the outside enclosure. This might be a moat or bank or fence, or a "Hedge of Quicksett verie thicke," or any combination of these all at once, for in the pictures there are often two or three layers one inside the other. Along the front of the house there was often a terrace which overlooked the whole enclosure, and round the garden there was generally a gallery or covered alley, formed either of pleached trees—yews or hornbeams or limes, like the modern one at Kensington Palace—or made by building a wooden scaffolding and covering it with "arch-hearbes"—vines or roses, "jacimine honeysocke or Ladies' Bower," which was a clematis. These walks were sometimes planted with scented herbs for the pleasure of their fragrance when they were trodden on, and the galleries were often enlarged into little arbours or "shadowe houses," arbours, says Parkinson, "being both gracefull and necessary." These shadow-houses were carpeted with grass, and Surflet tells us how to make the turf grow close and fine. The ground must first "bee cleansed from all manner of stones and weeds, not so much as the roots left undestroyed, and afterwards the floore must be beaten and troden downe mightily; then after this, there must be cast great quantity and store of turfes of earth full of greene grasse, the bare earthie part of them being turned and laied upward, and afterward daunced upon with the feet, in such sort as that within a short time after, the grasse may begin to peepe up and put forth like small haires; and finally it is made the sporting green plot, for Ladies and Gentlewomen to recreate their spirits in, or a place whereinto they may withdraw themselves if they would be solitarie and out of sight." The ladies of the Middle Ages would certainly have felt at home there.

The garden inside the surrounding green tunnels of the gallery was divided into more or less regular "compartiments" ("every man will please his own fancie"), and these were separated by paths and enclosed by hedges or palings, or perhaps by "Lattise worke continued into arbours, or as it were" (for they can never resist a fanciful idea) "into small chappells or oratories and places to make a speech out of, that many standing about and below may heare." I wonder what sort of speeches they made from such green pulpits.

Each of these small enclosures was a separate little garden, beds of flowers in one, "like a peece of tapestry of many glorious colours," and herbs perhaps in another. Herbs included what we should now call vegetables, and though they were sometimes grown separately in a kitchen or summer garden, there was no strict division, though "your Garden flowers shall suffer some disgrace," one writer warns us, "if among them you intermingle Onions Parsnips etc." There were gardens, too, for strewing-herbs—plants to strew on the floor instead of carpets, to "turn up the house," as they called it. The common ones were the aromatic plants we still call herbs today, but for honoured guests roses and violets were scattered where they walked, and Queen Elizabeth's favourite strewing-herb was meadowsweet.

Fruit trees might be planted in another division, or perhaps a nosegay garden, "with hearbes and flowers used to make nosegaies and garlands of." They give lists of suitable flowers, but "Beares eares or French Cowslips" (auriculas) are best of all, says Parkinson; "their flowers being many set together upon a stalke doe seeme every one of them to be a Nosegay alone of itselfe . . . with a pretty sweete sent which doth adde an encrease of pleasure in those that make them an ornament for their wearing." For what the seventeenth century calls a "nosegaie" we should call a buttonhole.

I have a friend who once kept a buttonhole garden in his gallant courting days, a little plot behind the house where he went every morning to choose a flower for his coat. And his favourite was love-in-a-mist—not for the name, as we might suppose, but because it grew its own green, a neat fringe of feathery leaves arranged like a ruff around the flower: the perfect buttonhole. I have felt more warmly towards him ever since, for nothing is more endearing than the rather ridiculous enthusiasms of our friends.

Most popular of all was the knot garden, and the books are full of patterns for them, page after page of "knots so enknotted it cannot be expres't," for who could resist drawing such very easy illustrations? Although these tortuous designs of hedges sound to us elaborately ugly (and quite shockingly wasteful of labour), yet they must have had a curious formal charm, like embossed velvet.

The paths dividing the garden beds are made of gravel, or sand beaten firm, or "the powder of the sawing of marble," and they are very narrow: "You shall marke out your Beds and Floores" (flower beds) "and the Pathes running along betwixt them. . . . And you must observe, that you make your Floores of such widenesse as that you may stride and reach your armes from one side to another, to the end that such as are to weed them, or to rake them, may from out of the said little Pathes be able to reach unto the middest of the Bed, and not to tread with their feet upon that which is sowne. Wherefore, if your said little Pathes be two feet wide, it will be ynough: for to make them anie broader, is but waste and losse of ground."

We can see why Bacon wanted space, and what he means by gardens "too busy and full of work," for these gardens were without lawns: the whole space was covered with beds and paths and hedges. The flower beds were often raised above the paths and edged with boards or tiles or pebbles or shells, or even by rows of sheep bones, "which prettily grace out the ground." "In places beyond the seas," so Parkinson says, they even use the jawbones of animals arranged in rows, but this he considers "too grosse and base." I suppose if they had had bottles or jam jars they would have used those, too, as cottage gardeners do still. In the beds they grew all the old-fashioned flowers of the mediæval gardens: Primroses, Cowslips, Rose Campions, Batchelours Buttons (which were double campions), Stocks, Wall-flowers, Violets, Columbines, Snapdragons, Larkes-heeles (or spurres or toes), Roses, Pansies, Poppies, Double Daisies, Marigolds, French Marigolds "that have a strong heady sent," Pinks, Peonies, Hollihocks, Sweet Williams and Sweet Johns, and "Daffadown-dillies which flower timely and after Midsummer are scarcely seen. They are more for Ornament than use, so are Daisies."

The most cherished flower of all, the "pride of our English Gardens," the "Queene of delight and of flowers," was the Gilly-

Master Tuggie his Rose Gilloflower.

flower or Carnation, which was brought to England by the Flemish refugees under Henry VIII, and for more than a century was the "chiefest flower of account of all our English Gardens." It was called Gillyflower or July-flower because of its season of blooming, and stocks were called Stock Gillyflowers for the same reason. But why wallflowers were called Wall-Gillyflowers I have never been able to make out, unless it was because they resembled single stocks and people had already forgotten what Gillyflower meant. The country folk of Sussex still call sweet rocket June Gillies. In any case, the old carnations can never have been so attractive as the names the gardeners gave them. I wonder what the Grey Hulo looked like, or Ruffling Robin, or Master Bradshawes Dainty Lady. But Master Tuggie was the famous name—"Master Tuggie his Rose Gilloflower," writes Parkinson under one of his illustrations, and later on, with growing enthusiasm: "Master Tuggie his Princesse." I hoped to find somewhere,

The Crown Imperial.

as the crowning happiness, "Master Tuggie his Queene," but if he ever raised anything finer than his Princesse, Parkinson does not tell us about it.

Besides these old favourites, there were hundreds of new plants from the enlarging world, from the "Indies, Americans, Taprobane, Canary Isles and all parts of the world." "Out-landish Flowers" Parkinson calls them, and they made the new gardens so beautiful, says one enthusiastic writer, that, compared with them, "the ancient gardens were but dung-hills" and even the Gardens of the Hesperides, he boasts, if set beside ours, "I am persuaded that an equal judge would give the prize unto the garden of our days." Parkinson gives a list of the Outlandish Flowers which were most successful and popular, many of them blooming in early spring when our own flowers were scarce. Daffodils, Jacynthes (hyacinths), Saffron-flowers (crocuses), Lillies, Flower

L. *Viola mariana*
G. *Mariettes*
A. *Couentry bells*

Drawing by Crispin de Passe.

de luces (irises), Tulipas, Anemones, French Cowslips or Beares eares, and Fritillaries, which included the Crown Imperial—a flower, says Parkinson, which "for his stately beautifulness deserveth the first place in this our Garden of delight." How I longed to say beautifulness when I was a child—it was so much more vivid than beauty, which was a remote and abstract word, the kind of word people put on monuments to the unreal dead. But beautifulness was the actual texture of the living petals in your hand.

The Tudor gardeners grew runner beans, not to eat but for their scarlet flowers, using them as "arch-hearbes" to train on trellises as we do sweet peas. Nasturtiums, too, were grown as climbers; they were one of Parkinson's favourite flowers. Indian Cresses he calls them, or yellow Larkes heeles: "the whole flower hath a fine small sent, very pleasing, which being placed in the middle of some Carnations or Gilloflowers (for they are in flower at the same time) make a delicate Tussiemussie, as they call it, or Nosegay, both for sight and sent."

Rosemary was the favourite shrub, and among its many uses were the making of bridal wreaths and the seasoning of food. They grew it not only as a bush, but trained to cover walls, or cut into topiary figures, strewing the scented clippings on their floors. Many of the flowers we still grow today the Tudor gardeners knew by other names. Lilac was the Blew Pipe-tree, cyclamens were Sowebread, monkshood was the Blew Helmet Flower, the gladiolus was the Corneflagge, Canterbury bells were Coventry Bells, winter aconite was Winter Wolfesbane, cornflowers were Blew Bottles or Sions, honesty was the Sattinflower, and pansies were Love-in-Idleness. The snake's-head fritillary they called the Checkered Daffodill, or the Ginny-hen Flower because the markings on the petals reminded them of a Guinea fowl's feathers; and tomatoes, which they grew for decoration, they called Love Apples because they considered them an aphrodisiac. Which lends a new interest to a respectable domestic vegetable.

They grew, too, many flowers which were merely curious, like the little trefoils called Snailes or Barbary Buttons from their oddly twisted seed-pods, "pretty toyes for Gentlewomen," and all kinds of curious primroses and cowslips: Hose-in-Hose, Curled Cowslips or Gaskins, and one they called the Foolish Cowslip or Jack-an-Apes-on-Horse-backe, a name country people used, so Parkinson says, for anything they found strange or fantastic.

In their delight in all things curious and fanciful, the Tudor gardeners persuaded even their fruit and vegetables to grow into strange shapes. The fruit was put in moulds while it was young, and "so you may have cucumbers as long as a cane or as round as a sphere; or formed like a cross. You may have also apples in the form of pears or lemons. You may have also fruit in more accurate figures, of men, beasts, or birds, according as you make the moulds." This advice is from Bacon, of all people, who despised knot gardens as no better than the pastry patterns on the tops of tarts.

There were aviaries in the Tudor gardens, but they loved best the "infinite number of pretie small Birds" which came freely to keep them company, "the gentle Robin-red-breast and the silly Wren, with her distinct whistle (like a sweet Recorder)." But the "chief grace that adornes a garden" was "a broode of Nightingales [whose] strong delightsome voyce, out of a weake body, will beare you company night and day."

Peacocks they kept both for use and pleasure, for "the peacock is a bird of more beautified feathers than any other that is, he is quickly angry, but he is far off from taking good hold with his feet, he is goodly to behold, very good to eat, and serveth as a watch in the inner court, for that he spying strangers to come into the lodging he failleth not to cry out and advertise them of the house." Thomas Tusser, in his *Five Hundred Pointes of Good Husbandrie*, complains that peacocks scratch up the seedlings, but his eighteenth-century editor tells us in a footnote what we must do. If you find your peacock, he says, in any part of the garden where he is not wanted, "with a little sharp Cur that will bark, tease him bout as long as he can stand, at least till he takes his flight, and he will come no more there." I dare say not.

These Tudor gardens are not very different from the gardens of the Middle Ages, but only grown more confident. They are still small, still rigidly enclosed, still divided up into little compartments without any idea of planning the space as a whole. Like the mediæval gardens, they are not a setting for the house but an extension of it—rooms for outdoor living—and almost as crowded, with their flowers and bushes and ornaments and "artificial inventions," and with the cheerful people who came to enjoy it all, for the people are gay now as they seldom were before.

If the gardens are still only a development from the Middle Ages, so, too, is the science behind them. Men still believed that plants were a spontaneous generation of the earth, and that any soil would bring forth the flowers inherent in it without the need of sowing seeds; "the great Mother of all living Creatures, the Earth, is full of seed in her Bowels, and any stirring gives them heat of Sun, and being laid near day, they grow," says Lawson, who is a better writer than he is scientist. But it is a belief easy enough to understand in any gardener who clears his own beds of the "weeds which earth utters forth of its own accord."

Nor had the Tudor botanists any satisfactory system of classifying plants. They group them as they please, by the shape of their leaves, or chance resemblances of their flowers, from the kind of places where they are found or by their habit of growing. So that Parkinson puts periwinkle with clematis and passion flower (which he calls the Virginia Climer) because they all need support. Neither did these early gardeners know anything of the pollination of flowers, and the results we get by crossing they believed they could achieve by grafting, a procedure in which they had an astonishingly blind faith. Fruit trees grafted on holly, they thought, might bear in the winter, a rose grafted on broom would have yellow flowers, a peach on an almond would obligingly grow a nut for a kernel; and an apple on a colewort or cabbage, so someone reported from the Low Countries (where all kinds of marvels seem to have happened in those days), "will bear a great flaggy apple, and the kernal of which, if it be set, will be a colewort and not an apple."

They had many other curious theories, just as easily disproved, so one would think, by simple experiment: that garlic planted round a rose-tree would make the roses smell sweeter by drawing away the bitter juices of the earth; that "Basill ill-tended" changed to rosemary; that two plants could be crossed by binding their young shoots together. The beliefs they profess in the virtues of herbs are so extravagant that we cannot help wondering whether they ever tried them for themselves, and if so, why they were ever ill. They even supposed that plants carried the sign of that part of the body they were intended to cure—what they called the plant's Signature. "Nature, or rather the God of nature," says William Coles, who was a religious man, "having stamped on them legible characters to discover their uses"—a principle which would prescribe kidney beans for the kidneys.

Drawing by Crispin de Passe.

Writer after writer makes the most surprising claims, but to quote only my favourite Elizabethan warning against lettuces: "The plentifull and dayly eating of the Lettuce of married persons is very incommodious and noysome to them, in that it not only doth diminish the fruitfulness of children, but the children often borne do become idle foolish and peevish persons." This is a sad prospect for vegetarians, though perhaps they are safe if they do not marry. Nor are all their suggestions so unlikely. To

soothe fretful babies, says one herbalist, make an infusion of
white garden poppies and give them to drink. We wonder if the
tired parents ever tried their own opium, and whether the fretful
babies had curious dreams.

Bacon's *Naturall Historie* is an astonishing book, for, although
we often think of him as the first of the modern practical scientists, he seems to believe every superstition he hears; that oak
boughs planted will grow into wild vines, and the stumps of
beech trees into birches. "It is thought by some," he says, "that
the ends of low rainbows fall more upon one kind of earth than
another: as it may well be." And he tells us "the old tradition of
a maiden that was fed with napellus, which is counted the strong-
est poison of all vegetables, which with use did not hurt the maid,
but poisoned some that had carnal company with her."

Parkinson is more sceptical about such stories: "I know none
such to be true, nor to be of any more worth than an old Wives
Tale, both nature, reason, and experience, all contesting against
such an idle fancy, let men make what ostentation they please."
"They are but men and have their Errors," Lawson had said
philosophically, but, for so mild a man, Parkinson is unexpectedly
sweeping in his condemnation of all the traditional science of the
old gardeners: "Without all doubt and question I will assure you
that they are all but meere idle tales and fancies, without all reason or truth, or shadow of reason or truth."

Even Bacon is doubtful of the "fabulous narration, that in the
northern countries" (I wonder if he meant the Low Countries)
"there should be an herb that groweth in the likeness of a lamb,
and feedeth upon the grass, in such sort as it will bare the grass
round about." As he says, a very fabulous plant, but one we can
see for ourselves on the title page of Parkinson's *Paradisus*, a
grazing lamb which looks very awkward and unhappy on the
top of its stalk.

Bacon's own observations, however, are scarcely more convincing. Most trees, he says, have no flowers, and elm and box
have neither flowers nor fruits. Yet every country child knows
the elm's paper shillings. Flowers can be made double, he tells us,

"by often removing them into new earth," "fruit-trees watered with warm water will bear fruit without core or stone," and he suggests extraordinary experiments for changing one plant into another—the Transmutation of Species, as he calls it.

It is very difficult to understand the mind of anyone who says, as Bacon does, that the differences between plants and metals are chiefly three: (1) metals are more durable, (2) more solid, (3) are "wholly subterrany," while plants are half above ground. To us this is the reasoning of a child or a lunatic, yet Bacon's curiosity about the physical world was an interest which was soon to develop into the scholarly work of the Royal Society, the birthplace of modern science in England. Besides, we should all be grateful to Bacon for being the first gardener to realize the value of leaf-mould: "it were good to try whether leaves of trees swept together would not make a good compost; for there is nothing lost so much as leaves of trees." What a relief it is to find something else recommended besides Willow-earth, that John Innes Compost of the old gardeners which they tell us to use on every other page: "the fine earth or mould which is found in the hollow of old Willow-trees, rising from the root up almost to the middle of the Tree, at least so far as the tree is hollow, for than this, there is no earth or mould finer or richer." I dare say not, but it is hard to believe there ever could have been enough hollow willow trees for all the Willow-earth we should need if we followed the instructions of Tudor gardeners.

If in the seventeenth century we are near the end of mediæval superstition, we are also near the end of gardens in the mediæval tradition. For under the Puritans the great Tudor gardens were destroyed. Only Hampton Court was spared because Cromwell lived there, and Nonesuch by an accident survived to be given by Charles II to his mistress, who, like the Puritans, divided it up and sold it to speculators. Hampton Court, Nonesuch, Whitehall, Theobalds, Wimbledon—these famous gardens of the Tudors had continued with little change under the Stuart kings, who took the same delight in them as their more exuberant creators.

But the Puritans angrily resented such pleasure-grounds, both as signs of royal privilege and because they were laid out so whole-heartedly for enjoyment. They belonged to the "serene time of Peace [when] the people, both poore and rich, did looke cheer-fully." But now, says Aubrey sadly during the Commonwealth, "the Countenances of the people [are] all changed, melancholy, spightfull, as if bewitched."

Yet Englishmen are natural gardeners, and even the melancholy Puritan intolerance could not wholly suppress an inborn delight in gardens as places of pleasure. Ralph Austen was both a Puritan and a gardener, as many others must have been, but he was also a writer, and in his books we can see the uneasy compromise between his natural spirit and his adopted convictions. *The Spirituall Uses of an Orchard of Fruit-trees*, he calls one book in a pathetic attempt to reconcile his opposing enthusiasms, but, reading it, we skip the spiritual uses and pick out the gardening, which is very easy, since the two parts are printed in different type as if to emphasize his divided mind. He was a true gardener, and loved his trees for their beautiful Blossomes even more than their useful fruits—"the trees in their Gallantries," he calls them —and his most un-Puritan delight was "to stand upon a Mount in the midst of a fair large Orchard in the spring time, and to be-hold round about a multitude of several sorts of fruit-trees, full of beautiful Blossomes, different in their shapes and colours, ravishing the sence with their sweet Odours, and within a while, turned into faire and goodly fruits of divers Colours and Kinds; the Fruit-trees gorgeosly arrayed with green leaves, and various coloured fruits, as with so many precious Jewels and Pearls."

But like so much else which they secretly desired, the Puritans were driven to destroy the Tudor gardens, and under Cromwell, Parliamentary surveys were made of the confiscated royal pleasure-grounds. These are unconsciously pathetic, for they show so clearly the authors' delight in what they are describing. They are not cold, business-like accounts of so many acres with so many fruit trees and so much timber, but appreciative descriptions of "a fair banqueting-house" or "an elaborate bird-cage, a great or-

nament both to House and Garden," a "very fair and handsome
fountain" with falls which "make a pleasant noise," a "fair walk"
of elms and lime trees, the covered alleys of gravelled earth "very
well ordered," and "one might walk," they say wistfully, "two
myle in the walkes before he came to their ends." We forget that
these are the men who hired ignorant vandals "for half a Crown
per Day, to break the painted Glass-Windows [of churches]
which were formerly fine." We forget that the writers are describing what they intend to destroy. And so perhaps do they.

"It is strange that men should rather be quarrelling for a few
trifling opinions wherein they dissent, than to embrace one another for those many fundamental truths wherein they agree."
Yes. It is very strange. But the gentle light of reason could not
reach the dark and deformed spirits of the Puritan zealots. Their
strangely twisted consciences kept them from joining Thomas
Hill's gardener who "turned to the prosperities of his hearbes and
flowers for the delight and comfort of his wearied mind, which
he may by himselfe or in fellowship of his friends conceive, in
the delectable sightes and fragrant smells of the flowers, by walking up and downe and about the garden."

Yet Ralph Austen knew very well what he meant by such delights. For in a garden, said this Puritan who was too gentle for
his faith, "a man enjoys pleasant quietnesse and tranquillity of
mind, which is seldom attained by those that follow State Imployments." But it is a hesitant voice, too quiet and too reasonable
to reach the violent men in State Imployments. The surveys are
drawn up, the royal pleasure-grounds destroyed, and although
the Puritans will be forgotten like an illness we have recovered
from, and fresh gardens laid out for men's pleasure, they will no
longer be the enclosed fantastic gardens of the Tudors. Once,
says Aubrey, the gay music of the pipe and tabor was common
through all England, "the Peasants danced to it on Holy days,
with joy and merriment." But now, he says, with a regret which
is only partly for a lost antiquity, "the Drumme and Trumpet
have putt that peacable Musique to silence."

CHAPTER FIVE

EARLY
SEVENTEENTH
CENTURY
GARDEN
LITERATURE

IN THE KIND OF BEST PARLOUR WHERE THE
piano had a white lace cover and family photographs on the
top, there were always two books in the small collection locked
away in the glass-fronted cupboard: the Authorized Version of
the Bible and the Works of Shakespeare. These are the unquestioned classics of English literature, and they both belong to the
early seventeenth century.

I suppose everyone makes their own arbitrary divisions of the
arts into periods, and for me early seventeenth-century literature
is not a space of time bounded by dates, but a period of writing
defined by qualities of thought and style. It begins towards the
end of the sixteenth century and ends somewhere in the middle
of the seventeenth, but it overlaps the periods before and after
like the fingers of clasped hands. It is an age when our literature
far surpasses the other arts, as indeed it generally has done in
England, but never more magnificently than in this seventeenth
century of our greatest glories. And because the level of writing
is so high, even among lesser authors, it is the only time when
ordinary books on gardening may perhaps be fairly considered
as literature. The poetry of Marvell and Herrick, the essays of
Sir Thomas Browne, are garden writing which everyone knows
of, but even the forgotten writers of handbooks share the early

seventeenth-century gift of prose which is a delight to read. They write clearly and vividly, often with the suggestion of beauty which is the true poetry of prose; they encounter their world as a direct experience, and describe it in exact and evocative phrases. At their best, as in the writing of Surflet and Markham and Lawson, they express almost unconsciously the curious wit and the brooding sense of strangeness which are the especial fascination of the early seventeenth century.

In the arts there seem to be particular states of consciousness and sensibility which can be expressed in different mediums depending on the nature of the artist—poet, painter, musician. Generally this particular way of feeling the world and expressing it in art is evident in artists of the same period. It is not only their own personal awareness, but the style (or whatever we choose to call it) of their time. They are great because their own consciousness corresponds to the consciousness of their age, and therefore finds its perfect expression in the forms and styles of art which they must use. So that they vary, not in the *kind* of art they produce, but in its quality; they are not so much different from other artists of their time, as better or worse.

This conception of the spirit of the age, as I suppose we might call it, must always be a very personal judgment, and may have no meaning for someone else who finds in the same artists quite different qualities; who sees perhaps the individual more clearly than the period, as we all do with art which is near to us in time. But for me, who have great difficulty in remembering music, even a completely unknown piece by Beethoven is easy to place because he reminds me unmistakably of Wordsworth and Constable. If I am out of sympathy with the art which develops from them, I even feel that the rot sets in with all of them, as someone said of Beethoven. It is not, certainly, that they are equally great, or can be expressed in terms of each other, but that the values they are conscious of in the world, the kind of beauty to which they are naturally sensitive, is the same for each of them.

But I think this same sensibility in the different arts need not always correspond in time or place. There is a special quality in early seventeenth-century writing which we come to recognize as the peculiar essence of the period. It is a particular kind of beauty, intellectual, subtle, rarified, and with a strange deliberate distortion which is of the mind and not the senses, as if emotion had been most curiously translated through intellect into art. We

Drawing by Crispin de Passe.

find it almost nowhere else in English literature, and for me the music which corresponds to this early seventeenth-century writing is Bach's in the eighteenth century, and the painting is Piero della Francesca's in the fifteenth-century Italian Renaissance. The special kind of rare and vivid pleasure I feel in reading Milton's "Ode on the Morning of Christ's Nativity" is the same as the pleasure in listening to the Brandenburg concertos or looking at Piero's "Baptism of Christ."

Nor is this correspondence perhaps so very unlikely. The sensibility of the early Renaissance was born in Italy, and took perhaps a century and more of bad communications to travel as far north as England and penetrate our vigorous and insular fashions. And if we think of the seventeenth century instead of the sixteenth as the early Renaissance in England, then the classicism of the late seventeenth and eighteenth centuries follows as an echo of the Italian High Renaissance and our eighteenth-century architects go naturally to Palladio's sixteenth-century villas for inspiration.

If it is true that art generally expresses the character of its period more clearly than that of its particular author, it is certainly so in early seventeenth-century literature. Here we recognize the period unmistakably and only afterwards the author. Even Shakespeare, who transcends all rash generalizations, has more in common with other poets and playwrights of his day than we realize in our first dazzled delight. We recognize him (when we *do* recognize, for the scholars differ) not by any particular style, but by his excellence. For he has a hundred different styles, as he has a hundred different characters, and Shakespeare as an individual is inscrutably universal. What we do unmistakably recognize is the style of the early seventeenth century, the quality of the *period*, the way many men's minds worked at that time, the way they looked at things and expressed them in words, the kind of beauty which satisfied them. It is not simple, for their minds are strange and intensely poetic, their knowledge is a fruitful transition between mediæval superstition and modern ideas, they take pleasure in a curious wit of words and conceits, and for all their age of stormy passions, they have an intense brooding quietness, a sense of strangeness underlying the everyday world.

"Spirit" is a word of such vague meaning that we need to define it for ourselves if we are going to use it. We can say that it is a part of man's consciousness lying beyond his emotions and his intellect. These are specialized and limited activities of his mind which the spirit transcends, and it is when a man succeeds in conveying the experiences of his spirit that his art is valid. For the direct expression of emotion is not art, nor is the statement of intellectual conceptions—neither weeping nor the multiplication table—but the experience of the spirit in these activities is the material the artist works with.

Although this universally authentic region of the spirit is the realm where all great art belongs, there are various ways of reaching it. For much of the nineteenth century, for instance, it is through the emotions. They love or hate or are pitiful or angry, and though much of what they produce is no more than the out-pouring of their feelings, now and again they crystallize out the spiritual experience which will go on living long after their (or our) love or hatred is dead. Renoir, for example, painted women with desire—he tells us so in unequivocal terms. His nudes are soft and warm and delicious, they are a generous flowering from a rich and solid earth. But in his greatest pictures he paints not simply a woman he has desired, but the lovableness of all women. Our reactions are not of the senses but of the spirit, and we look at his finest nudes not with desire, but with a kind of pity. We are moved in the same way as we are moved by tales of generous or noble actions, by fine architecture or music or poetry.

The seventeenth century approached this realm of the spirit not through the emotions, but through the intellect. From a steady level of mental activity they suddenly take wing and soar to the higher air. Their problem is not to find solid rock in the swirl of their emotions, but to make their intellectual conceptions live, to feel them as vividly as we all feel hate or anger. So that where the nineteenth century degenerates into sentiment, the seventeenth century degenerates into pedantry. There are pages and pages which affect us only as an intellectual exercise, which we read with the same limited attention which the non-musical like myself bring to Bach's *Art of the Fugue*. We keep alert whatever faculty of our minds it is which responds to artistic excellence, but the pedestrian stretches between the high flights we let pass over us as a kind of technical chatter. So that, reading idly through the curious pedantry of the *Garden of Cyrus*, we are suddenly startled by a thunder of magnificence: "Providence hath arched and paved the great house of the world." Or "All things began in order, so shall they end, and so shall they begin again." Or "Darkness and light hold interchangeable dominions."

But before we consider the fine flowers of any garden, we need to know something of the soil they grow from, the ordinary prose style of the time. This is necessarily the medium of the writer, the stuff from which he must create his masterpieces. He may mould the language of the day, use it and make it his own, but still it is the raw material he starts with, and Shakespeare would not have written as he did at any other time than the early seventeenth century. We must forget, then, Sir Thomas Browne on gardens, and listen to the ordinary prose of the day simply giving instruction with no other thought than to make the meaning clear. Here are three passages from handbooks on gardening and other country occupations, for they are all set out together—husbandry, gardening, hunting and hawking, angling, cock-fighting, and the keeping of bees.

First an early account of smoking tobacco: "The inhabitants of Florida doe feed themselves a certaine space with the fume of this hearbe which they take at the mouth by meanes of certain small hornes . . . the truth whereof we gather by mariners comming daily from the Indies, which hanging about their neckes little pipes or hornes made of reeds or rushes, at the ends of which little hornes there are put and packt manie drie leaves of this plant, writhen together and broken. They put fire to this end of the pipe, drawing in with their breath at their mouth wide open, so much of this fume as possibly they can, and affirme thereupon that they find their hunger and thirst satisfied, their strength recovered, their spirits rejoyced and their braine drencht with a delightsome drunkennesse."

Then how to tell a mad dog: "The first sign to know is a melancholy separating himself from other Dogges, and walking up and down alone, oft casting up his head into the wind, and looking upward, his tayle at the setting on, rising upward, and the rest hanging down, his Mouth will foam and be full of slaver or white froth, as he runneth up and down he will hastily snatch at everything that he meeteth with, yet, but only give one snatch and away, his eyes will be red, and more fiery then other Doggs, and his breath will be strong and of a filthy savour."

Then a sentence on so-called "English flowers": "Those flowers that have been usually planted in former times in Gardens of this Kingdome, have by time and custome attained the name of English flowers, although the most of them were never naturall of this our Land, but brought in from other Countries at one time or other, by those that tooke pleasure in them where they first saw them."

The first thing we notice is how alive the writing is, how straightforward and decisive, how clearly the language says what it means to say. In fact, how excellent it will be for the discourses of the Royal Society when Charles II blesses it in 1660. And it has a vividness and immediacy which few scientific writers have achieved since:—"one snatch and away"—four very simple words, but anyone who has seen a dog in a fit will realize how exactly and economically they describe its restless maniacal activity.

This is almost the first common English prose which is sufficiently developed to express a complicated meaning clearly and simply. The passage on English flowers, for instance, the latest of the three and written in 1629, is a complex sentence of clauses and conjunctions, the meaning is involved and subtle, but it is set down with such an easy use of language that we read it as a simple statement of fact. Yet prose is a later development than poetry (which seems an odd contradiction, as if one should dance before walking), and this is the first time ordinary Englishmen have written their language easily enough to concentrate on what they want to say instead of how to say it.

In the sixteenth century, English was newly accepted as the official language of England, for since the Conquest the court had used French, and scholars Latin. But as a literary language

English prose in the sixteenth century was still in an awkward stage of growing up. As a development from the language of the people it was too racy and vernacular for quiet writing, while as used by scholars accustomed to Latin it was stilted by classical constructions alien to English ways of language. Then, too, modern English is almost without inflections; we use conjunctions and new arrangements of words to express the meaning which was once clear from the endings. But in the sixteenth century these new ways of expression were not clearly worked out; the conjunctions seem to us haphazard, and the meaning often doubtful. The quoted passage on tobacco is the earliest of the three, and we can see that there is still some uncertainty in how to connect the phrases logically.

But by the seventeenth century these growing-pains are mostly over, and a new literary prose emerges, confident and vigorous and clear. So, too, may be the writing of other periods, but the quality of early seventeenth-century literature is essentially poetic, and as at no other time, the prose-writers express this poetry supremely well. This, too, seems a curious contradiction, yet Traherne, writing of the same subject in verse and prose, produces only mediocre poetry, but superbly poetic prose: "You never enjoy the world aright till the Sea itself floweth in your veins, till you are clothed with the Heavens, and crowned with the Stars: and perceive yourself to be Sole Heir of the whole world." But in verse this is reduced to two lines from a mid-Victorian hymn:

> *Nor till* His *Works* my *Wealth became*
> *No Lov or Peace did me enflame.*

Sir Thomas Browne writes prose with the same poetic power, and Donne in his sermons, and so, too, in a faint echo, do the writers of handbooks.

It is difficult to define what we mean by poetry in prose, but we might say that it is the evocation of beauty beyond the actual theme (a too vague definition which could equally apply to good painting). It would be easy to quote page after page from the famous writers, but here is forgotten Gervase Markham on "the best season to Angle in":

"If the day be darke, close and lowering, or have a gentle whistling and playing upon the water, it is good to Angle in, and the Fish will bite with pleasure; Nay, if a fine mizling dew of Rain fall gently, without violence, they will then bite the faster: Also after Floods are gone away, and the Rivers are come within their own Banks, the first cleerness recovered and the water pure, then is it good to Angle."

Or frosts come, he says, "the aire being calme and quiet, and in faire nightes."

Or again, he tells of a fish called the Luce "which haunteth the broad and large Mears, which are miles in compasse, being deep and still, and ever lodgeth in the bottom thereof, amongst the Roots and Tufts of Sedge and Bulrushes, being quiet and least troubled." A most poetic fish, and worthy to haunt the waters of the silver lake with Milton's fair Sabrina. Piero della Francesca can paint a dog with the same suggestive poetry.

The writers of the early seventeenth century also have a particular gift for what we have since learnt to call *le mot juste:* for finding the one word which exactly expresses the particular essence of the experience they are describing. Milton, in lines we all learnt at school and scarcely thought about, stands on a little hill looking at the summer landscape. He sees the towers and battlements of a country house set among trees—'Bosom'd high in tufted trees," he says, and we must all have seen quite often the kind of scene he describes in his short line. But let us forget for a moment his two triumphantly right words and try to find them for ourselves: forget *bosom'd* and *tufted.*

It is summer, we know from the rest of the poem. In a landscape with trees the house stands out head and shoulders high, as a bather stands in water. But how to get it into a single word? *Breast-high* perhaps? But breast will not do. It is too firm and active a word, with its associations of breasting the waves. This is soft and leafy summer, the house stands serenely among its garden trees, not breasting waves of encroaching forest. The trees are not enemies, the tree-tops are soft, bosomy, vaguely rounded. There it is: *bosom*—"bosom'd high"—the gentle but luxurious English summer scene, the height and shape of the trees against the house, the peaceful setting, all in a word.

But now for the trees themselves. He might have said *summer* trees, or *leafy* trees, or a dozen other obvious adjectives of two syllables to fit the metre. But Milton is a great poet and adjectives must be felt. So now for the trees. As a setting for the house they may be vaguely bosomy, but in themselves they are strong living structures. Under the leaves are hard twigs and firm branches. For all their soft outline, each leaf is attached accurately to the tree, they are growing. But the word? *Branching* trees perhaps? No—that would do for winter, but not summer with the branches hidden. *Billowing* trees? No. It gives no feel of their growing structure. Perhaps some word suggesting a fountain? It is very difficult. Let us sit on our hill and look at the view again.

It is like an aerial photograph of woodland, a survey of jungle seen from above. And what was it the trees reminded us of when we saw the photograph in the newspaper? Of paint-brushes. Of hundreds and hundreds of paint-brushes with their bristles in the air. Now, to describe paint-brushes is easy: they are *tufted*. And there is our word: "tufted trees." The leaves are loose and soft like the tops of the brushes, but firmly attached beneath to a strong upright trunk. *Tufted*—the softness, the firmness, the feeling of growing.

"Bosom'd high in tufted trees"—it is an earned and permanent pleasure, for we often have to earn our pleasures in the seventeenth century. Which is not to suggest for a moment that this is how Milton wrote his poem, but only that it is the kind of effort we must make to understand it. It is no use sitting back and letting the words flow vaguely over us, as we can with so much modern verse, or nineteenth-century music, or the painted ceilings of the eighteenth-century mansions. Being a great poet, Milton probably perceived with the intense poetic concentration which strikes out at once the right evocative word, as Shakespeare, they said, never stopped to blot out a line of his thousands of lines crammed with *mots justes*. Indeed, Shakespeare scarcely can have done much blotting out to write such an enormous amount in one lifetime. But we, being no poets of any kind, must work hard to follow them.

This struggle to find the right word or phrase is not so much a search as an intense effort of concentration, a deliberate attempt to escape our own identity, to feel the scene as a direct contact with something outside ourselves: to experience it, not as it stimulates our own reactions, but as it exists in itself. And although this is nonsense, and a human being can never feel how a tree exists, nor a house, yet we can try to experience them directly through our senses, without the quite irrelevant interpretation into our own life and personality. We can concentrate on the impression which comes to us from the house and the tree, and not on the associations which we supply from ourselves. We try, that is, to isolate the quality of the scene which is authentic, which is not a personal interpretation only valid for ourselves but an essential part of the scene itself and therefore valid for everyone who looks at it, as is all great art.

We look at dew on grass, for instance, as Surflet did, and are half conscious of some particular experience we would like to define exactly. The morning is damp and chilly, but that is our own reaction, it has nothing to do with the dew. The dew is clear, it sparkles, but that is not what we noticed this particular morning. It is something to do with the shape of the drops, their close tight outline, and even more to do with the way they are arranged like beads on the tips and edges of the leaves.

Now is the moment for the final effort. We must pass beyond our personal reactions of freshness and coolness, all our vague poetical associations. We must ignore all qualities of the dew which do not directly lead to this particular experience. By a trance-like concentration we must isolate the exact impression of the dew-drop on the tip of a grass-blade like a bird on a twig. There. The dew-drop *perches* like a bird—"doth pearche unto the grasse," says Richard Surflet, a Practitioner in Physicke who translated the *Countrey Farme,* and how delighted he (or his

French original) must have been to find his word, a tiny treasure of experience securely caught. And he did better than Andrew Marvell, who only got as far as the dew "scarce touching where it lyes."

There are single words from the seventeenth century which everyone remembers—the liquefaction of silk, the tempestuous petticoat, feathered rain, a cold quicksilver sweat, the poor crooked scythe, and many more. The gardening books, too, are full of such felicities: the arched petals of irises, the cornered twigs of broom, the furrowed stone of a peach, the branch-songs of birds, the purr of the springing partridge, the hawk which weeds the wood of pheasants, the nets of spiders, the curious architecture of bees, the soft mossiness of their bodies, the swarms which come forth mustering and knit together. On every page there are phrases as evocative as the phrases of poetry, vivid metaphors expressed in a single word.

Another quality of early seventeenth-century writers which we only realize by comparison with other periods, is that they write about themselves without self-consciousness. They write to make their meaning clear, not to express their own personality, and although to the reader the personality of the early seventeenth century is more alive than any other period, it is because their view of the world is so intensely their own and because they have expressed it so vividly, not because they intended to write about themselves. Even when they describe their own emotions, as they often do, they are the universal emotions of all men—joy, melancholy, repentance, love, delight in beauty, grief that youth passes—not the emotions of their individual lives and personal moods. The world they describe is outside themselves, however strongly it may be coloured by their own peculiar vision. And for our introspective age it gives their writing great force and authenticity. Writers who look inward describe a world which is valid for themselves, but only incidentally so for other people. If Milton's *bosom'd* had described his relations with his wives, and not the shape and texture of summer trees, it would be of no particular interest to anyone but his biographer. For if we are interested in the lives of human beings, artists are unlikely to be very rewarding subjects. Poets and painters are preoccupied with poetry and painting, not with living. They are unique as artists, not as human beings.

The seventeenth century constantly enlarges our vision of the world, as lesser writers only occasionally do. Our age could not produce Shakespeare for the parlour bookshelf, nor the Authorized Version of the Bible, whose translators, as if by a deliberate effort of inspiration, transcended their own identities and let the subject speak through them for itself, simply, magnificently, and timelessly. This preoccupation with their subject leads to a different kind of unselfconsciousness in the garden writers. In the great it is part of their universal quality, but in these lesser people it shows as a most endearing unawareness of the impression they may make on the reader. It is Pepys's greatest charm, that and his unfailing *joie de vivre*. For he has no idea at all of being funny (indeed, he is almost completely without any sense of humour) when he tells us how his midnight singing delighted the neighbours: "It being a very fine moonshine, my wife and Mercer come into the garden, and my business being done, we sang till about twelve at night, with mighty pleasure to ourselves and neighbours by their casements opening."

He has no more suspicion of seeming absurd than George Herbert, who wishes to be an orange tree to praise God more busily:

> *Oh that I were an Orange-tree,*
> *That busie plant!*
> *Then should I ever laden be,*
> *And never want*
> *Some fruit for him that dressed me.*

It is simply that they are untroubled by our exaggerated dread of looking silly. Ridicule is not an enemy it has ever occurred to them to fear or even notice. So Pepys tells us happily about his new clothes: "Up, and this day put on my close-kneed coloured suit, which, with new stockings of the colour, with belt, and new gilt-handled sword, is very handsome." Of course we feel the same in our own new clothes, but once grown beyond child-hood, we are too self-conscious, too anxious to seem sophisti-cated. We would never begin our diary for the year as Pepys does: "Myself in a most handsome and thriving condition." But he is not boasting; it is rather a kind of innocence, which we have lost. He is equally frank about the house where he was "most prince-like lodged, with so much respect and honour, that I was at a loss how to behave myself."

So Surflet, telling us how to trim our trees into topiary balls, says we must take extra trouble to cut them neatly on the outside hedge where people see them—"You must cut them for the sight of the Countrey, as round as ever you can." And Evelyn, after an exhausting list of varieties of fruit trees, tells us that he only put them in to make a show, and there are no more than five worth growing—"Now of all these Fruite-trees which I have named for pomp and variety, the very best are those under named, almost all the others hardly worth the Curiosity." And "this is a noble ex-periment," says Bacon, that Machiavellian figure of the *Essays*, describing how he made seeds grow more quickly in a hot-bed, "but there doth not occur to me, at this present, any use thereof for profit; except it should be for sowing of peas, which have their price very much increased by the early coming." And "All to bed," says Pepys, "without prayers, it being washing-day to-morrow."

But these writers are not childish because they write inno-cently. They are men at peace with themselves and the world, so that they feel no need to be on their guard, and care not at all if they seem sometimes absurd. Indeed, in the seventeenth century they may not have seemed absurd at all, for their carefully com-posed title pages are an especial pleasure: "A Way to Get Wealth . . . gathered for the Benefit of Great Brittain . . . a Work very necessary and useful for Gentlemen . . . Gathered to-gether for the general Good and Profit of the Common-wealth, by exact and assured Experience."

As people, the seventeenth-century writers are so delightful that, above all others we have met, we would wish to keep them as our friends. "To the Friendly Reader" they address their books, and that is exactly what I am; not a Dear Reader or a Courteous Reader or an Ingenious Reader, as they will call me later on, but a Friendly Reader, happy to be in their company and sorry always to leave them. If we wished to convert an unbeliever to Christianity, we might well send him to read the seventeenth-century religious writers: Herbert's *Temple*, Jeremy Taylor's *Holy Living*, Browne's *Religio Medici*, Traherne's *Centuries of Meditations*. They are such charming people, they are so lovingly concerned for our soul's happiness, that one might well turn Christian simply for fear of hurting their feelings. Certainly they would not convince our intelligence with their unquestioning acceptance of miracles, but they are so gentle, so good, above all so happy, that we feel the Christian belief must have some intrinsic virtue for human beings beyond its doubtful value as truth. But then we remember that they believed in a savagely vindictive hell, and that Sir Thomas Browne, who was proud of his tolerance, caused women to be burned as witches. It is safer, after all, to share their harmless delight in gardens, and their charm is just as vivid.

"The most pleasant and delectable thing for recreation is our Flower Garden, to behold out at a window faire and comely Proportions, handsome and pleasant Arbors, and, as it were, Closets, delightfull borders of Lavender, Rosemarie, Boxe and other such like: to heare the ravishing musicke of an infinite number of pretie small Birds, which continually, day and night, doe chatter and chant their proper and naturall branch-songs upong the Hedges and Trees of the garden: and to smell so sweet a Nosegay so neere at hand: seeing that this so fragrant a smell cannot but refresh the Lord of the Farme exceedingly, when going out of his bed-chamber in the morning after the Sunne-rise, and whiles as yet the cleare and pearle-like dew doth pearche unto the grasse, he giveth himselfe to heare the melodious musicke of the Bees, besides the Borders and continued Rowes of fragrant hearbes, the sight and view whereof cannot but give great contentment unto the beholder."

They have such enthusiasm, such curious and enquiring minds, they ride their hobby-horses with such zest. It is a pleasure simply to read a list of the titles of their books:

A most excellent and Perfecte Homish Apothecarye
The Gardener's Labyrinth, a discourse of the Gardener's life
A perfite platforme of a Hoppe Garden
Joyfull Newes out of the newe-founde worlde
The Garden of Health
The Jewell House of Art and Nature
The Fruiterer's Secrets
The Perfect Use of Silk-Wormes and their benefit
An Olde Thrift newly revived
The Inrichment of the Weald of Kent
A Way to get Wealthe
A Discovery of Infinite Treasure, hidden since the Worlds beginning
Cornucopia, a miscellaneum of lucriferous and most fructiferous Experiments
The English Vineyard Vindicated
England's Happiness Increased, or a sure and easie remedy against all succeeding Dear Years. By a plantation of the roots called Potatoes

We want to sit down and read them all at once. For what could promise more pleasure than the *Joyfull Newes?* or more tempt our curiosity than the *Discovery of Infinite Treasure?* And then to have all our troubles cured by potatoes!

Much of the information in the old gardening books is repeated from one to the next, for the authors borrow from each other in an easy way which seems very shocking to our anxiously individualistic age. These early writers cared dearly for their subject, but very little for the fame of authorship. Sometimes their books are anonymous, and often signed only with initials H. F. or W. S. or Master W. L. No one seemed to mind if you used sections of someone else's book to make your own; there was no question of plagiarism. Existing writing was a common fund of material for all to use and do with as they pleased, recent writing just as much as the Classics, and there seem to have been very few dogs in seventeenth-century mangers. A good story is told and retold so often in one book after another that we cease to care who first thought of it. It belongs to whoever can tell it most vividly or use it most aptly. No one, after all, calls Shakespeare a plagiarist for taking his plots from Boccaccio, nor Racine for using the stories of Greece and Rome, though instructions for catching moles in a garden are not perhaps exactly comparable.

Of all the plagues which infest a garden, moles for me are the greatest annoyance, and in each book I turn hopefully to headings like "Offences of Moles. The Cure," hoping to find some forgotten easy way of ridding the garden of "this harmefull blind beast which turns up Garden-grounds to the great griefe and paine of the carefull Gardener." "More molehills, more ground," one writer tells me, but it is doubtful comfort, and I prefer my ground flat. The books offer a fine variety of "Cures," like burning brimstone at their holes, or "perrofin," putting onions or garlic in their runs, catching a weasel and training it to hunt them, or inviting boys to play football on any grass where moles are known to be, so that they are driven away by the thumping of so many feet. But, as for that, I would rather have my moles than the footballers. The remedy I like best of all is the "easie practice" of using a live female mole as bait to attract the others. It is a popular remedy (at least on paper), so that, reading the different versions, we become connoisseurs of the story.

"Take a live one in March, when they are a-bucking, and put the same into a verie deepe and hollow bason at night after Sunne set: burie the said bason in the earth up to the brims, so that the Moules may easily tumble into it, when they heare the captive crie in the night time: for all such as shall heare her (and this kind of cattell is of a verie light hearing) comming neere to their food, they will into the bason one after another: and by how many moe goe in, by so much will they make the greater noyse, not being able to get out againe because the bason within is smooth sleeke and slipperie." That is Surflet's version, and I think he should be given the story (though I am not sure he ought to call the mole's lady-love his "food") if only because he says brazenly that he has seen dozens together taken in this way.

But Thomas Hill, whose *Gardener's Labyrinth* appeared in 1577, is his close rival as a story-teller, and he has no equal for his remedy against frogs, which keep him awake at night with their croaking. "The Frogges which in the summer nightes are wont to bee disquieters to the husbandmen wearied through their daily labour, by chyrping and loude noyse making. Let the Husbandman set on some banck a Lanthorne lighted, or on some tree so hang a light that by the brightnesse of the same light, it may so shine upon them, as if it were the sunne, which will cause them to leave their chirping and loude noyse making." They must have had very impressionable frogs in the sixteenth century, and snakes, too, for the cure of serpents is to burn old shoes, whose smoke will not only drive away all snakes from the garden, but also bring up those which men have swallowed through sleeping carelessly with their mouth open. "By making a smoke with olde shooes burned, the serpents incontinent speed away, nore those onely flie out of the garden ground, but such as are entered into men dead sleepe in the Sommer, in sleeping open mouthed in the field, do like come forth with the said smoke."

Sometimes we are tempted to suspect that he is as amused as we are: "Barley boiled in wine and sprinkled abroad doth defend the seeds from the injurie of birds. Those being starke drunke, he" (the gardener) "willeth then to hang up by the legges, on a long rodde sticked in the earth, to the terror and fearing away of all other birds comming to the place."

But I suppose he meant it as serious advice, for it is easy to believe all sorts of extravagances of a Thomas Hill who, finding his first book a popular success, grew dissatisfied with so homely a name, and for his next book swelled Thomas Hill to Didymus

Mountain. If the world had neglected him, would he have shrunk to Tom Molehill, I wonder?

Nor was he any more credulous than Bacon, whom we think of as the father of experimental science because he died of a cold caught on Highgate Hill while he experimented with preserving a dead chicken in snow. The proverb *"Africa semper aliquid monstri parit"* (Africa is always bringing forth something monstrous), he says, "cometh for that the fountains of waters there being rare, divers sorts of beasts come from several parts to drink: and so being refreshed, fall to couple, and many times with several kinds."

The gardening books commonly include accounts of other country pleasures and occupations, and anyone with a taste for pornography might well try the seventeenth-century books on hawking—an irreproachable interest to which not even the most squeamish censor could object. Yet they have a subtly sexual intensity, these accounts of taming the beautiful fierce creatures who are trapped and tethered and sold to men for their pleasure.

The master has power of life and death over his captive hawk, but what he desires is the dominance of his will over her rebellious spirit, and that he must work for. So the strange wild creature is disciplined by darkness and captivity, by hunger and habit, sometimes by force, but chiefly by a most determined patience. Until at last, with her fierce spirit unbroken, the wild bird becomes utterly subservient to the man.

For the books speak constantly of "the man"—seldom the master or the falconer, but quite simply the man, just as the hawk is always "she."

"All Hawks generally are manned after one manner—by watching and keeping them from sleep, by a continuall carrying them upon your fist, and by a most familiar stroaking and playing with them, with the wing of a dead foul, or such like, and by often gazing and looking them in the face, with a loving and gentle countenance, and so making them acquainted with the man."

"The onely maine poynt," says Bert, is "to have his hawke in love with him," and the man must blame himself if "instead of gaining her love by fair Allurements he hath converted it into Hatred Abhorrency and Disdainful Coyness." For even if she is proud and coy, you must not "disoblige her with unkindnesse,"

Hawking.

but give her "all the content and satisfaction imaginable," even though at first you "get no more from her than what you extort by force." (I wonder if Shakespeare thought of manning hawks when he wrote *The Taming of the Shrew*.) You must never neglect your hawk and so "tempt her to play the wanton," but "attend her pleasure with patience" until, says Bert, "she be farre in love with my voyce" and "so familiarly made as that she is well pleased with my loving dealing with her, and will attend my comming in to her, not fearing anything so I be by her: so would I have her wholly to relye upon mee, and be confident that when I come unto her shee shall have her desire satisfied."

At night hawks become curiously docile, and by candlelight the falconer may do as he will with her, unsealing her eyes, putting the hated hood on and off, fondling her head and wings. But this is a candlelight courtship, and in the morning she may well be as wild and coy as ever.

This fine temperamental creature must be treated with the greatest circumspection to keep her goodwill. If she is angered by any accident, her keeper must not let her catch his eye, lest she should blame her discomfort upon him and dislike him for it. "If she be so angry as that she stare thee in the face upon any such accidentall occasion, or sodaine thought of her present bondage, owne it not, see it not, and by all means possible carry thine eye from looking upon her, for that will worke her more dislike towards thee."

It is a delightfully ridiculous picture of the man afraid to meet his hawk's eye, like Gerard de Nerval, who bought in Cairo a slave girl for his pleasure, but she soon became so completely mistress of her situation that even to set out on a journey he hesitated to wake her if she happened to be asleep. "The slave was in a bad temper," he says, and like the falconer he has no remedy but to avoid her eye.

For whatever reason we read these books, they are a pleasure for their fine English and their vivid background of country life. *Country Contentments* Markham calls his volume, or the *Husbandmans Recreations. Containing the Wholesome Experience, in which any ought to Recreate himself, after the toyl of more Serious Business. Newly Corrected, Enlarged, and adorned with many Excellent Additions, as may appear by the Mark.* And the Mark follows—a plump and very rustic-looking hand, with one finger pointing, and the drawing cut off firmly at the wrist by what I think is meant to be a lace cuff, but which looks more like a paper pie-frill. And sure enough, every so far through the book this busy hand interrupts us, pointing firmly from the margin to some Excellent Addition.

But though the hand is somewhat unconvincing, the Contentments are authentic enough. The consciousness of life in the country is so intimate, the writing so vivid and direct, that we can almost smell the background of the green English country-side.

When your hawk is ready, Markham is going to tell us, choose a fine day, take her to a stream, and encourage her to bathe. Those are the bare instructions as a townsman might give them, but Markham is a countryman. "You shall spy out a fair day when the weather and aire is most temperate, and carry your hawk to some fair, little, shallow, sandy, running brook (or Run-dle) where the water is quiet and still, and where your hawk may stand up to the mid thigh therein, and having prickt her down, and made her fast hard by the verdge thereof, you shall take off her hood, and go a little way from her and see whether she will bathe therein; but if you find her fearful of the water, you shall with a little stick paddle in the water a while before her, and then depart from her again, and let her then bathe therein as long as she pleaseth." He might have said "on a fine day take your hawk to a stream and let her bathe," but instead he has given us an intimate scene of a country gentleman's life. He is conscious of the weather, watching the clouds perhaps the night before to tell whether the morning will be fair or wild, going over in his mind the different streams of the countryside, remembering their sandy beds and the slope of their banks and whether the water runs swift or slow. Then in the warm morning he sets out alone with his hawk, very gently lest he alarm her, and tethers her in the shallow stream, so that her hooked feet are covered as they grasp the yielding sand. Then he goes away a little distance to watch, the hawk wary at first, the man curious and intent, and all around this strange preoccupied pair lies mile after mile of green country, and in the warm stillness the birds singing one beyond the other until their calls blur in a distant haze of high sweet sound.

And if the hawk still hesitates, the man goes quietly back and paddles the water gently with a little stick, so that the bird is fas-cinated by the glittering drops, and stirred by some dim instinct of her wild kind, bathes herself therein, and "this bathing giveth a hawk courage, boldnesse and great appetite."

Early seventeenth-century literature has a peculiar quality for which we have no exact word, and, for want of one, we call wit. But it is a very different quality from our present-day wit; ours is worldly, often malicious, intelligent rather than intellectual, amusing, and quite without poetry. It is the wit of Dryden, Pope, and Horace Walpole. But the wit of the seventeenth century is not concerned with amusing us or making clever epigrams; its aim is to give us pleasure of a very particular kind. It is the creation of a peculiar beauty by means of curious intellectual conceptions. At its best it is a form of poetry, but it need not be limited to words: Bach's music and Piero della Francesca's painting, for me, are witty in the same way as Milton's early poetry or the strained conceits of Donne. It is a very conscious distortion, often of things already beautiful, to create a rarer, more particular, more intellectual beauty. Milton ends his "Ode on the Morning of Christ's Nativity" with a sudden picture of the angels filling the stable where the child lies. A magnificent glory, we might think, but this is how Milton describes it:

> *And all about the Courtly Stable,*
> *Bright-harnest Angels sit in order serviceable.*

It is a very curious ending, as if he had deliberately spoiled any effect of the grand or sublime by his two surprising adjectives, *bright-harnest* and *serviceable*. But it is a highly wrought art, and although its beauty is not obvious, it is nonetheless intense. For our own age, which understands visual effects more easily than verbal ones, it is easier to see the beauty of Piero's angels than Milton's, and they are all of the same rare family. His picture of the Baptism of Christ hangs in the National Gallery, and every time I go to look at it it seems to me the most beautiful picture I have ever seen (but so do a hundred others if I look at them for long enough). Christ stands in the middle, pale as a corpse, like all Piero's people, his flesh shadowed with green. A figure with awkward legs pours water over him from a little basin, and above his head a snowy dove hovers against a sky of that ethereal roof-less blue which only Piero can paint. To the right a man is pulling a shirt over his head, and on the left, between trees, are the three angels. There they stand, with rather sulky faces, solid, heavy, on thick legs and flat feet, essentially serviceable. And they are bright-harnessed, too, dressed in blue and pink, with rainbow wings and tight uncompromising wreaths of flowers set firmly on their heads. Yet we see, as we look longer, that in the atmosphere of the picture they are astonishingly beautiful: noble and serene and real. And so are Milton's angels. They are seventeenth-century wit at the highest level, where it becomes poetry. It is the same curious conception of beauty which makes Botticelli draw Venus' neck as if it were dislocated, and paint the completely satisfying understatement of her eyes, the pupils dull gold like her hair, the whites greyish-blue like the sky behind.

Sir Thomas Browne, in defending the animals commonly considered ugly, makes a curious statement: "I cannot tell by what Logick we call a Toad a Bear or an Elephant ugly. . . . There is no deformity but in Monstrosity; wherein, notwithstanding, there is a kind of Beauty: Nature so ingeniously contriving the irregular parts, as they become sometimes more remarkable than the principal Fabrick."

Deformity, a kind of beauty, ingeniously, irregular, more remarkable—he has himself given us words to describe the peculiar quality of his time's wit and his own. "Methinks I have out-lived myself, and begin to be weary of the Sun: I have shaken hands with delight, in my warm blood and Canicular days, I perceive I do anticipate the vices of age; the World to me is but a dream or mock-show, and we all therein but Pantalones and Anticks, to my severer contemplations."

But Browne's quality is rather strangeness than wit, and it is the poets and dramatists who illustrate his definition most constantly. When Macbeth speaks his over-quoted lines:

> *. . . this my hand will rather*
> *The multitudinous seas incarnadine,*
> *Making the green one red.*

Or:

> *Sleep that knits up the ravell'd sleave of care,*
> *The death of each day's life, sore labour's bath . . .*

or almost any other of his famous utterances, that is the wit of the seventeenth century, and he would not have talked in such a way if he had come to life at any other time. For Shakespeare finds his perfect expression in this concentrated and intellectual manner, seventeenth-century wit being not something added to the subject to enliven it, as we might supply a few witty epigrams, but an inherent way of thinking and feeling.

> *Our eye-beames twisted and did thred*
> *Our eyes, upon one double string.*

> *At the round earth's imagin'd corners*

Dead bodies: *"the shells of fledge souls left behinde"*

The *"quaint enamald eyes"* of flowers

Flowers that their gay wardrop wear

But best of all I like that treasure of understatement which at the end of a hauntingly beautiful lyric sums up the legend of the dead Narcissus: "Nature's pride is now a wither'd daffodill." Following the echoing loveliness of the lines before, it is the quintessence of all the laments ever written on the age-old theme of the passing of spring and youth and beauty.

Sometimes, indeed, the wit does not convert the deformity to beauty. To talk of "sepulchrall bone-fires" is a ghoulish pun, and near-puns on the name of Jesu hardly seem in good taste. It is absurd to write poems in patterns like Alice's mouse-tail, rather horrible to call the blood flowing from a martyr's wounds his "purple wardrobe," unsympathetic at the least to address a drowned scholar:

> *in thee*
> *Neptune hath got an University.*

And Sir Thomas Browne's question seems scarcely pious, when he asks whether Lazarus, coming back from the dead, had a lawsuit with his heirs.

But this is only the doubtful fringe of a peculiar way of feeling and thinking which has left us the concentrated treasures of seventeenth-century writing. It is a literary and highly wrought style hardly suitable for works of instruction, but it is so widespread that there are echoes even in the gardening books. The hedgehog has his "naturall fortifications," moles are "blind velveteers," the woods in Autumn "quit their leavie pretences and come to the naked truth." The Garden of Eden, says one writer, "is the world's most antient Monument," "God's own plantation wherein he gave intertainment to our first Parents," to Adam and Eve in their "imparadised condition." And once, in a forgotten country church, above the grave of a forgotten country gentleman, I found an epitaph which Donne might have written and Shakespeare not have been ashamed of:

> *Tis as you see nought but the Spoiles of Death,*
> *Gods High Controler and Impartial Taker;*
> *Free hold wee had of Land but none of Breath,*
> *All one day must resigne unto their Maker.*

But the supreme quality of the early seventeenth-century writers, which gives their work such depth and mysterious splendour, is their sense of strangeness. It is not fantasy nor madness nor fanciful invention; not Xanadu nor Kafka's nightmare world nor the enchanted forest of the *Faerie Queene;* but an authentic strangeness, a quality of real things, a sense that they exist in another dimension than the familiar world of daylight. It is a deeply felt emotion of serious men, a depth they sense behind the surface of living, as when two mirrors are set opposite each other, and beyond the infinitely repeated reflections, at the dim end of the long arcade of receding forms, we can half make out some ultimate mystery, some glimpse of another, stranger world.

"I have found," says Traherne, "that things unknown have a secret influence on the soul, and like the centre of the earth un-

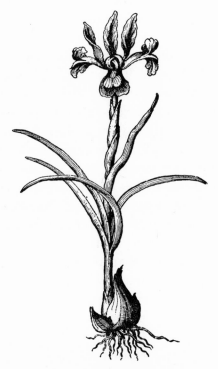

The iris or fleur de luce.

seen, violently attract it. . . . There are invisible ways of conveyance by which some great thing doth touch our souls, and by which we tend to it." And standing alone one evening in a field, he is bewildered by strange fears: "Another time in a lowering and sad evening, being alone in the field, when all things were dead and quiet, a certain want and horror fell upon me, beyond imagination. The unprofitableness and silence of the place dissatisfied me; its wideness terrified me; from the utmost ends of the earth fears surrounded me. How did I know but dangers might suddenly arise from the East, and invade me from the unknown regions beyond the seas?"

In Sir Thomas Browne we feel this strangeness at its most intense and poetical. He will write about the Garden of Cyrus, he says, and we are all ready to listen. Then comes his first sentence: "That Vulcan gave arrows unto Apollo and Diana the fourth day after their Nativities . . . may passe for no blinde apprehension of the creation of the Sunne and Moon, in the work of the fourth day; when the diffused light contracted into Orbes, and shooting rayes, of those Luminaries." It is his own unmistakable music, but nothing to do with gardens, even in the development. It is as incomprehensible in its context as the end of the same essay: "But the Quincunx of Heaven runs low, and 'tis time to close the five ports of knowledge. We are unwilling to spin out our awaking thoughts into the phantasmes of sleep, which often continueth præcognitions; making Cables of Cobwebbes, and Wildernesses of handsome Groves." We only understand that in all beauty there is a certain strangeness, and that Sir Thomas Browne gives us both in full measure.

Yet it is an ordinary homely garden which shelters this strange exotic flower. Browne was a busy Norwich doctor with a wife and family and many friends. He collects coins, he gardens, he prescribes for Mr. X's stone, he writes affectionate and sensible and quite undistinguished letters to his son in France, telling him to practise the language, to learn not to be a country bumpkin, to put on his winter underclothes in good time. And his wife adds postscripts about their little grandson Thomas—that he is sick, is better, is longing for his first breeches.

"But I am in the dark," says Browne, "to all the world, and my nearest friends behold me but in a cloud," the dark cloud of his "retired and solitary imagination" from which he utters his curious masterpieces. For suddenly the friendly chatter fades, the cheerful domestic hubbub, and in the silence we hear his strange tranced voice telling of half-apprehended visions in some far country of his mind.

This awareness of mystery in ordinary life underlies the finest

thought of the seventeenth century. It is the strangeness behind
Lear's madness and Hamlet's and Macbeth's; it is the background
of Prospero's island, the darkness of Webster's tragedies, the
Eternity which Vaughan saw

> *the other night*
> *Like a great Ring of pure and endless light*

—Eternity, says Traherne, which is "a mysterious absence of
times and ages: an endless length of ages always present, and for
ever perfect." It is the strangeness of the curious light and perspectives of Piero della Francesca's "Flagellation of Christ," of
the mysterious woodland gathering of Botticelli's "Spring." Our
English strangeness is darker than Italy's, for we live where a
doubtful sun leaves too much of the year in gloom, but it is essentially the same. It is the sympathy which translates with such
power the more mysterious passages of the Bible—the still, small
voice, and Jonah in the belly of hell—and gives sometimes a
depth of poetry to gardening books which were written only
for instruction. "These are the signs of wind," says Surflet. "If
the Clouds in a faire Season and beautifull Skie be carried on
high: gathered together as they were Flockes of Sheepe; if Forests and the high tops of Mountaines doe make a noyse: if the
starres of Heaven runne everie way: if the sound of Bells be
sometimes heard very easily, and by and by not to be heard: if
the webs and small threads of the Spyders do flye in the Aire: if
the Duckes doe spread and flicker with their wings often and a
long time together: if the Heron crie toward night as he is
flying."

   We feel, not that the wind is simply a change of weather, but
some mysterious presence which disquiets the natural world. And
Lawson, writing of the sap in orchard trees, feels the strangeness
of this invisible flow beneath the bark—"the sap is the life of the
Tree, as the blood is to man's Body; neither doth the Tree in
Winter want his sap, no more than man's Body his blood, which
in Winter, and time of sleep, draws inward: so that the dead time
of Winter, to a Tree, is but a night of rest."

Then hunting, says Markham in the middle of a matter-of-fact treatise on country sports, "hunting is a curious search or conquest of one Beast over another." And we suddenly see Uccello's painting in the Ashmolean Museum at Oxford, a strange picture of a hunt at night. We remember the mysterious gloomy vistas between the trees, the curiously spaced figures of men and beasts, the strange preoccupied excitement of this scene before they all disappear into the searching darkness.

It is as if beneath the flowery gardens of the seventeenth century lay some dark realm where urns are buried and trees are rooted, where herons cry at nightfall, and the stars of heaven run every way, and homely Norwich doctors hear dim incantations of mysterious splendour, repeating them Sybil-like for our delight and wonder:

"The Huntsmen are up in America, and they are already past their first sleep in Persia. But who can be drowsie at that hour which freed us from everlasting sleep? or have slumbering thoughts at that time, when sleep itself must end, and as some conjecture all shall wake again."

Chinese Landscape. "Spring Dawn by the Lake," by Chao Ling Jang, A.D. *1080–1100.*

"Paradise Garden," Cologne School, c. 1410.

The Mediæval Heroine.
From a rubbing of a fifteenth-century brass.

"Portrait of a Young Woman,"
by Roger Van Der Weyden.

The Tradescant Dodo.

Henry VIII's garden at Hampton Court,
with the Tudor palace behind and the Wren block on the right.

Tudor gardeners making an arbour,
AND
A Tudor gardener bedding out flowers.

Piero della Francesca's "Baptism of Christ."

ERTVS CHESEMAN
ANNO D M

TATIS SVÆ XLVII
M D XXXIII

One of Henry VIII's hawks. Painting by Holbein.

Bramham Park.

A garden in a bosquet. *Hedges used as architecture, fountains, orange trees in pots,* parterres de broderie.

ABOVE: *a fancy in a* bosquet *at* Versailles—*the swans, reeds, and central tree in bronze, the tree a fountain raining water from its leaves.*

BELOW: *the* Fountain of Flora *at* Versailles. *Hedges forming an order of field architecture. The fountain figures from a design by Le Brun.*

THE ROYALL PALACE OF HAMPTON COURT

The French-style gardens at Hampton Court. Henry VIII's gardens are in the background between the old palace and the river.

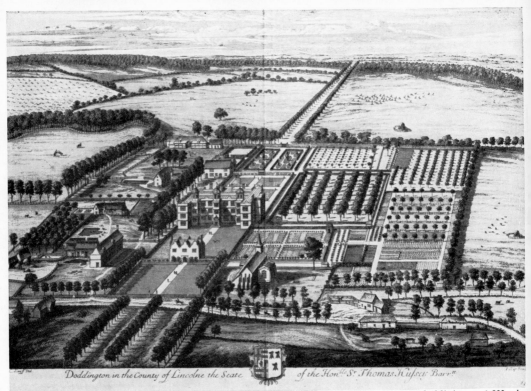

Kip's view of a country-house garden laid out in the seventeenth century.

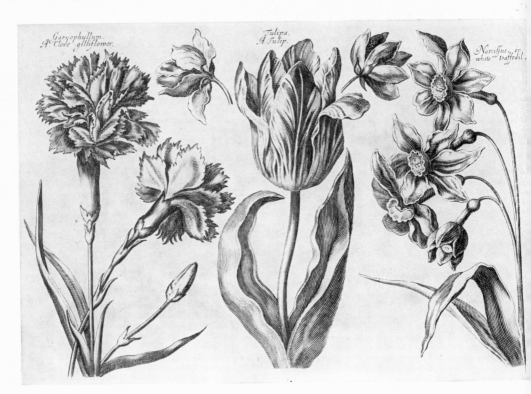

Favourite flowers of the seventeenth century.

The first pineapple grown in England is presented to Charles II by his gardener.

Seventeenth-century London gardens round Saint James's Park.

A view of the seventeenth-century canal in Saint James's Park.

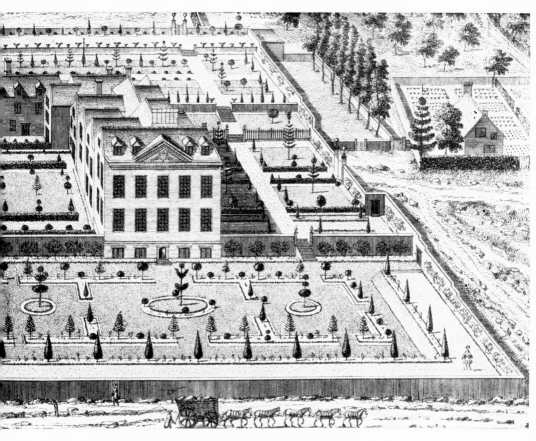

Topiary gardens (the best tree is in the hedge of the gardener's own cottage).

Inside an orangery.

The "new mode of gravel-walks and grass plots, ornamental shades, fountains and other Magnificent Ornaments."

BEFORE

AFTER

The countryside converted to a landscape park. From Repton's Theory and Practice of Landscape Gardening.

The decline of the formal garden: Kensington Gardens in the early eighteenth century.

The transition from formal to landscape gardens at Chiswick House.

The landscape style perfected.

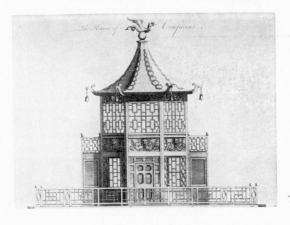

THE HOUSE OF CONFUCIUS

THE MOSQUE

Follies in Kew Gardens.
From Views of the Gardens
and Buildings at Kew in Surry,
by William Chambers.

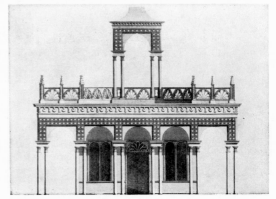

THE ALHAMBRA

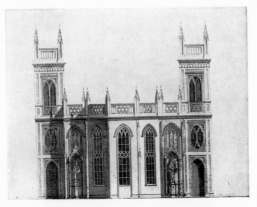

THE GOTHIC FAÇADE

Eighteenth-century flowers.

*X-ray photograph
of philadelphus.*

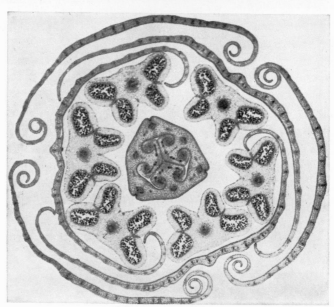

*Cross-section
of a tulip bud.*

The farmer's landscape: "Flatford Mill," by Constable.

Tea in the Garden. "The Picnic," by Tissot.

CHAPTER SIX

LES
JARDINS
DE
L'INTELLIGENCE

WHEN I WAS A HALF-GROWN GIRL MY FAM-
ily left the town and went to live in a cottage by a
stream. There, as I wandered about the surrounding countryside,
I discovered near by a great empty park with tall trees over high
walls, and a strange air of remoteness. Cautious but curious, I
climbed in to look, watching nervously for the slightest sign of
human beings, startled by any sound however distant, ready at
the least alarm to slip back into the trees and rush pell-mell for
the boundary wall. But I never saw any trace of life, not even
a wheelbarrow or the smoke from a bonfire, and I came back
often, drawn by an indefinable sense of difference, a consciousness of a life foreign to any I knew, alien, but unmistakably authentic.

I remember, from so long ago, no flowers in those gardens, no
bushes, no familiar tangle of undergrowth in the woods, but only
long avenues between tall trees, stately urns presiding at the end
of vistas, and sometimes the gleam of formal water. Even over-
grown and neglected, the gardens kept an unmistakable imprint
of order and meaning. The trees, I realized, had not been planted
to be admired as separate living entities, as trees were for me, but
as the living material to express a new conception. Once over the
wall, I felt, I was in a different country of the mind. Not that I

could have explained the significance of this scene, which I would suddenly remember for years afterwards in the bustle of school-days and the troubles of growing up. I was only convinced in an unreasoning way that the people who created it did not speak English. Nor did they: they spoke French. For the garden was Bramham Park, and the inspiration was Le Nôtre's. For, whether or not this supreme *"architecte des jardins"* ever did come to England and design gardens on the actual sites, Bramham Park is unmistakably a garden in the French grand manner of the seventeenth century.

An orangery. The plants carried out for the summer.

The French are very conscious of their own good qualities—*"les qualités proprement françaises de limpidité et de netteté dans la langue, d'esprit de finesse et de naturel dans le style, de vérité profonde dans l'analyse. Nous sommes un peuple que 'la raison à ses règles engage,' ennemi de toutes les extravagances de l'imagination ou du cœur, épris d'idées claires et universelles."* (I suppose they have no need of modesty in such a dower of virtues, but still it might be very charming.)

Les Jardins de l'Intelligence

Like all generalizations, it forgets the awkward facts which will not conform: ignores almost the whole of nineteenth-century French literature. But most people would feel that Molière is more typical of the French spirit than Victor Hugo, and unless we risk a few rash generalizations we shall get no further in trying to link the different styles of gardening with the other arts of the same time and place.

"At war with all extravagances of the heart and imagination, in love with clear and universal ideas." It follows that the greatest achievements of the French genius are logical, that their quality is intellect, raised at its finest to the power of poetry, but still the underlying spirit is logical and intellectual. Man is great, said Pascal, because he thinks. *"L'homme est fait pour penser,"* c'est *"toute sa dignité et tout son mérite."* It is not the whole truth, since human beings may be great in ways as various as their various natures, but it is one of the Classical truths, a conception of man as a rational creature considering the world about him by the steady daylight of intelligence.

No one by taking thought could achieve the poetic quality of early seventeenth-century English literature. And if we could, it would not help us to lay out cities, build palaces, plan gardens, or order our lives with dignity. But the French delight in intellectual clarity is a condition of the mind which can be fostered in civilized people: by taking thought we can achieve some degree of their clear-sighted logic. And it is a conception which can be referred to in the ordinary affairs of life, used as a logical framework for creating all kinds of works of art: architecture, town-planning, and the manners of the Salons, as well as the plays of Molière and the paintings of Poussin. Le Nôtre is related to Corneille in spirit as well as fact.

So that the seventeenth century in France is a noble flowering of all the arts together in the first fine weather of modern man's intellectual confidence: the pure arts, the applied arts, and the arts of living all combined in a harmonious whole, each interpreting the others. If everything of seventeenth-century France were to disappear and leave us only the gardens of Versailles, we should still understand why the age which produced this noble landscape of the mind was called *Le Grand Siècle*.

In England, too, the seventeenth century was our age of giants: Shakespeare, Milton, Purcell, Wren. But we do not think of it as our Great Century, for it is not a unified whole held together by an intellectual conception. The different arts do not interpret each other: seeing a seventeenth-century English garden, we could never infer Shakespeare, as we can infer Corneille from Versailles.

No one would say of the English that we are enemies of all extravagances of the heart and imagination. Such extravagances, indeed, have often been the finest inspiration of our arts. We have never much cared for the intellectual order of Versailles, for, not being an inherently Classical people, we tend to look at the Classical tradition from the outside, as the established status quo of European culture. Too often it does not seem to us a vital creation of man's imagination, but an order of nature which exists inevitably by its own laws. Only once, looking over a formal seventeenth-century French park from a high window of the house, I left my Englishness behind as I climbed the stairs, and the great garden, which till then had seemed only an unexceptionable dull exercise in planning, suddenly became the expression of a poetic ideal of order which haunts the shadowy minds of men, a vivid intellectual creation which they only precariously achieve from chaos. The perfectly proportioned spaces, the serene vistas, the regular avenues of trees—these were suddenly no more than a faint and beautiful pattern laid by a visionary upon the underlying landscape, and the order which had seemed inevitable was now as strange and fleeting as the shadows of the clouds upon the hills.

For me, at least, the Grand Manner is not poetic in its parts but only as a whole, as Paris is mostly unremarkable in separate detail but incomparable as a city. It is the conception which is beautiful, not the incidentals—quite contrary to England, where our finest things so often seem almost accidental.

Les Jardins de l'Intelligence

For us the Classical tradition lacks romance, and the English, so everyone tells us, are incurable romantics. It is too logical for us, too unassailable, too clear. We feel with Bacon that "there is no excellent beauty that hath not some strangeness in the proportion." But it is because we do not stand far enough off; we should look at it from a top window of the house. Seen in its setting of alien nature, the formal garden becomes high poetry; for surely it is both strange and romantic that a race of puny animals should dominate their world simply by the force of their spirit, should mould the indifferent landscape to this aristocratic order only to express their conception of man as a noble creature, as "*l'animal qui pense.*"

Versailles, someone said, "*est la squelette fossile d'une vie,*" and the life is the courtly ceremony of Louis XIV. For the original palace was too small to be a fitting background for royal functions, and the gardens were laid out as an appropriate setting. We should think of the long alleys as crowded with the aristocracy of France, the formal spaces as the scene of magnificent ceremony, the green enclosures of the *bosquets* cheerful with people, gay lively intelligent people who would dispel with a witticism the air of tranquil melancholy which haunts the park today.

This court life which surrounded the King was as formal and ordered as the gardens it was set in, and weary of the impersonal etiquette, Louis would escape from time to time to his house at Marly, where ceremony was forgotten and everyone mixed with easy familiarity. The more conventional were uneasy—"I find great difficulty in getting used to this confusion," said a visiting duchess, shocked because she could not tell the Queen from her ladies when they walked together in the gardens. And indeed the seventeenth century is too early for this sophisticated game of the Simple Life in Satin Slippers. It needs for background the landscape gardens of eighteenth-century England and Marie Antoinette's *hameau*. In Le Nôtre's gardens it must have been embarrassingly difficult to keep up the pretence, and Marly changed from an informal country house to Marly-le-roi, the most magnificent of all the royal pleasure-grounds.

There is a pleasant story how one fine day four friends drove to Versailles in the same carriage, made a tour of the gardens (avoiding the water surprises), then sat down beneath the trees to listen to a poem in praise of the beauty of the place. The friends were Molière, Racine, Boileau, and La Fontaine, who wrote the verses, and I dare say no other carriage has ever carried such a load of genius. For Versailles was a magnet which drew the talents of the age: Molière wrote plays for the garden fêtes, Lully composed music, Le Brun designed scenery, and Le Nôtre created green theatres in the *bosquets*. There is a painting of one of these performances, which were often the central point of the royal entertainments. It is warm night and leafy summer. The stage is brilliant under the high shadowy trees, the faces of the watchers vivid against the darkness. To English eyes the scene is unmistakably Romantic, and the play we think of in such a setting is *The Tempest*, with Prospero's poetry, Ariel and the island full of noises, and the loves of Ferdinand and Miranda like a forced exotic flower.

But it is not *The Tempest* they are watching in their green enchanted theatre, nor Milton's *Comus* nor Ben Jonson's *Sad Shepherd*. Instead it is that level-headed satire to banish all dreams of summer nights, Molière's *Le Malade Imaginaire*.

Most of us nowadays have an unquestioned idea of a garden as a place for growing flowers. But it is a humble conception, and we must get rid of it before we go to Versailles or we shall certainly be disappointed. Versailles is not a garden in this sense, but rather a work of art which uses plants as its medium, as a painter uses the appearance of objects, and a poet the words of human speech. Like most other mediums of art, it is impure: gardens *can* be used for growing flowers in, as words are used to state facts and painting to illustrate views. But none of these functions is art. Of all the mediums of artistic expression, only music is pure in this sense that it has no other meaning, and all art, says Pater, "constantly aspires towards the condition of music. For while in all other kinds of art it is possible to distinguish the matter from the form, and the understanding can always make this distinction, yet it is the constant effort of art to obliterate it." So that it is as perverse to go to Versailles to look at the plants as to use Cézanne's landscapes as guide-book illustrations to Provence, or Shelley's "Ode" as a scientific statement of the habits of the sky-lark. We must think of Versailles as music. The great central vista is the main theme, an untroubled progress to the horizon, simple, noble, and mysterious. Then there are variations, developments, lesser themes, smooth passages of water, gay effects of flowers, fanciful interludes in the *bosquets*. But all is music, calm and confident, with no doubtful effects or random charms, no chance felicities which may or may not succeed. We share the intellectual tranquility of perfection, a conviction of the inevitably right, which sways our spirits to peace, as Duns Scotus swayed Hopkins.

But I am incurably English. I do not like Versailles except to think about at a distance. I do not particularly enjoy the sensation of being what Corneille calls *saoul de gloire;* for me the peace too easily becomes boredom. I believe that Le Nôtre is the greatest of gardeners, but it is a judgement outside my personal liking.

"The basis of all artistic genius" (it is Pater again) "lies in the power of conceiving humanity in a new and striking way, of putting a happy world of its own creation in place of the meaner world of our common days." Most modern artists seem to ignore the happy, but certainly Versailles puts a world of its own creation in place of our meaner one. But how does it create this other world? Its finished order may seem inevitable, but even an imitation of the Grand Manner is difficult for those not born to it, as we can see by considering the fussy and pretentious triteness of most public parks and formal gardens laid out in England since the early nineteenth century.

The Theory and Practice of Gardening is a large French treatise credited to Le Blond and translated into English by John James. It is a full and clear account of the principles which underlie Versailles, the rules which Le Nôtre formulated and followed in the famous gardens which he laid out all over France, and which were copied for the next hundred years by a Europe dazzled with their magnificence.

Le Blond leaves us in no doubt from the beginning about the exalted qualities needed in a good gardener. "A fine Garden," he says, "is no less difficult to contrive and order well, than a good Building. . . . A Man should know something of Geometry and Architecture, and be able to draw well; he should understand Ornament, be acquainted with the Properties and Effects of all the Plants made use of in fine Gardens; should design readily; and with all this, have a right Judgement and natural good Taste, form'd upon the Contemplation of Things that are excellent, the Censuring of those that are ill." This is a long way from any English idea of a gardener, and he would certainly dismiss our garden literature as the work of "the very meanest Gardeners, who laying aside the Rake and Spade, take upon them to give Designs of Gardens when they know nothing of the Matter." Yes. But it is exactly that, the smell of the earth on the spade, that we read their books for.

It is most important, says Le Blond, "to form a right Taste of what concerns the general Disposition of Gardens," and he gives us "Four fundamental Maxims to be observ'd."

1 "Art must give place to Nature." This seems to be a constant claim of all styles of art, however artificial they seem to us, and we should never guess that it was the first fundamental of Versailles. But we can see what he means. Water should be in hollows, woods cover hills, and there should not be too much architecture or ornaments (statues, etc.), since this "has nothing of the Air of Nature, and falls very short of that noble Simplicity we should aim at."

2 "Gardens should not be made dull and gloomy, by clouding them with Thickets and too much Cover. Fine Openings should be preserved about the Building, and in other places where the Prospect of the Country can be seen to advantage."

3 "Gardens should not lay too open, so that it is needless to go into them to see them; you discover the whole at one View

Les Jardins de l'Intelligence

from the Vestibule of the House without troubling yourself to walk in them. The pleasure of a Garden is to have the View stopt in certain places, that you may be led on with Delight to see the more agreeable Parts of it, as fine Groves of Woodwork, Green-Halls adorned with Fountains and Figures etc. Those great flat Parts rob us of the Woods which make the Contrariety and Change in a Garden, and which alone make all the rest valuable."

Seventeenth-century roses. Drawing by Crispin de Passe.

4   "A Garden should always look bigger than it really is." To show it all at once makes it seem smaller: on the other hand, it is made to seem larger by "artfully stopping the Eye" with hedges, woods, etc., before it reaches the boundary. Also, Prospects should be opened into the surrounding country so that it seems part of the composition.

After these rather general rules Le Blond becomes more explicit.

The length of a garden should be one and a half times the breadth.

The principal walk should lie direct from end to end of the garden in front of the house.

A cross-walk should lie at right angles to it, and all these walks should end in Prospects with "wet ditches" replacing the walls of the garden (long before the ha-has of the eighteenth century).

There should be a descent of at least three steps from the house to give a "general Prospect."

Before the house should be an open space, laid out as a parterre which can be appreciated from the windows.

The rest of the garden is to be laid out with "Designs of tall Groves, Quincunxes, Close-Walks, Galleries and Halls of Verdure, Green-Arbours, Labyrinths, Bowling-greens, Amphitheatres adorned with Fountains, Canals, Figures etc."

In the layout there must be careful contrast of flat spaces and raised areas such as woods. To set a grass plot beside a Parterre of flowers, for instance, "would be one gap against another."

Designs of gardens, although formal, should only be symmetrical "in open Places, where the Eye, by comparing them together, may judge of their Conformity." Otherwise there should be variety, as groves, for instance, which have the same outward shape, must be different within. "For it would be very disagreeable to find the same thing on both sides; and when a Man has seen one, to have nothing to invite his Curiosity to see the other; which makes a Garden, so repeated, justly reckoned no more than half a Design."

The general impression of a garden must be magnificent, and "should studiously avoid the Manner that is mean and pitiful, and always aim at that which is great and noble. 'Twere infinitely better to have but two or three Things somewhat large, than a dozen small ones which are no more than very trifles." (Alas for the Tudor gardeners!)

"Before the Design of a Garden be put into Execution, you should consider what it will be in twenty or thirty years to come, for very often a Design which looks handsome and of good Proportion when it is first planted, in process of Time becomes small and ridiculous." For Le Blond is not merely gardening for pleasure, but creating a work of art for posterity.

As he goes on, we begin to understand how Versailles was

made, and to realize the intellectual discipline which controls these noble garden landscapes. They should be large, he says; thirty or forty acres is the best size, but even in "so small a Garden as five or six acres" we must still aim at that "Air of Magnificence," must forgo all fancies and "chuse a plain Regularity, not clutter'd and confus'd, which looks much more noble and great."

The careful spacing and proportions of walks is of great importance, for "Walks in Gardens, like Streets in a Town, serve to communicate between Place and Place, they conduct us throughout a Garden, and make one of the principal Beauties. The Breadth of Walks should be proportioned to their Length, for in this lies their greatest Beauty." Short walks must not be too broad, nor long ones too narrow, but the rules of Proportion be exactly observed.

Woods, too, are an "essential Part of a Garden," for they provide the necessary height and mass to contrast with the flat lawns and flower beds and formal waters. "Woods and Groves make the Relievo of Gardens and serve infinitely to improve the flat Parts. Care should be taken to place them so that they may not hinder the Beauty of the Prospect."

As for the Prospect—or view, as we should call it—"The Prospect is the most valuable Thing about a Country-Seat. I esteem nothing more agreeable in a Garden than a fine View and the Prospect of a noble Country." For though we of the twentieth century may grow weary of such constant nobility, man has at last outgrown his garden walls, he no longer shuts himself in with his treasures safe from a hostile world outside, his garden is no longer a retreat, but an expression of the order he can now impose on chaotic nature—"*ce plaisir superbe de forcer la nature.*" The whole world is his intellectual province, and the vistas to the far horizon are the noblest part of these noble gardens. They imply even more than they declare; offer new realms of knowledge, of opportunity without limit. They are the use of silence and mystery and suggestion. As in the pictures of Claude, this empty space is the one essential which we remember. We may forget the foreground, we may never have known what subject was intended, but we never forget that mysterious recession into the far distance which is the real subject of Claude's pictures.

From the children holidaying in France we had excited letters, made even more breathlessly enthusiastic by a most sparing use of punctuation. "Dear Dardy Last night I ate the biggest supper I ever have. I have had great fun with my butterflies I caught four clouded yellows and four pale clouded yellows another stick insect and another fritillary which is the same as the other and I think they are both heath fritillaries which in England are rare . . ." and so on. Then here it is. "I enjoyed Versailles a lot we went in through an arch and saw a beautiful view to begin with there was a blaze of flowers then a long strech of grass after that a lovely lake after that it rather peatered out but there must have been something there sometime because it was so empty-looking."

Fine vistas, the use of silence, it peatered out—we all mean the same thing, and it is stated with such perfect clarity that it is unmistakable even to a schoolboy preoccupied with catching butterflies and eating large suppers.

As for the details of these gardens, they were often fanciful, for although Poussin might declare that *"les plaisirs de l'intelligence sont les premiers de tous,"* everyone's taste was not so austere, and within the formal framework there were all kinds of frivolous inventions. The *bosquets*, especially, sheltered a wealth of delightful absurdities which have long since disappeared. "The French call a Grove Bosquet," says Le Blond (the English spell it *Boskett*), "from the Italian Word Bosquetto, a little Wood of small Extent; as much as to say, a Nosegay, or Bunch of Green." Inside these Nosegays were hidden a great variety of constantly changing fancies: mazes and labyrinths with high hedges, grottos and green theatres, and little rooms for open-air meals. There were fountains everywhere: fountains which played music, or balanced balls on their jets, or threw up coloured water; fountains in the shape of trees or rushes, raining water from their leaves; rows of fountains forming arches where one could walk unspotted; fountains which drenched the unwary visitor—the "water-surprises" we know already. "Decidedly it was an ignoble form of humour," said Henry James later on of a similar practical joke, but, none the less, the Roi Soleil's courtiers thoroughly enjoyed it. The Trianon de Porcelaine and its garden (they are long since gone) were decorated with plaques and seats and urns in blue and white porcelain, and the flowers which filled its beds were grown in greenhouses in pots which were buried in the soil of the garden and changed every day, so that the scene was always brilliant with flowers at their most perfect. (We cannot help shuddering now at the expense of it all.) There was a Cabinet de Parfums surrounded by sweet-smelling flowers, where one could sit and enjoy a planned harmony of fragrance; this was a fancy which particularly delighted the Eastern ambassadors.

The open walks and parterres were more decorous, and the hedges which bordered them were simply cut. The word *parterre*, says Le Blond, who has a liking for rather unreliable etymology, "comes from the Italian partiri—to divide." It is used for a design not unlike the Tudor knots, though larger: a flat bed, generally square, divided into symmetrical patterns which were repeated in each quarter, and planted with low shrubs or flowers divided by narrow paths. "Formerly," says Le Blond, "they put in the Heads of Greyhounds Griffins and other Beasts; which had a very ill Effect, and made Parterres look very heavy and clouterly." Curious to see what *clouterly* translated, I looked up the French version, but there is nothing. "*Très-lourds*" it says, and *clouterly* is James's own addition to show his scorn of Tudor absurdities. But James often amuses himself quietly, sometimes at the expense of the over-confident Le Blond. *Boulingrin* is the French version of our word *Bowling-green*, and is a name they used for a round hollow lawn of grass, often broken up with flower beds. "The Word Bowling-Green or Boulingrin," says Le Blond, who seems never to have heard of Drake or Plymouth Hoe, "comes to us from England, from two English Words; namely from Bowl, which signifies a round Body; and from

Green, which denotes a Meadow, or Field of Grass; probably because of the Figure in which it is sunk, which is commonly round and cover'd with Grass." James translates without comment.

What the French did admire in our English gardens—and it seems to be the only thing—were our grass lawns. "In England their Grass-plots are of so exquisite a Beauty that in France we can scarce ever come up to it." It is still true.

But what about flowers in these grand pleasure-grounds? Is there no place for this chief preoccupation of English gardeners? If I ask the children what they would like for lunch on their birthdays, they are always ready with an enthusiastic list of chocolate biscuits, cream cakes, sugar buns, jelly with fruit in, and ice-cream in three different colours. Only very half-heartedly they sometimes add at the end clear chicken soup, or stuffing out of a goose, or sauce with shrimps in it. Children plan their meals in puddings, and the English plan their gardens in flowers. We have the indiscriminate sweet-tooth of the child whose palate has not developed. Yet adults often ignore the pudding altogether, choose cheese instead of ice-cream, and the late great gardens in the French Grand Manner are almost flowerless. For the English gardeners, fine flowers make fine gardens, but for Le Blond it is not so simple. "The fine Lines and Views from one end of the Garden to the other, and the Harmony of the Parts, together with what one discovers in the several Alleys . . . is sufficient to satisfy anyone in its Disposition, Variety, and Distribution of its Ornaments and Water."

In such a composition flowers have no real place. Their prettiness is a distracting chatter. If they are used in so large a setting they must be massed as uniform blocks of colour, and if we no longer have a sweet-tooth we may prefer the more restrained and suggestive colour schemes of trees and sky and water, as Le Nôtre did. Parterres, he said, are only good for nursemaids, *"qui, ne pouvant quitter leurs enfants, s'y promenaient des yeux et les admiraient du deuxième étage."*

Les Jardins de l'Intelligence

The treatment of the open space which lies in front of the main façade at Versailles shows how the taste for "noble Simplicity" rejected the fussy formality of parterres. There were at least six different designs before the present perfection was achieved: patterns of beds and borders, elaborate parterres of flowers and hedges and water, topiary, statues and fountains, until at last Le Nôtre swept it all away and made the two simple parallel pools which still reflect the palace, and surrounded them with reclining statues too low to disturb the clear wide sweep.

Yet some of the green parterres of box have a certain beauty when used against the high walls of the *bosquets*, whose lower branches are cut back to form a vertical hedge. They give a deep rich texture to the flat ground, like the pile of an elaborate carpet, and they make an interesting foil for the satin-smooth water of the basins. Le Blond warns the Reader "against the Notion some People have got, that Parterres are the most difficult things to invent. Parterres are as small Matters of Invention, compared with the Dispositions and general Distributions of Gardens. All Parterres are near alike. Perhaps the Reason why these Persons make a Mystery of designing a Parterre, is that they are not capable of anything else; and that a general Plan will presently put them to a nonplus." Which is probably an attack on English gardening books, if he ever bothered to read them.

In his own book no plants of any kind are mentioned until he has written us one hundred and sixty-four pages of Dispositions and general Distributions. Then he begins with trees: horse chestnuts, limes, and elms are the favourites, and for hedges hornbeam is best, then beech or maple. Evergreens are valued highly, and flowering shrubs commonly grown, but any shrubs used in parterres must be clipped ruthlessly low to keep the clear contrast between horizontal parterre and vertical groves. Flowers get only twenty pages, compared with thirty on the use of water in pools and fountains. Le Blond's garden is no home for flowers, but a strictly disciplined country where they must live by rigid rules if they are to be admitted at all. It is no place for Master

Tuggie's Princess. Even the trees are not allowed to develop their own personality, but must combine in formal avenues and *bosquets*. Existing woods were disciplined by the cutting of glades in a logical pattern. The goose foot was often used: a plan of avenues radiating from a focus like the toes of a bird. At Chantilly the alleys met at a central view-point, so that anyone standing there could watch an entire stag-hunt through the woods with no more effort than a turn of the head as the hunt crossed each logically radiating glade.

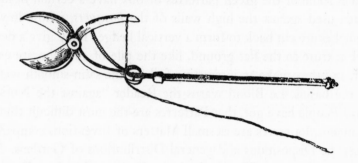

The species of trees chosen for planting are valued for their regularity, and because they will suffer pruning and clipping to form green walls: "These Decorations in Green compose a kind of Order of Field Architecture." When I saw the avenues at Versailles I recognized again the trees I had seen long ago in Bramham Park, for although Versailles is pruned chestnuts and Bramham freely growing beeches, they are unmistakably of the same race of orderly beings. After the Italian Art Exhibition, so they say, all the fashionable women of London looked like the figure of Botticelli's "Spring." I dare say they did, for fashionable women are astonishingly versatile, but it seems even odder that after Le Nôtre all the fashionable trees of Europe should look like Versailles.

What of this "famous Monsieur Le Nostre" himself, whose "ingenious skill gave the last perfection to Gardening" as Evelyn said? He was born of a well-known family of gardeners, but his training for Versailles was not in grafting rose-trees or layering gillyflowers. He studied first to be a painter—an enthusiasm which never left him, for he collected many fine pictures, especially by Poussin who, as we might guess, was his favourite artist. I also enjoy Poussin in my own way, but I doubt whether it is Le Nôtre's way. He reminds me always of fair-grounds. For so often his pictures are constructed in a revolving movement round a central focal point, a stately and inevitable circling in space, like a most wonderfully dignified merry-go-round. And then there are his horses, so nobly posed, so magnificently monumental, the real authentic Grand Manner in the very best sort of rocking-horses.

From painting Le Nôtre turned to architecture, a training which must have suited his formal sense of balance and proportion. But neither of these arts was his proper medium, and eventually he was given a post in the royal gardens, where *"la grande capacité qu'il a à dessiner"* was soon noticed by Louis XIV. He reduced the haphazard landscape to three main elements: flat ground or water, walls of trees or architecture, and the open sky. With these essentials he composed, eliminating detail, keeping a clear order for the eye and the mind.

> *On crut qu'il avait le pouvoir*
> *De commander à la nature*

said La Fontaine.

The Tuileries Gardens were laid out by Le Nôtre, and though the details have changed since his time, the main plan is still the same. On a stretch of awkwardly sloping land he found an untidy confusion of buildings and gardens which Evelyn describes in one of his letters. There was "a building in which are kept wild beasts for the King's pleasure, a beare, a wolfe, a wild boare, a leopard etc." There was also "an artificial echo redoubling the words distinctly, and it is never without some fair nymph singing in it. Standing at one of the focus's, which is under a tree or little cabinet of hedges, the voice seems to descend from the clouds; at another as if it was underground." (I wonder if it was as hard to find a nymph to sing to the echo as it was later on to find a hermit to live in the cells in the eighteenth-century wildernesses. And I wonder what songs they sang.)

This engaging muddle of the old Tuileries, Le Nôtre cleared and levelled and laid out with noble avenues aligned on the palace of the Louvre. But this was not enough. *"Il ne pouvait souffrir les vues bornées,"* said one of his contemporaries, and the outlook from the Tuileries Gardens was bounded by the city wall. So in the waste-land beyond the town he planted avenues of trees which climbed the opposite hill and carried the view calmly and confidently to the horizon—an avenue we still admire as one of the great beauties of Paris, and we call it the Champs-Élysées.

Le Nôtre, for all his clarity, is an ambiguous figure, for with his stately grandeur of mind went a warm and spontaneous personality. He was generous and straightforward, with simple informal manners and a cheerful enthusiasm in all he did. In an audience with the Pope he was so delighted with the aged prelate that he jumped up and embraced him warmly, a story which astonished the ceremonious French courtiers, but not King Louis, for Le Nôtre often kisses me, he told them, when I come back from campaigns. And the King seems to have returned his affection, driving with him alone in the park, urging him to come and live at Versailles because he liked his company, giving him a princely pension when he retired, offering him a coat-of-arms. But I have one already, said Le Nôtre, whose head was not at all turned by his fame: *"trois limaçons surmontés d'une tête de chou."* But Louis was not to be gainsaid, and presented him with a crest of three silver snails.

For with Le Nôtre the somewhat unsympathetic figure of the Sun King shows at his most attractive. His delight in his park at Versailles is an enthusiasm every gardener will understand, and, anxious that visitors should come upon its glories in the proper order and see the layout from the view-points best suited to its display, he worked out an itinerary for "doing" the house and grounds (we are reminded of Henry VIII), writing it out in his own large awkward hand. *"Manière de Montrer Versailles: En sortant du chasteau par le vestibule de la cour de marbre. . . . Il faut aller droit sur le haut de Latonne et faire une pause. . . . Ayant tourné à gauche pour aller passer entre les Sfinx, on ira droit sur le haut de l'orangerie d'où l'on verra le parterre des orangers et le lac des Suisses."* And so on and so on, from one famous view to the next. Yet at the heart of this formal grandeur, warming it with a humanity which can appreciate the inspired common sense of Molière and the friendly world of La Fontaine's fables, stands the cheerful figure of Le Nôtre, the simple happy man whom everyone loved—*"plus agréable vieillard qui ait peut-être jamais été, toujours gaillard, propre, bien mis, d'un visage agréable, et toujours riant."*

It is an old age which every gardener must hope for.

CHAPTER SEVEN

GARDENS

OF

SEVENTEENTH

CENTURY

ENGLAND

THERE IS NOTHING MORE USEFUL FOR FACING danger or hardship than an engrossing interest in something else. If we are preoccupied enough with some enthusiasm, we brush away incidental difficulties which would certainly daunt us if we ever gave them our attention. A child intent on reaching the top of a tree ignores cuts and bruises which would overwhelm it with misery on the ground. Botanists in search of flowers scramble absent-mindedly over mountains so alarming that they would never think of attempting them as climbers. If we rode our hobby-horse furiously enough, we might pass through the Valley of Death and never notice.

Darwin, so he tells us, at ten years old had a single-minded ambition: to know something about the history of every pebble in the gravel outside the front door. For Darwin's first enthusiasm was geology, and it led him with only two native companions through the wild mountains of South America, through hardships and dangers he scarcely noticed. "The worst passes in the Cordillera," he says, "but their danger has been much exaggerated." The worst pass of all he never even knew he had crossed until a day later; but the scenery, he complains with feeling, "was very uninteresting." It is an enthusiasm which engrosses him equally in the company of dinner-parties. One evening there occurred what he calls "a sharp earthquake," and he is delighted with this unexpected geological demonstration. "Strong Earthquakes useful to Geologists," he writes in his notebook. "I heard the forecoming rumble, but," he says crossly, "from the screams of the ladies, the running of the servants and the rush of several gentlemen to the doorway, I could not distinguish the motion."

Once, indeed, affected perhaps by the lack of oxygen, he is detached enough to laugh at himself. Climbing a high mountain range made it difficult to breathe the rarified air, a condition the natives call *puna*. "The exertion of walking was extremely great and the respiration became deep and laborious." But, "finding fossil shells on the highest ridge," says Darwin, "I entirely forgot the puna in my delight. The inhabitants all recommend onions for the puna," he adds; "for my part I found nothing so good as the fossil shells."

In the seventeenth century an equally enthusiastic Englishwoman rode side-saddle from end to end of England, from Newcastle to Land's End, from the Lake District to Kent, ignoring the very real hardships and dangers of seventeenth-century travel. And for what? For domestic curiosity: she liked to look at other people's houses. She wanted to see how they arranged their rooms, what colours they chose for curtains and covers, and whether they had laid out their gardens in the new fashion. Driven by this housewifely interest, she set off lightly on her heroic journeys, risked being robbed on the roads or lost among the precipices of the Peak or drowned in the treacherous crossing of the Humber.

Celia Fiennes is a somewhat monotonous writer; her highest praise is "neat," and her particular abhorrence is pictures of Venus with no clothes on—"a fine picture of Venus were it not too much unclothed," and "fine pictures, but they were all without Garments or very little, that was the only fault, the immodesty of the Pictures, especially in my Lord's appartment." But despite her limitations she gives a first-hand account of the houses and gardens of England in the late seventeenth century, seen through the mind of a lively, curious, and not very intelligent woman of the lesser aristocracy.

As in every age, she has no liking for the fashions of the period which is passing; "good but old-ffashioned," she says often, "in the old fashion," "all in an old fform and mode." These old-fashioned gardens which Celia Fiennes briefly dismisses are the gardens in Tudor style, which had so well suited the English idea of what a Garden of Pleasure should be like that they were loved and tended right through the seventeenth century. There must even have been gardens newly laid out in "the old mode," for writers like Rea and Meager give plans and instructions for making gardens scarcely different from those of Elizabeth's day; they have only been pruned of their more extravagant fancies by the bleak weather of the Commonwealth, "that dismal interval"; and "since our long Winter is so well over," says a Restoration writer, gardening is an occupation more beloved than ever before.

These old-fashioned writers cared nothing for Le Nôtre and his Grand Designs. "What some modern Authors mean by putting Gentlemen upon Grand Designs, and vilifying all others as *crimping, diminutive* and *wretched Performances,* I could never understand," said John Laurence as late as 1716. "Nothing hath more tended to the Ruin of brave Estates than a fond Affectation of imitating a vain People in what they call La Grand Manier." Rea was no more enthusiastic—"I have seen many Gardens of the new model," he says, "that a green Meadow is a more delightful object." "A choice Collection of living Beauties, rare Plants Flowers and Fruits, are indeed the wealth glory and delight of a Garden," he says, and we know at once that we shall not be expected to understand the perspective of vistas.

Leonard Meager is too humble to criticize anyone; he even warns the Friendly Reader that his book is hindered by "want of time and want of Learning," and that he has "set it down very plainly, whereby it may become very useful for all sorts of practitioners, yea though of very weak capacities." But his title page places him at once with the early seventeenth-century gardeners, although he wrote in 1670. "The ordering of the Garden of Pleasure, with variety of Knots, and Wilderness-work after the best fashion, all Cut in Copper Plates—likewise several other very useful things—fitted for the use of all such as delight in Gardening, whereby the meanest capacity need not doubt of success."

The gardens these writers describe are the ones we know already: small (thirty yards square is big enough for a nobleman), full of flowers lovingly tended, divided up into quite separate compartments (Rea even shares Henry VIII's liking for rails), and still completely shut in by an encircling wall or hedge. For small boys still came scrumping apples, it seems, though Laurence has an ingenious new remedy. "At my first coming to my Parish" (for he was a clergyman, like many gardeners since) "I found some difficulty to preserve my Fruit from Robbers: Hereupon I resolved upon this Stratagem. I ordered the Smith to make a large Iron Trap with formidable Teeth to close one within another, which was to be called a Man-Trap. This was hung up several Weeks at the Smith's Shop *in terrorem*, giving it out, that now there would be great danger, if any one should attempt to rob my Garden. This, without setting the Trap, succeeded according to my Wish, and I have not been since robbed these twelve years." "*Note*" (he adds at the bottom), "Restrain'd, I hope too, not altogether by Terror, but from better Principles."

We cannot help wondering what his parishioners thought of a preacher of brotherly love who planted his orchard with man-traps, but I dare say they found him as disarming as we do. "Advertisement," he writes on a spare page at the end of his book: "Lordships Surveyed and Maps Drawn of the same" (a Lordship not being a lord's person, but his land) "by Edward Laurence, Brother to the Author of this Book. He is to be heard of when in London at Mr. Senex's at the Globe in Salisbury Court. *N.B.* In Winter, and at such Times as he is not Surveying, Gentlemen may have their Sons or Daughters Taught Accompts at their own Houses, with the Use of the Globes and Maps, and all other useful Parts of the Mathematics."

It is odd how these old-fashioned gardeners of the second half of the seventeenth century share with the early ones, not only their taste in gardens, but also their charm of personality. "I forgot to mention it before," says Meager endearingly, and he ends a list of evergreens "with many other sorts which at present I cannot call to mind." "In three Books, as in so many Beds," says Rea, who wrote *Flora Ceres et Pomona*, "have I lodged Earth's Beauties." And again: "It is impossible for any man to have Plants to prosper, unless he love them: for neither the goodness of the Soil, nor the advantage of the Situation will do it without the Master's affection."

These men write, too, in the simple vivid style of the early seventeenth century, and though they seldom suggest the poetry or strangeness of writers like Markham and Lawson, they flower into happy phrases quite unlike the pretentious manner of many minor writers of the time. "Let not your Walks be too little, neither too big, like a small City with over-large gates," or "The Sun hastens flowers to perfection, causing them quickly to flower and quickly to fade," and they call anemones Parsley Roses because of their fringed leaves.

But Celia Fiennes has no taste for these out-of-date gardens. She likes the new style, what she calls "the London mode," and the gardens she considers worth describing in detail are all much the same: "a very fine parke which is full of deer and fine rows of trees; you ascend to the house thro' the midst of rows of trees, on either side a very broad Glide or Visto that looks finely to the River and to the adjacent hills, a distance clothed with fine woods . . . the house looks very nobly, the Gardens very fine . . . deck'd with all sorts of trees and greens, very fine Gravel walks and Grass squaires with Statues and fine Grass walks . . . very fine fountains . . . the prospects very delightful." Hampton Court is also "very fine" (there is only one higher level of praise, and that is "very neat"), for the new gardens laid out with the new palace were in the latest "London mode." That is, they were French gardens: the parterre in front of the Wren block, the goose-foot of lime avenues, and the long tree-bordered canal across the park. The parterre has been altered since the seventeenth century, and the long herbaceous border is new, but they still keep much of their early atmosphere. Whether Le Nôtre ever came to England we do not know, but this has always been considered as one of his gardens, and certainly there were French gardeners in England who worked in the authentic French style. The French complained that the rest of Europe never understood Versailles, that they copied the form and missed the spirit, but "the English fall more into our manner of Gardening," says Le Blond patronizingly, "having had Designs sent over to them from hence, which are well enough performed; and have also had French Architects and Gardeners in their Country, who have left their Productions behind them." London and Wise, the most influential gardeners of the day, were among the followers of Le Nôtre, and the seventeenth-century gardens at Stowe, Blenheim, and Greenwich were French-style productions, as well as Bramham Park, and Chatsworth which Celia Fiennes admired for its fountains.

"The French," says one writer, "are very prodigal in their Expences about Fountains," and so these gardens in the French fashion are full of water: simple fountains, multiple fountains, fountains of every imaginable ingenuity, and, of course, our old friends the "water surprises," which Evelyn, travelling about Europe, reports with enthusiasm everywhere he goes. He particularly enjoyed a very up-to-date one of two "musqueteers" (who) "shot us with a streme of water from their musket barrells. The viewing this paradise," he says appreciatively, "made us late." The English gardeners have their own suggestions. "A Statue of a Woman," one recommends, "that at the turning of a private Cock, shall cast Water out of her Nipples into the Spectators Faces" (there is a picture, explicit but wonderfully dignified). Or, again: "Secret Pipes may be under the ground, the ends not appearing above it, that when any Ladies unawares or casually walk or stand over them, by the turning of a stop-cock you may force the Water upright under their Coats to their sudden surprise." The crudely childish taste of the Tudor gardeners has become crudely adolescent. But it will soon be outgrown altogether, so we must enjoy the joke while we still may, and only be thankful for the ladies' sakes that their men had no petrol or electric motors to make the surprises even more efficient and disconcerting (though I would have liked to be there when "the Muses plaied to us on hydraulic organs").

"To recompense the loss of past pleasures, and to buoy up their hopes of another Spring," says one writer, "many have placed in their Gardens, Statues and other curious pieces of Workmanship." He goes on to give us help in placing our statues to the best advantage: "Statues are commendable in the midst of Fountains, in Green Squares, in Groves, and at the end of obscure walks." But we must be careful to give them an appropriate background, for "a Neptune in a Dry Walk, and a Vulcan in the middle of a Fountain, are shocking to common Sense."

But where were they to come from, these sculptured figures which lay in wait at the end of every avenue and bathed endlessly in fountains without number? Italians had only to dig, for the soil of Italy to produce antique figures as plentifully as cypresses for their Renaissance gardens, and Louis XIV's sculptors provided good groups as they were needed. But English soil held no such treasure, nor did the English court harbour fine sculptors. The wealthy brought back good pieces from the Continent, and some of the small lead figures we still have from seventeenth-century gardens are as delightful and unpretentious as the gardening books themselves, but we cannot help suspecting that most of the ambitious marble works of art were quite often, and quite simply, bad. "Statues etc.," warns Rea, who cared only for flowers, "are excellent ornaments and marks of Magnificence; so all such dead works in Gardens, ill done, are little better than blocks in the way to interrupt the sight, but not at all to satisfie the understanding."

Another writer is so concerned by the low level of statuary in England that he wants the King to set up an academy "for its Improvement, and for a Nursery for young ingenious Men;

which when they have learnt to Draw and Carve well, might be distributed amongst the Nobility and Gentry, who most of them stand in great need of these noble Decorations of Statues about their Country-Seats. 'Tis certain there can be no better Method to furnish themselves with Statues than by continually employing four or five Masons, and as many or more Carvers in that Work: 'tis inconceivable what a Show such a number of Men will make in four or five Years time: and the Expence in keeping, no more than that of other common Servants, Wages excepted." He gives us no help about the Wages, but only tells us to put our young sculptors "under the Care of some solid sober Man" and to keep them "as far as possible from all Tipling-Houses, the Bane of all Ingenuity."

However, gardens which were copies of Versailles never really took root in England, any more than Italian gardens like Wilton, which were similar to the French though rather theatrical than intellectual. We lack what Laurence calls La Grand Manier (I would like to know how he pronounced it). Louis XIV had played at being informal and found he was not very good at the game: with Charles II it was not a game at all, but his natural behaviour—too natural, thought Pepys, and he was scarcely a prude. A visiting Italian nobleman has left us a guarded account of his experiences in England. "The King's house" (at Newmarket) "does not deserve the name of a royal residence," and though he scarcely likes to make the same comment on the English court, we can feel his surprise. "The King had left on foot to take exercise . . . in a plain and simple country dress, without any finery." And if Charles had no liking for ceremony, his people had no particular liking for gardens in the fashionable style of Versailles. But in our long history of invasions we have had such practice in adopting the ideas of our conquerors and acclimatizing them to the mild air of England, that this robust intellectual digestion might almost be considered our greatest artistic gift: certainly it has given us a language which is unsurpassed for poetry. So we took the French ideas and translated them into

English as confidently as we changed a foreign-looking word like *jets-d'eau* into the comfortable English *jeddows*.

The gardens we planted in the soil newly enriched by Le Nôtre were in a new style which one writer happily describes as "rural and extensive." They are large and simple, parks rather than gardens, making full use of our English wealth of trees and fine grass which Le Blond so admired. There is a certain formality, a restful order; the trees are planted in avenues, the woods divided up by regular rides, and the water confined in formal basins. But there is no feeling of nature being forced: these gardens are not dominated by the power of Le Nôtre's controlling conception. They are orderly without being logical; they are English, and the tune their musical fountains play is no grand French march, but the cheerful air of "Lilliburlero. "When they please," says Celia Fiennes, they "play Lilibolaro on the chimes," as the pipe and tabor played it before them.

Pepys, who was a shrewd and sensible man, saw how well suited this style was for England. "Walked to Whitehall . . . up and down with Hugh May, who is a very ingenious man" (for in the seventeenth century ingenious and ingenuous both mean intelligent). "Among other things, discoursing of our present fashion of gardens to make them plain, that we have the best walks of gravell in the world, France having none nor Italy; and our green of our bowling allies is better than any they have. So our business here being ayre, this is the best way, only with a little mixture of statues and pots, which may be handsome." Flowers and fruit, he thinks, are best grown by themselves, and the garden kept clear for walking in the open air, "leave the walking Garden only for that use." The gardens of Whitehall, where Pepys was discoursing, adjoined Saint James's Park, whose seventeenth-century layout (the present one is in the eighteenth-century manner) is sometimes said to have been by Le Nôtre, though it was in a very simple style more English than French. In Charles II's time a long canal was made from one end to the other where the lake now lies, an avenue was planted along the

north side where the King played Paille-Maille, and another on
the south where he kept his bird-cages, looked after by Mr.
Storey. The space between was rough grass for walking, and
near the Admiralty Arch was a small enclosure called Spring
Garden because of its fountain. We still have the names. Saint
James's soon became the most popular parade ground of fashionable London. "Some Gentlemen, who have been abroad, have
told me, that there is no publick Place for Walking in any City
on this side Italy, that is so pleasant as St. James's Park . . . of
a large Extent, and disposed in handsome Walks of Lime-Trees
and Elms, a large regular Canal, a Decoy for Ducks . . . the
wild Fowl, such as Ducks and Geese, breed there." There was a
rookery in Carlton House Garden, and a pelican, as there still is
—"a melancholy water fowl," said Evelyn, "between a stork and
a swan, brought by the Russian Ambassador." But Evelyn had
little love for the Russians. Peter the Great had rented Evelyn's
house and garden at Deptford so that he could be near the dock-
yards, and it was there that he performed his famous feats of
barrow-wheeling over lawns and flower beds and especially
through holly hedges. Poor Evelyn had a particular liking for
holly bushes. "Is there under heaven," he asks in *Sylva*, "a more
glorious and refreshing object than an impregnable holly hedge,
about four hundred feet in length, nine feet high and five in di-
ameter, which I can show in my now ruined gardens at Say's
Court (thanks to the Czar of Muscovy). It mocks the rudest assaults of the weather, beasts, or hedge-breakers." But it did not
mock the assaults of Czar Peter, who enjoyed being pushed
through it in a wheelbarrow. He was obviously no meek garden-
lover to be daunted by a few prickles, and the damage he did at
Sayes Court (it included three wheelbarrows) was assessed by
Wren at £150 and paid by the Government as a kind of war
damage. "A right nasty tenant," said Evelyn, and though we
sympathize with him, we feel less indignant than we should if
Peter had destroyed Mr. Meager's garden or John Rea's; for,
with all his ability, we do not find Evelyn a very sympathetic
personality, any more than Pepys did. But he had a wide knowl-

edge of trees and their culture, which makes him an important figure in this age of gardens where trees and grass are the Chief Beauties.

One of the pleasures of living in the country is the auction sales of furniture in old houses. We see a notice in the county newspaper and plan our week to allow the day off. Away we go after breakfast, promising ourselves that this time we really will buy only the things we need, but all the while following notices "TO THE SALE" nailed crookedly on trees at the corners of lanes. "SALE THIS DAY" it says finally in red letters across the notice on the gatepost, and no three words could promise greater pleasure. For it is not only that we find treasures for a song, it is also the fun of going through other people's belongings, of feeling the intimate atmosphere of someone else's life, even, if we are lucky, the life of a different age. It was this, after all, which drew Celia Fiennes along all her muddy miles of roads.

We arrive with our catalogue and our lunch in a basket, and when we have been through every room of furniture, looked through every drawer and cupboard, every table crowded with china and ornaments, then we go back to the marquee on the front lawn and settle down expectantly like children at a pantomime, comfortable in the rows of odd chairs which will later on be sold.

The Auctioneer is our host, and he knows he is there just as much to keep us all happy as to sell the furniture in the house behind him, for if we are not happy we shall go home, and then there will be no one to sell it to. "Good morning, ladies and gentlemen," he greets us, and makes a welcoming speech about how lucky we are to have a fine day, and how there will be an hour off for lunch, and cups of tea for 2d. in the back garden—for all the world as if we were on holiday and out for pleasure, which of course we are.

Then the show begins, and relays of porters carrying the various lots appear through the flaps at the back of the tent like actors from the wings. Such astonishing things people have in their houses, such unlikely objects they collect, such incongruous oddments someone has put together on a tray to be sold as one lot. And I think how eccentric my own household might seem if it were sold up like this at random (especially the things I have bought in sales).

The Auctioneer is a cross between a prima donna and a master of ceremonies, and he is a tireless performer. He encourages us, he appeals to us, he scolds us for being slow, he tells us we don't know the value of good things, he works up a repertoire of re-curring jokes which everyone laughs at every time. "This elegant chaise-longue," he says, and points to my chair. "The lady will tell you how comfortable it is." And I stand up while he sells the chair from under me, and I assure the audience, who know per-fectly well that every spring is broken, that "Yes, I have never sat in a chair so comfortable." It is all the greatest fun, and at the end we go home laden with unexpected treasures, and (for all our resolutions) with extraordinary white elephants we cannot imagine any possible use for.

Once in a sale at an eighteenth-century mansion I bought a pile of old pictures, so velvety with dust that I could make out nothing but black and gold frames, and lines on old paper which might be maps or might be drawings. When I had washed them clean of a century or so of dirt, I found they were engravings by Kip of English country-seats and their gardens at the begin-ning of the eighteenth century. They are bird's-eye views, half map, half picture, and they have a most intriguing air of sophisti-cated naïveté. There are Rural Seats, said Evelyn in his *Sylva*, "dispersed through the whole nation, conspicuous not only for the structure of their houses, built after the best rules of architec-ture, but for situation, gardens, canals, walks, avenues, parks, forests, ponds, prospect and vistas, groves, woods, and large plan-tations, and other the most charming and delightful recesses, natural and artificial." Well, there they are in Kip's drawings, and I never pass them, hanging now on our London staircase, without saying to myself: "Rural and extensive," for it perfectly describes them. Extensive they certainly are, for they include woods for timber and orchards for fruit trees as well as the approaching avenues and the formal gardens near the house. And they are just as certainly rural. By "rural" the seventeenth-century writer meant an easy lack of formality: the walks of the avenues left simple grass, the vegetable garden planted near the house for convenience, a walled-in space for favourite flowers and bother the plan. But they are rural, too, in our rustic sense of the word. Versailles might be anywhere—even in the middle of Paris, if there were space enough and vistas—but, looking at these pictures, we know at once that they are in the country. Much of the area is no more than fields crossed or bordered by rows of trees, and in the meadow between, animals graze unconscious that they are in an English version of Versailles. The neatly planted "bosketts" only repeat the pattern of the neatly planted haycocks over the hedge, where men and horses are working in the summer fields. The round haystacks are as much at home, and as decorative in the picture, as the round clipped trees. There can never have been a pleasanter way of laying out English gardens, and the French can complain as much as they please that we never understood the spirit of Versailles. Though of course they are right and we never have done. We disturb our green vistas with coloured flowers, blur the edges of formal pools with water lilies—there are lilies in the canal at Hampton Court —troubling the serene outlines, weakening to prettiness what should be noble and austere.

What we did learn, however, and very thoroughly, from the French in the seventeenth century, was to plant trees in rows. "We have been to Boughton," wrote Augustus Hare, "the great desolate house . . . built by the Duke of Montagu, who was ambassador to Louis XIV, and the King lent him a French architect and gardener. He made it as like a French château as possible. Then he told his friends that he must plant an avenue to drive to London by, and when they remonstrated that an immense part of the way to London did not belong to him, he said 'Well, at any rate I will have an avenue of the same length,' and he planted seventy-two miles of it in his park. These trees, hemming in the view in all directions, make the place indescribably dull."

The Dutch style of gardening, which became popular in England with Dutch King William towards the end of the seventeenth century, was another variation in misunderstanding of the French Grand Manner. Le Blond had seen quite clearly the dangers of the French style: that it might become too fiddling and too artificial, too much divided up, too cluttered with ornaments

Avenues run wild at Badminton.

and fussy detail. The Dutch gardens proved him to be perfectly right. In a small space, he said, we must be content with a few simple things on a large scale, but this was exactly what the Dutch were not content with. Into gardens much smaller than the smallest Le Blond ever considered, they crammed everything: canals and fountains, walks and hedges, statues and topiary, trees with trunks painted in coloured stripes, and, above all, parterres—beds and flowers planted with meticulous exactness, measured out to the half-inch. These were no longer gardens for palaces, but for doll's houses—"The Dutch Taste, of which the

People of the common level of Understanding grew so fond; being delighted with little Niceties and fantastical Operations of Art, always thinking that the finest, which was least natural." For even while they were popular, men of taste considered these gardens absurd—not only Le Blond, who dismisses them in a phrase: "the whimsical Designs of Holland and Flanders."

There was much water in the Dutch gardens, but they ladled out Le Nôtre's wide levels into little basins and toy canals of no particular plan. And their gardens were always "stuffed too thick with Box," a shrub they valued highly because it was "tonsile" and "patient of the sissors," an excellent bush for clipping into tiny hedges and for the topiary work in which they delighted. The Dutch gardeners could never leave anything alone, but "Our Trees," complains one writer, "rise in Cones Globes and Pyramids," and "a Citizen became no sooner Master of a Pair of Yews, but he entertained Thoughts of erecting them into Giants like those of Guildhall."

The favourite flower of these gardeners, as we could guess without knowing, was the tulip, and trade in tulips became as fantastic a speculation as the South Sea Bubble later on. The "broken" tulips which they chiefly prized, their petals streaked and flamed with a contrasting colour, were of a style exactly to suit their taste for the artificial, the bright and fussy. And florists' tulips are the ideal tidy flower for the tidy-minded to marshall into exact rows: from each bulb one flower, all the same size, all the same shape, held rigid on stalks like so many green pokers. They are the most uncompromising of flowers, and difficult to place in any natural garden arrangement. But, dull as they are, the coarse floppy leaves have a waxy bloom which is attractive, and, bundled together, the stalks make the same leathery creaking noise which delighted Gerard Manley Hopkins in bluebells: "a brittle rub and jostle like the noise of a hurdle strained by leaning against."

Of the culture of their tulips they made the most absurd mystery. "I was forbid," says the author of *The Dutch Florist*, "as it were by the Inspiration of a Divine Genius to declare this Mystery to any but the Knowing, that it might not be defiled by the Profane and Vulgar," and there follows a lunatic abracadabra about the Strength of your Mother and the Ashes of her Bones and the Ground shall be filled with Oysters. Which tells us one thing very clearly: that it is a characteristic of small minds to love secrets, and to make mysteries of simple things.

Though perhaps we should never mock any gardener, and besides, the Dutch gardens are not so very different from the Tudor ones; it is only that they lack their curious charm. But the seventeenth-century Dutchman was, in any case, impervious. "A Dutch merchant's accounts and his garden were kept with the same degree of accuracy and attention," says one critic maliciously, scorning his art and commerce both at once. But the Dutch gardener would have welcomed his remark as warm praise. "Beds," he says, "must not be broader than two Foot and a Half, that you may divide them into Rows five Inches Distance from each other, as well in Length as Breadth: which is the most regular Way, for Tulips ought to be planted at an equal Distance from one another. The Beds being so prepared, you must make use of a Line to strike the Rows equally distant in Length, and of a Rule to divide them exactly square in Breadth; remembering always to leave two Inches and a Half at each Edge of the Bed. Tulips planted in so regular an Order shew the Ingenuity of the Gardener." They do indeed. "You must also observe, when the Tulips are planted, to put on one Side of the Bed as many small Sticks as there are Roots, and not let them stand above two Inches above the Ground: Let every fifth Stick be bigger than the others; and continuing thus from one Hand to the other, and from one Row to the other, set down the Name of each Tulip on the Stick, that at one Cast of an Eye you may presently tell the Name of any Flower, be it the first, second, third, fourth, or fifth Row, before any one shews itself above Ground, which will be a great Satisfaction to the Florist."

"Flowers," says John Rea, who was not Dutch but English, "are the wealth glory and delight of a Garden." It is a judgement which our gardeners have seldom quarrelled with, for we have seldom considered gardening as one of the fine arts. So the seventeenth-century gardener turned his back on Le Nôtre's noble vistas to "delight in the fairness and trim growing of [his] Flowers," and in the significant silence of the perfectly planned spaces, we hear his homely gentle voice telling us how to make our Gilliflowers open equally without splitting the green cup of their calyx: "Save the Wesand-pipe of great Fowls, as Geese etc. and

Bowling green and drying ground in a formal garden.

being cut into several rings, put over the pods of the flowers, thereby causing them to blow round and handsome."

In France, too, there were plenty of gardeners who loved flowers and ignored planning. Quintinye was the chief authority on practical garden work, and was constantly quoted in English translations. He begins with a very shrewd account of the qualities to look for in a good gardener, and one most desirable virtue is a hard-working wife who will take his place when needed: it is a very different list from Le Blond's. Among our English writers, Parkinson was still much respected, but so many new flowers had been discovered since his time that new books were needed. "I easily perceived Mr. Parkinsons Book to want the addition of many noble things of newer discovery, and that a multitude of those there set out, were by Time grown stale, and for Unworthiness turned out of every good Garden." But for all the "vast Perfection we in this Island are arrived at in Gard'ning," our climate hinders us. France and Italy can grow flowers which will not prosper with us, for their summers are reliable, "as those that are upon Terra Firma do observe," says one writer, for all the world as if England were not solid earth at all, but only an island floating in the sea, like the whales which sailors mistook for land in old sea-stories.

The flowers these gardeners list include many new plants from both East and West, but the favourites are still the same. The long-loved Gilliflower is still cherished, being "no less profitable than pleasante, they do not only preserve the bodies of men" (when used in medicines) "but also doth keep the minde and spiritual parts from terable and fearfull dreames through their heavenly savour, and most sweet pleasant odor."

But the newer-fashioned preferred the tulips of the Dutch gardens, and there are long accounts of how to grow them to perfection. Poor ground makes flowers light-coloured, good ground dark: all the writers affirm this so confidently that perhaps it is true. But then I remember the Cures for Moles, and I wonder. They tell us, too, what we should do to make them break into the flamelike streaks which were the love of fashion. We know now that the breaking of tulips is a virus disease, but the seventeenth century knew nothing of viruses; they only knew that this flaming was not a reliable beauty in any tulip, but would often disappear, especially in the largest and healthiest flowers, and that growing them in poor conditions encouraged it.

Auriculas were still popular, and Emines or Animons or Anemonies (Meager is no more confident about his spelling than I am). In the seventeenth century the first flower-shows began, with prizes for the best blooms. These were humble competitions and encouraged the love of flowers in ordinary people who had no parks or greenhouses, but only back gardens. Later on, different districts specialized in different flowers, and from my North Country childhood I remember a tradition for growing auriculas still alive in back yards and window-sills—an unexpected enthusiasm of the drab little Northern towns, like keeping whippet dogs and canary birds and singing *The Messiah* at Christmas.

The seventeenth-century gardeners valued their evergreens as we do. Greens or Perennial Greens they call them, "it seeming

Drawing by Crispin de Passe.

from these to be summer all the winter." Laurustinus, which they call the Wild Bay, was their favourite, as it was the Tudor gardeners', and they also prized cherry-laurel, privet, holly, pyracantha, and phillyrea, which they spell Filaree. They grew exotics in tubs which were wintered indoors, especially orange trees, Le Nôtre's favourite, but also lemons, pomegranates, aloes,

. 189 .

and even bananas and pineapples. There is a curious picture of a
kneeling gardener presenting the first English pineapple to King
Charles II, against the background of a formal garden with fountains. But it is hard to understand how they ever managed to
keep alive plants which needed shelter in the winter, for these
were kept in large rooms heated only with charcoal and a very
inadequate flue. The only thermometer was a bowl of water set
on the floor: if it froze, it meant the weather was cold; if it did
not freeze, it drowned the mice who came to drink. Nor were
their orangeries any better lit than heated. They had windows to
the floor, but no glass in the roofs, and it is not surprising that the
gardeners complain of their plants turning yellow. But it was for
want of air, so they thought, and they recommend a great deal
of opening of windows. They boxed up their tender flowers
against the winter cold, they brought in potted shrubs as "chimney plants" to fill their empty hearths in the summer, and when
these poor prisoners languished in the dark, it was not, so the
gardeners thought, because they were starved of light which is
the life of a plant, but because they lacked fresh air, "they want
the free Circulation of the Atmosphere." Food, water, and air—
these they knew a man must have to live, and so, they reasoned,
must a plant. But that light is almost more vital than any of these,
they had no idea, so that they advise all kinds of unlikely garden
practices, like burying plants in roofed-over pits to shelter them
from the "murd'ring Winds of March." Though even then, they
say sadly, many plants will "die and pine away." But since air
and light often go together, much of their advice is still useful.
Plants should not be set between high walls or they will languish,
and pot-plants in the hearth must be often set out in the open to
recover from their confinement.

If we know more about light and virus diseases than the seventeenth century, they knew ways of handling plants which we
have forgotten, "secrets not till now divulg'd." The pictures in
the gardening books show workmen transplanting trees of a
truly heroic size which we should never dare to attempt. Two or
three times the height of a man, with a trunk as thick as his body,
they dig them up confidently and plant them somewhere else.

Perhaps the trees were hardier then, like the people. At Hampton Court a row of limes was moved forty years after they were planted, and fully grown forest trees were carried in hundreds to Versailles (where three quarters of them died and were replaced). Even as late as the nineteenth century in England, huge conifers were carried from Kent to the Rothschild manor at Waddesdon so that the new grounds should look immediately ancestral; and the long trucks they were carried on held up all the traffic in the Strand as they came through London.

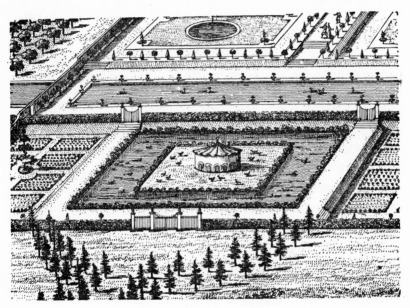

An Aviary on a Formal Island.

The books give various "secrets" for moving large trees. The most reasonable is to dig round them a year before they are to be moved, cutting through all the large roots, so that they produce a close mesh of new fibres which will hold a ball of undisturbed earth when the tree is transplanted a year later. Another way, which sounds too ingenious to be true, was to dig a trench round the tree in frosty weather and drench the roots with water. When this froze, the tree and its roots could be lifted as a solid block. An even more hazardous method was for moving trees in full summer leaf. A hole was dug for the coming tree and filled with fine earth and water, which was stirred round to make a kind of mud porridge. The leafy tree was then dug up and plunged into this "pap," as the writer calls it, where it grew, so he assures us, even more vigorously than if it had never been moved, producing a fine crop of fruit the very same year.

The trees to be moved were often fruit trees, for the seventeenth-century gardeners lavished their greatest care on orchards. The purists might scorn them as "Rather a confused Chaos of Fruit-Trees than a Regular Garden," but the ordinary gardener went on happily with his pruning and took no notice. Sir William Temple wrote an essay of "Gardening in the Year 1685." "Few countries are before us," he says, "either in the elegance of our gardens, or in the number of our plants." He has a certain talent for boasting without offence, but as a gardener he cares little for the elegance of planning, and even less for growing flowers, "which is more the ladies' part than the men's," he says, and we wonder if Dorothy Osborne kept the flower garden. His real love is for his fruit trees, and these, says Evelyn, were "most exquisitely rail'd and train'd, far better than I ever noticed elsewhere." Even the Puritans, who were doubtful whether flower gardens could be justified since they were only for pleasure, encouraged orchards both for Pleasure and Profit.

Almost as important as the orchard was the Garden for Herbs. Our idea of a herb garden is a small and somewhat self-conscious plot outside the windows of a country tea-shop. It is set with clumps of neat plants like thyme and marjoram, to be used doubtfully as flavourings by vegetarian cooks in skirts of hand-woven tweed. But a seventeenth-century herb garden was quite simply a vegetable garden, and there is nothing quaint about the lists of "divers sorts of herbs" which they recommend: "Beetes, Carrots, Garlick, horse-radish, Cabbages, Colliflowers, Parsnips, Pease and Spinage, Potatos, Rubarb and Hartichoaks."

Two famous gardens which still survive from this time are the Chelsea Physicke Garden in London, which I have only seen through the locked gates, and the Botanical Garden at Oxford, which was built in 1632 on the site of a Jews' cemetery, five acres of ground given by the Earl of Danby, and enclosed by fourteen-foot-high walls which cost £5,000. The gateways were a further £500, and were paid for by a fine levied on the Oxford antiquary Anthony à Wood for libelling the Earl of Clarendon. They were designed by Inigo Jones, and I think there can be no more inviting entrance to any garden. The pillars which hold up the pediment are sliced with alternate layers of rusticated stone, which stand out like the tufts on the legs of fashionable poodles. On each side of the entrance arch there is a figure in a niche—Charles and Danby, so the inscription says, both dressed up in delightfully theatrical armour and boots like the Principal Boy in a pantomime, both short-legged to fit their niches, one bewigged, the other crowned with laurels, both making fine heroic gestures whose effect is somewhat subdued because both lack an arm. The garden inside its fourteen-foot wall is the pleasantest place in all Oxford, though I have been there many times and never found the "intelligent assistant" promised me by an early nineteenth-century guide-book: "Persons who are fond of the study of botany may receive minute information respecting the plants in this Garden from the intelligent assistant to the Professor, who is always on the spot for the purpose of conducting strangers to the different walks, the Green-houses and Hot-houses."

Beyond the old walled garden is a new one open to Christ Church Meadow which lies beyond, a calm green sea of level grass with walls for cliffs. Even the seats round the edge share this illusion of water, raised on steps, like boats drawn up the beach beyond reach of the tide. And from the tall trees the nuthatches whistle like boys.

The seventeenth and early eighteenth centuries are, above all others in England, the age of popular gardening. Not only did every cottage have its garden, but every town house, too, however humble. "There is scarce an Ingenious Citizen that by his confinement to a Shop, being denied the priviledge of having a real Garden, but hath his boxes, pots, or other receptacles for Flowers Plants etc. In imitation of it, what curious Representations of Banquets of Fruits, Flower-pots, Gardens and such like are painted to the life, to please the Eye, and satisfie the fancy of such that either cannot obtain the Felicity of enjoying them in reality, or to supply the defect the Winter annually brings." It was still the same in 1722 when Thomas Fairchild wrote *The City Gardener:* "I find that almost every Body, whose Business requires them to be constantly in Town, will have something of a Garden at any rate." Or if they had not so much as a square yard of earth, then they "furnish their Rooms or Chambers with Basons of Flowers and Bough-pots, rather than not have something of a Garden before them."

We often talk as if the smoke and soot of London were modern plagues unknown before the Industrial Revolution, but Parkinson lamented the "smoake of sea coales" which "of all others is the worst, as our citie of London can give proof sufficient, wherein neither herbe nor tree will long prosper; nor hath done ever since the use of sea-coales beganne to be frequent therein." Evelyn is almost violent about the "clouds of smoke and soot, over and above great cities and other volcanoes, continually vomiting out their acrimonious and sometimes pestiferous fervour, infecting the ambient air, as it perpetually does about London and for many miles adjacent." (I wonder what he meant by other volcanoes.) After the Great Fire he suggested a plan for London as a garden city surrounded by plots of thirty to forty acres, planted with shrubs and sweet-smelling flowers whose fragrance would be "perpetually fanned" over the town.

Fairchild gives lists of plants which will grow even "much oppres'd with the London Smoke." Flowers and deciduous trees are easy, for flowers can be renewed each year, and most deciduous trees will grow if they are not cut about. The difficulty with the garden of a London square, he says, is "how to make it look well in the Winter, and that Part of the Spring, when Persons of Distinction are in Town." And, reading him, I suddenly remembered a village woman who used to come and help me to clean. She had been a maid once in a big London house of balls and dinners and entertainments, and her year, too, had its seasons, as important as the gardener's: "You'd hear them crying Lavender in the streets outside, and you'd know the Season was over."

So it was no use, said Fairchild, planting a fashionable square with the flowers of late summer, "for the Persons of Distinction . . . will not pay for a Thing that they have no Benefit of, or Pleasure in." And we think how often our own borders have flowered for themselves alone while we were away on summer holidays. Nor is Pepys's plain style of trees and grass suitable, Fairchild thinks, for a small London square: "Wilderness-Work" of trees and flowering shrubs, cut through by walks and edged with flowers, will "divert the Gentry better than looking out of the Windows upon an open Figure." London gardens should be planted with bulbs and spring flowers, and above all with evergreens, he says, and tells us which will grow. The vine, too, "will do very well in London," and so it still does. I grow one in a tub which ripens small black grapes, and the children eat them with ostentatious pleasure, though I have tried, too, and they taste very little of anything at all except soot.

Fairchild had a high reputation among gardeners of his day, and his name appears over and over in their books. He could, so one writer tells us with awe, strike a laurustinus bush from a cutting of a single leaf. He kept a nursery garden at Hoxton, where he sold all kinds of shrubs and flowers, and he warns us against buying plants in shops and markets, where they have been long out of the earth: "I have seen Plants that were to be sold in the Markets, that were as uncertain of Growth as a Piece of Noah's Ark would be, had we it here to plant."

The seventeenth-century Frenchman thought. He thought about Life, one supposes, and about Man (certainly they would both have capital letters), and he made Versailles with all it stood for. The seventeenth-century Englishman also thought, and his thinking was just as much a journey from the old world

to the new, but by a different road. The French are a Latin
people with a natural sense of form. We are not. But we are
practical if somewhat eccentric scientists, and when Newton sat
in a garden he thought, not about the laws of classical proportion,
but about the law of gravity. Science was very close to the
garden in the seventeenth century, as it no longer is in our days
of atom-splitting and electron microscopes. Scientists now seem
remote technical creatures who use elaborate apparatus as extra
senses beyond our human seeing and hearing and feeling, but in
the seventeenth century they were ordinary intelligent human
beings who sat under a tree and watched apples fall with eyes
the same as ours.

Newton had many other theories even closer to gardening;
he thought, for instance, that the seeds of plants like holly, which
normally passed through the body of a bird, might need similar
conditions if they were to germinate quickly, and he suggested
they should be kept in wet bran before they were planted. The
more thoughtful gardeners were constantly experimenting—on
the action of roots, the transpiration of water through the leaves,
the different effects of different soils, and, above all, on the
circulation of the sap, which they tried to explain by Harvey's
discovery of the circulation of the blood. The Royal Society was
extremely active, botany was developing as a science, the Society
of Apothecaries was founded and went "herbalizing" in the
fields round London, and intelligent men spent their leisure in
scientific experiments, exchanging their results in long letters.
The gardening books constantly address "the Curious" or
"Curious Gentlemen," meaning this active audience of intelligent
amateurs.

Objective observation was a growing habit, yet there were
still plenty of superstitious ideas difficult to uproot. Perfectly
sensible people still believed that seeds should be sown by the
phases of the moon, that the earth produced the plants natural
to it, and that soil could be prepared which would bring forth
corn of its own accord without planting seed. Moss, says one
writer, was a "spontaneous excrescence . . . proceeding from

the natural inclination of the matter on which it grew, animated by the Celestial influences." Evelyn did not believe it, affirming that all plants "had their original from seeds. And I think the same of all animals, even to the minutest worm and insect." Certainly Isaak Walton would not have agreed with Evelyn, for did he not breed maggots for bait simply by hanging meat in the sun? But many of the Curious knew he was right. "A learned Virtuoso, by the help of a Microscope hath observed the Seed-cods of Moss to contain Seeds in them no less wonderful for the greatness of number than the smallness of bulk, which seed Vessels when ripe, he pressing them pretty hard, found that there was a small dust went out of them, which seemed to vanish into the Air; pressing and squeezing others of them upon a black plate, and examining the Powder with a Microscope he found it to be a great heap of exceeding small Seeds. These seeds being thus small may be carried into the Air from place to place, even to the tops of the highest Towers or places remote and be there sown."

But the old-fashioned were not convinced. How are heavy seeds carried? they asked, as if they had never seen a bird or a squirrel. How do oaks and beeches and hollies appear in cleared woodland? How is it that "so great a quantity of Erysimum or Irio should be sown in the Ruins after the late great conflagration in London, where it was observed that more of it grew there than was known to be in all Europe besides"?

Irio we know as London rocket, a cornfield weed of the East brought to England in imported grain. When the docks were destroyed by fire, the seeds escaped from the corn stored in the London warehouses and spread over the burnt-out city, as rose-bay willow-herb has comforted the Ruins of our own "late great conflagration."

The Art of Gardening in Three Books, by J. W. Gent, was published in 1677, and J.W. is John Woolridge. He covers all the seventeenth-century garden styles: French planning and English adaptations, Dutch niceties and city gardens; he is interested in flowers and fruit and herbs, in old superstitions and new experiments. He is all the seventeenth-century gardeners in one.

The First Book, says the title page proudly in fine large print, "Treateth of the Excellency, Scituation, Soil, Form, Walks, Arbours, Springs, Fountains, Waterworks, Grotto's, Statues and other Magnificent Ornaments of Gardens."

The Second Book, in medium-sized print, as being a humbler division of the art, "Treateth of all sorts of Trees planted for Ornament or Shade, Winter Greens, Flower Trees, and Flowers, that are usually propagated and preserv'd in the Gardens of the best Florists."

The Third Book, in such humble small print that we can scarcely read it, "Treateth of the Kitchin Garden, and of the great variety of Plants propagated for food or for any culinary uses."

"Illustrated with Sculptures" (by which he means copper plates, but there are none) "representing the form of Gardens, according to the newest Models."

From which survey we might guess that Woolridge's garden would be a compromise between the formal grounds of France and the English love of flowers, "the affections of our Country-men so naturally tending that way." And so it is: a most success-ful compromise.

"Gardening," he says, "is the beautifying of Seats with in-vegetate Ornaments," and what we notice first is that when he takes trouble his style is most unfortunate. Yet he means well; his "stile is plain," he says, "and suited to the Vulgar." But he talks about Sedentary Repasts and calls gardening books Hortu-lane Tracts. Yet even an educated man like Evelyn is sometimes no better, and from now on we must forget that ordinary gar-deners once wrote fine English, and think instead about what they have to say. Though mercifully they often forget to be literary and write simple and sometimes vivid prose.

Woolridge is very thorough in his advice, and begins with the improvement of soil, though here he is brief, he says, because "that most learned of Hortulane Authors, Evelin, hath lately been very copious on the same subject." (This was the *Discourse of Earth* delivered to the Royal Society, and I, too, found it very copious.) He then gives advice for laying out "A Complete Garden with its Magnificent Ornaments, its Stately Groves," and so on—we know the list by heart by this time. "A plain level is best for a Garden," he says, though the eighteenth century would soon deny it, and "Woods and Water two of the best Ornaments of the Seat." But though he approves of "the new mode of Gravel Walks and Grass-plots . . . with those Ornamental Shades that now are become common," he loves flowers, and is sad that "Many stately Country Residences have banish'd out of their Gardens Flowers, . . . but it's hoped that this new, useless and unpleasant mode, will like many other vanities grow out of Fashion."

"In your Garden of Pleasure," he says, and he might be talking directly to our labourless age, "you aught to be frugal of cost and pains," and he advises us against such Tudor pleasures as trellises and fanciful hedges. As for the arbours so beloved since the earliest mediæval gardens, they not only need too much work to keep them, but they are damp and airless, he says, and a movable seat set under a tree for shade "is much more pleasant than to be hood-winked in an Arbour." Of course it is, but we must beware of growing too reasonable or we shall give up gardening altogether and sit in the fields instead. However, we need have no fear for Woolridge: he has a reassuringly fanciful taste in grottoes and "fountains to sing like birds," and his cure for caterpillars is worthy of Thomas Hill: "To destroy Caterpillars on Trees . . . make a Ring of Tar towards the bottom of your Tree, then hang a bag full of Pismires on the Tree that they may easily get out, and when they cannot get down by reason of the Tar, rather than they will starve for hunger, they will eat up all the Caterpillars." But he does not tell us how to get rid of the ants. Perhaps we simply take away the Ring of Tar and they will all go home again.

Although we may know simpler ways than Woolridge for discouraging our twentieth-century caterpillars, we have none better for laying out gardens. First, he tells us, plan the garden

as a whole, then plant it with trees and shrubs, especially evergreens, and last of all set flowers "in the intervals that remain
and the borders of the Walks." Evergreens he values highly,
since half the garden year is winter—"Winter," he says, "that
seems elsewhere most barren, here amongst these Greens appears
like a perpetual Spring." He has a fancy, too, for variegated
shrubs, and thinks that the Gilded-leafed Plants should be
grouped together to make a Golden Grove. Flowering shrubs
are "Flower Trees," and he recommends them because they
need little attention. I think of our modern fashion for flowering
shrubs, and I suspect that there are no new ideas in gardening,
just as there are no new ways of making love, since both have
been going on so long already, ever since Adam and Eve and the
Garden of Eden.

As for flowers, they are "the best Ornaments, the Miracles of
Nature," and Woolridge cherishes them as children. "Cherish
your Gilliflowers" (from too much sun) "by some artificial
Skreen," and from bad weather in a "Cave or Pitt, for there no
Winds nor severe Frosts can annoy them, the driving rains also
cannot much offend them." Gilliflowers (they were sometimes
called carnations now, a name used because the original ones
were flesh-coloured) are still his most treasured flowers, though
tulips are almost as precious. Ranunculas, anemones, and cyclamens are still favourites, and auriculas, he says, "considering
their size are the finest Flowers the choicest Garden holds."
London pride he calls London Tufts or Pride of London, and
"Colchicums are called Naked Boyes because they appear naked
out of the Earth and are withered and gone before the green
leaves appear." He writes well enough, after all.

The French gardens often had aviaries of singing birds, but
Englishmen have not much liked wild birds in cages, and Woolridge feels as the Tudor gardeners did before him. "One of the
pleasures belonging to a Garden is an Aviary, but we are rather
for an Aviary at large, that the whole Garden with its Groves
and Avenues may be full of these pretty singers." As for the

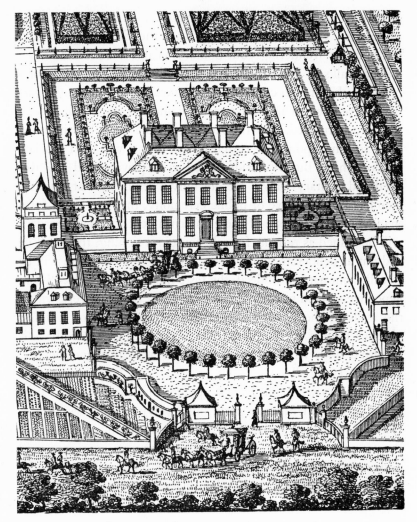

A seventeenth-century entrance court.

vista, "your principal walk," he says dutifully, following the French model, "should extend it self as far as you can in length," and he mentions "the priviledges and advantages of Air and View." But his heart is not in it: he talks too often and too eagerly of "Solitary repose," of "Retired and Solitary walks" (Solitary is honoured with a capital S, even though it is only an

. 201 .

adjective), and summer-houses "private . . . from frequent disturbances." Open fences certainly leave the view open, he says, but only by "rendering your Solitary Walks less private."

The walks of Versailles were not Solitary; privacy was not a privilege the French court set much store by, and the royal gardens were open to all who cared to come and stare: "all accesse is freely permitted." By the Revolution the gates had been set open so long upon their rusted hinges that it was then too late to close them. But Woolridge liked to be private, and his "Retired and Solitary walks" are not only a reminder that Englishmen had no great love of public ceremony, they are also a foreshadowing of the taste of the eighteenth century. Soon gardens will be valued as retreats for self-conscious sighing; they will be laid out as deliberate wildernesses, and the highest praise will be to call them natural. Indeed, the taste has begun already. "From hence we walked into the Parke, which for being intirely within the walls of the City is particularly remarkable; nor is it less pleasant than if in the most solitary recesses, so naturally is it furnish'd with whatever may render it agreeable, melancholy, and country-like."

It is not, as we might have supposed, the late eighteenth century praising a landscape park, but Evelyn writing as early as 1641. Agreeable, melancholy, and country-like. Capability Brown was not, after all, so revolutionary an innovator, and perhaps all fashions only interpret into popular language the changes which have already taken place in sophisticated taste.

CHAPTER EIGHT

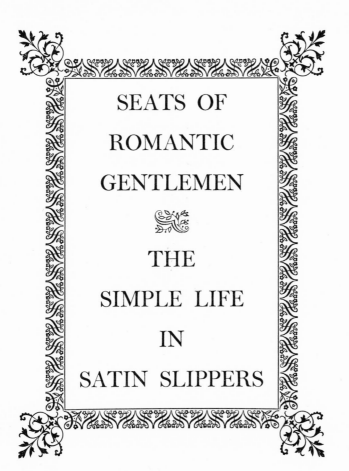

SEATS OF

ROMANTIC

GENTLEMEN

THE

SIMPLE LIFE

IN

SATIN SLIPPERS

WHEN I WAS A CHILD WE LIVED IN THE MID-
dle of a sprawling industrial city, and because I longed
for the far-off country, I hated parks. For parks, I felt, promised
to be country, but when you came to know them were as
artificial as gardens, and without the flowers. For the parks of
industrial cities are the grounds of eighteenth-century mansions
laid out in the style of Capability Brown, and bought by the
Corporation when the resident family retreated before the
industrial flood. They are not country preserved, as I thought
they were, seeing them for the first time, but deliberate works of
art, and I cared nothing at all for works of art. I wanted the
simple country.

"Small paths to the greenwood"—it was a line I had found in
an old poem, and I used to say it to myself over and over, until
it became a magic spell which I need only repeat under my
breath to follow in fancy a narrow turf path which led to the
edge of a remote and flowery wood and disappeared among the
leafy summer trees, a green and secret invitation.

"Small paths to the greenwood . . ." I said it often as I followed eighteenth-century paths through eighteenth-century
landscapes, and when I found in the end only some contrived
and public view, some shabby Classical temple with initials

scraped in the plaster, I was every time most wretchedly dis-illusioned. For the "carpet walks" of the landscape parks have no intention of losing us in the greenwood. They are as carefully planned as Louis XIV's tour of Versailles, to lead us to the best view-point for admiring a landscape deliberately laid out as a work of art. But I never recognized the art, only the artificiality, for I think children have very little æsthetic feeling before adolescence, and when their taste corresponds with ours, as in the modern fashion for the paintings of very small children, it is for reasons other than æsthetic.

So I hated all parks when I was a child, all but one, and that was too small to promise anything, for you could see right across it and through the railings at the other side. It was called Charlie Cake Park, though I never knew why unless it was the shape, an acute triangle of land wedged between two converging roads and laid out as a garden of trees and shrubs and flowers, and grass not to be walked on. It was exactly an acre, so someone told me, and because we remember everything from our child-hood as wonderfully large, my idea of an acre will always be a triangular area of a most unlikely size; even now, when someone says "a field of ten acres," I do a jig-saw puzzle in my head, fitting together ten narrow triangles to make a square.

This park I loved because it was a garden, but all the rest I hated, for children are violent in their affections and the world is black and white. The other parks were shams, I thought; their promises were lies, like the highly decorated cream-cakes which are sawdust inside. In the end—and it was a milestone in my growing up—I accepted the unhappy truth that I should never find a primrose on their banks, or cowslips in their meadows, or bluebells in their woods, but only docks and nettles and grass without flowers.

"An open country is but a canvas on which a landscape might be designed." So said Horace Walpole, and it is easy to see why I mistook my parks for country. "Any tract of land whose characteristick expressions have been strengthened by art, and in which the spontaneous arrangements of nature have been improved by the hand of taste, ought to be considered as a Garden."

This was a conception completely new in the West, though in China it was so old that no one remembered its beginnings. Marco Polo had come back from the East with descriptions of gardens which we recognize at once as landscape parks, enclosed in a wall eight miles on each side, "ornamented with many handsome trees, and meadows in which are kept various kinds of beasts." But no one believed him, for he invented his fine stories, they thought, and Sir John Mandeville, who repeated his tales, discredited him still further, for the bogus Sir John was quite simply a brazen liar. "I have seen with my own eyes full many times," says this arm-chair traveller who never went beyond France.

Sir William Temple in the seventeenth century had looked curiously at these irregular Chinese gardens "that may, for aught I know, have more beauty than any of the others. . . . Their greatest reach of imagination is employed in contriving figures, where the beauty shall be great, and strike the eye, but without any order or disposition of parts, that shall be commonly or easily observed. And though we have hardly any notion of this sort of beauty, yet they have a particular word to express it . . . Sharawadgi." But these irregular gardens are too difficult for us to attempt, he warns us; "they are adventures of too hard achievement for any common hands; and though there may be more honour if they succeed well, yet there is more dishonour if they fail, and 'tis twenty to one they will; whereas in regular figures, 'tis hard to make any great and remarkable faults."

But revolutionaries are seldom troubled by the difficulties of what they undertake, and the landscape gardeners did not hesitate to sweep away the formal gardens and lay out the ground according to their own theories. Moreover, they were wonderfully satisfied with the results. "We have discovered the point of perfection. We have given the true model of gardening to the world," Walpole boasts as confidently as Le Blond had boasted of his now discredited gardens. "It is surprising how much beauty has been struck out," Walpole goes on, "with how few absurdities." But we shall see later on about the absurdities.

The ideal garden, so they decided, had already been described by Milton in the Garden of Eden, and they quote him time after time. A garden was nature improved, a landscape made more beautiful by art. For certainly, they thought, nature needed improvement: "the scenery of a Garden should differ as much from common nature, as an heroic poem doth from a prose relation." And most improvements are "artificial," for "nature produces nothing either boiled roasted or stewed, and yet we do not eat raw meat." None the less, art must be concealed, for "all forms that are unnatural displease," and "Art should never be allowed to set a foot in the province of nature, otherwise than clandestinely and by night."

The improvements which Art is to undertake in this rather furtive way are to enhance the natural style of the given landscape. "Ground should first be considered with an eye to its peculiar character; whether it be the grand, the savage, the sprightly, the melancholy, the horrid, or the beautifull. As one or other of these characters prevail, one may somewhat strengthen its effect." This division of gardens into various moods is much insisted on by the eighteenth century, and comes from the Chinese; so said Sir William Chambers, a successful architect who shared with Adam the practice of eighteenth-century London. He had been to China, and came back enthusiastic about Eastern gardens, encouraging Englishmen to copy their natural felicities.

But the various atmospheres of eighteenth-century gardens, if they ever existed outside the owners' fancy, are lost now in the unmistakable common style which they all share, the enhanced natural landscape of trees and grass and water. "We have returned to simplicity by force of refinement," said one writer: a statement as deceptively simple as the simplicity it qualifies. Simple, then, serene, and curiously elegant: as a style for parks it is of unsurpassed beauty, even though I still prefer the greenwood, and could never feel, as one enthusiast did, that the view of Blenheim Park from the entrance drive is the most beautiful scene in the world.

"Nature abhors a straight line," said Kent early in the eighteenth century. It is a new and simple and completely revolutionary statement in garden design. Versailles is dismissed in five words, five words which seem to have the truth of an undeniable natural law. And not only must Versailles go, but every other style of garden which Europe has known till this time. None of them will do, they are all of them unnatural, all planned in the straight lines which nature abhors. From now on all level ground must be broken up, all avenues must go, all hedges be destroyed, all drives must wind, all trees be planted naturally in woods and clumps, all water be left with irregular curving edges. It means, in fact, the eighteenth-century landscape park instead of the seventeenth-century formal garden, and though it seems a simple rule to produce such a sea-change, it is the one fundamental difference.

Naturally the new gardeners despised the old, just as Celia Fiennes had done, but the eighteenth century is much more articulate than she was, and has a gift besides for destructive ridicule which laughed away the old formal gardens with surprising thoroughness. The Chinese, so Temple had told them, "say a boy that can tell a hundred, may plant walks of trees in straight lines," and therefore, they argued, he could very well lay out Versailles; "in short, 'tis a garden for a great child," said Walpole, whose own garden was Strawberry Hill. Chambers denied that it was a garden at all; it is a "mere city of verdure," he said, with hedges for walls, walks for streets, open spaces for squares, and statues for people, ranged "in regular lines like soldiers at a procession." Too great regularity, says another writer, "stupifies and dulls the Senses as bad as the constant Noise of a Mill, or turning round for half an Hour would do." Yes, agrees Chambers, and even the great size of formal gardens is only the sum of many small gardens repeated, "like the honest batchelor's feast, which consisted in nothing but a multiplication of his own dinner: three legs of mutton and turneps, three roasted geese, and three buttered apple pies." They are all agreed and repeat in chorus: "Whatever seems the most natural is the grand Taste, whatever possesses formal Regularity is the Mechanical Taste." Nothing, in fact, could be more ridiculous and vulgar than Versailles; Addison said so in the *Spectator*, and we can only be thankful it did not lie in England, to be swept away like the delightful lost gardens of Kip's engravings.

Fashion, like the wind, blows where it fancies. Though the wind, indeed, blows where it must; nor can we help looking for reasons to explain this complete change of heart. And since it is a style which never really flourished outside England except for a few fashionable imitations, the reasons we find must be English reasons. Politically we had been at war with France, and so might well despise our enemy's gardens. But fashion cares little for politics, and the original gardens laid out round Blenheim itself, that monument to our victory over Le Roi Soleil, were gardens in the style of Versailles. So that it is more helpful to look for reasons inside our own country.

The seventeenth century had been an age of political revolution, but the agricultural and industrial revolutions of the eighteenth century had a far more direct effect on the setting of people's lives. The new advances in farming, "the prevailing rage for agriculture," and the final enclosure of the old open common land created a new orderly landscape, and overlaid the scenery with the new patchwork of fields which to us now is so familiar that we think of it as "the country." But to people used to the old countryside of woods and commons, it was altogether too neat and regular and tame, too much like domestic animals whose ears, says one writer without in the least meaning to be funny, are "to receive the Word of Command from their Masters."

From this too tidy country the Masters turned deliberately to the wild and the "natural." The seventeenth-century gardens seemed to them too like the new countryside. There were hedges now round every field; they wanted none in their gardens. "Hedges are universally bad," and so are all the neat enclosures which they surround. Besides, "civil peace and personal liberty were more secure than in any previous age" (it is Trevelyan speaking this time, and not the eighteenth century), and country life was becoming as orderly as the country landscape. There was no need of formal gardens to make visible man's conception of order, just as there was no need for an enclosed garden to make him feel safe. The side of his complicated soul which he now wanted to express in his gardens was not his need for safety or discipline, but his longing for romance and adventure. Mountains were coming into fashion, Salvator Rosa's theatrically wild land-scapes were stylishly popular, by the end of the century *The Mysteries of Udolpho* was a best-seller, and landscape gardens were the height of good taste. It is a natural reaction from formality, and even Louis XIV had felt it strongly enough to try careless week-ending at Marly. Besides, for people who were not princes, "the fine Sett Gardens are so very Expensive in the making and keeping that very few Gentlemen can alienate so much Yearly Revenues towards the Maintenance of those prodigious Gardens." "I will be bold to affirm," one writer assures us, "that £10 will go as far in this" (landscape gardening) "as £50 will in the Methods commonly taken." "Those that would appear splendidly frugal" should follow the new style, for they will find that the "Decoration and Improvement of a Country-Seat will not be that expensive Bug-bear it may of late have appear'd to be."

Bacon had said that gardening follows, not leads, the other arts, but he could not foresee an eighteenth century which would create romantic wildernesses in a classical age. For the eighteenth-century landscape parks are the beginning of the Romantic Revolution, its earliest expression and its most English. Secluded on our islands from the culture of southern Europe, we have been more naturally romantic than classic, we are also gardeners and country-lovers, and from this peculiarly English mixture the eighteenth century created what might well be considered a new form of art, the landscape park.

There are still views beyond the boundary, but they are no longer Le Nôtre's logical vistas of the mind; they have blurred now to the hazy blue distances of romantic painting. Vistas have changed to Prospects, and "Prospects," said Shenstone, "should take in the blue distant hills, but never so remotely that they be not distinguishable from clouds." Garden history, social history, and æsthetic history, too, all are ready for the landscape style.

"I don't see what good it is learning Geometry. I don't see what *use* it is," said one of the children, annoyed that he must finish his homework and not make paper darts to aim through the banisters. "Well, I don't know," the other answered thoughtfully. "It would be very useful for making flower beds in lawns." Euclid might not have agreed, but the Victorians certainly would, and so indeed did the formal gardeners of the beginning of the eighteenth century. For in the Dutch style the regular garden reached depths of triteness which even carpet-bedding could scarcely surpass. "New Improvements," one gardener writes at the head of a chapter which describes a "New Invention for the more speedy Designing of Garden-Plotts; whereby we may produce more Variety of Figures in an Hour's time, than are to be found in all the Books of Gardening now extant. The best Designers may improve their Fancies by it, and may with more certainty hit the Humour of those Gentlemen they work for, without being at the trouble of making many Varieties of Figures or Garden-Plotts, which will lose time, and cause an unnecessary Expence, which frequently discourages Gentlemen from making up their Gardens." This wonderful invention, which he calls a Glass, is simply a kaleidoscope, and he describes enthusiastically, both in words and pictures, how it will produce endless patterns without any effort from the designer. "I think it may not be improper to advertise that the Publisher of these Papers is provided with Glasses of several Sizes ready fitted up for the Experiment at the following Prices: the small sort at three Shillings, and the other at five Shillings."

Small wonder then that intelligent fashion was out of love with formal gardens, that they felt "the want of something at once more grand and more natural," and that the old gardens were swept away, good and bad together, to make way for the new style of nature (more or less) unadorned.

The true eighteenth century, says Trevelyan, does not begin till 1740, and neither, till somewhere about that date, do the true landscape gardens. For they do not arrive all at once with their lawns and clumps and serpentine waters. Temple's *Sharawadgi* was written as early as 1688, and the first gardener of note to follow the Chinese principles was Kent, who leapt the hedge, said Walpole, "and saw all nature was a garden." Perhaps he did, but it was still a fairly formal garden, as we can see at Chiswick House. The pattern is not so much swept away as loosened; the paths are curved instead of straight and there are irregularities in the symmetry, but even in my most hopeful childhood I should never have dreamt of looking for bluebells under Kent's trees.

Richard Bradley, F.R.S., was the first garden journalist, and as early as 1724 he recommends the new style, though rather for snobbery than pleasure. "The more agreeable to Nature our Gardens are made, so much more beauty do they contain, and come nearer that elegant and polite Taste which at present is working in Gardens. . . . Good Judges will judge of Gardens as they do of Pictures, the more free and lively Expression is always preferr'd before the more stiff and formal. . . . The most beautiful Gardens may be made where the Ground is the most irregular and uneven, where there are Hills and Pits: these unlevel spots dictate to Men of Taste those Varieties, which by discreet Management, will afford the greatest Beauties in a Garden."

In the eighteenth century we soon grow as weary of the "Man of Taste" as we do of the "Nobility and Gentry," and we sigh again for the Curious, and the Friendly Reader. All the writers are not such snobs as Bradley, but they are bad enough and we miss our old friends. Philip Miller, F.R.S., was Gardener to the Botanick Garden at Chelsea, and he wrote a *Gardeners Dictionary* which is still useful. The style of the garden which he suggests owes much to the seventeenth century, but he has some new ideas of his own. "The most polite Persons of this Age" (this is his variation of the Man of Taste) prefer gardens "design'd from Nature, so whatever has the stiff Appearance of Art does by no means correspond therewith." Too formal and trite . . . too stiff and formal . . . dismal clipt hedges . . . unnatural bad taste—we are already used to the fashionable abuse. But Miller is not always so vague, and some of his advice might have been written especially for us. "In small Gardens there may be some rising Clumps of Evergreens placed just beyond the plain Opening of Grass before the House, where the Eye will be carried from the plain Surface of Grass, to the regular slope of Evergreens, to the great Pleasure of the Beholder: but if there is a distant Prospect of the adjacent Country, then this should not be obstructed, but rather a larger Opening allow'd for the View, bounded on each side by these rising Clumps. And on the back Part may be planted the several Kinds of flowering Shrubs. In Wildernesses there is but little Trouble or Expence after their first planting, 'tis no wonder they are so generally esteem'd, especially when we consider the Pleasure they afford." Yes. It is only that we now say shrubbery for Wilderness.

The new-style gardeners, although they all condemn the formal, were far from agreeing about the natural. Civil wars are the bitterest of all quarrels, and the only arguments more acrimonious than those between next-door neighbours are those between people who share the same house. It is a truth which I realize every week-end when I read the latest village quarrels in our local country newspaper. So the different practitioners of the different varieties of the landscape style never miss a chance of abusing each other for lack of taste. Capability Brown, so we imagine, was the unquestioned king of eighteenth-century gardening. But not at all.

"Mr. Brown. I very earnestly desire that I may die before you."

"Why so?" said Brown.

"Because," said he, "I should like to see heaven before you had improved it."

As for why he was so disliked, his rivals considered him too genteel, too mild and tame and insipid. His grass was "neat

bowling-greens," his houses rising from meadows were "dia-
monds set in lead," his empty sweeps were only the "carcass of a
garden," and as for his much-praised "Purity," plain water is
pure, said Chambers, and "a little simplicity will go a very great
way."

Brown we might call the Serene Style, for his scenes are always peaceful, and his bitterest enemies were the supporters of
the Picturesque. These sought to change the gentle English country into wild scenes of horror, mystery, and "that terror which is
so nearly allied to sublimity," and if their landscapes seem to us
as serene as Brown's own, it is because two centuries of the English climate are a far more powerful influence than any fashionable theories of the Sublime.

The third style of landscape is much less clear, the Liberal beside the Conservative and Socialist, uncertain which side to join.
It is the Chinese school led by Chambers, who built at Kew the
Chinese Pagoda, which once had a gilded dragon on every angle
of its charming roofs. His attitude is more frivolous than his rivals', for he studded his gardens with fanciful buildings (the
ruined arch at Kew is also his) and had a weak fondness for flowers. At the end of his *Dissertation on Oriental Gardening* he
added an "Explanatory Discourse by Tan Chet-qua, Gent."
which begins by introducing the Chinese author. "Chet-qua had
three wives, two of whom he caressed very much, the third but
seldom, for she was a virago and had large feet. He dressed well
. . . wore nine whiskers and four long nails . . . and every
other ornament that Mandarins are wont to wear." He was a
"pretty general scholar, and, for a heathen, a very compleat gentleman. He composed a billet-doux at pleasure, recited verses and
sung love-songs in many languages. He likewise danced a fan-
dango, played divinely upon the bag-pipe, and made excellent
remarks."

This very compleat gentleman lodged in the Strand, and,
among other things, he talked of gardens till "the audience fell
fast asleep; for the tone of his voice was like opium to the hearers." Chet-qua has a fine high-spirited scheme for turning all

England into a garden. We should set every roadside with flowering shrubs and blossom trees, he tells us, plant our commons with flowers, turn all our bridges into triumphal arches, set the tombs of our ancestors along the highways, and "the whole Kingdom might soon become one magnificent vast Garden, bounded only by the sea."

But alas, he remembers, the people of England are wantonly destructive. They would cut down the trees, pull up the flowers, kill the birds, and throw stones at at the statues; such, he says, is their "destructive brutality. Would to Heaven! . . . as I say to the mistress Chet-quas in a morning, would to Heaven my ducks, we were all at Quang-chew-fu again, with all our long nails and all our whiskers about us."

I wish our own gardening books were half such fun, but we have lost the sophisticated high spirits of the eighteenth century, and our gardens, as well they might be, are nearer the humble retreats of the Middle Ages than to these grandiose but light-hearted follies. For the landscape park is essentially a sophisticated taste—a decadent taste, I dare say the moralists would call it if they ever thought about it. Rousseau "made the dawn visible to people who had never risen till noon, the landscape to eyes that had only rested on drawing-rooms and palaces." Bored with their palaces, the fashionable created artificial wildernesses for their amusement; tired of drawing-rooms, they developed a taste for the Alps—"Precipes, mountains, torrents, wolves, rumblings, Salvator Rosa. Here we are," says Walpole, "the lonely lords of glorious desolate prospects."

Real wildernesses are peopled by Robinson Crusoes or by depressed natives even less civilized, but the wildernesses of the eighteenth century are the setting for the loves of Paul et Virginie, for Marie Antoinette playing at milkmaids, and for "Dowagers as plenty as flounders." There is a very simple way of telling at a glance real country people from those who only play at the Simple Life. Country folk use up old clothes for dirty work; followers of the Simple Life wear special clothes for the occasion. Farm labourers work in navy-blue trousers once long ago their

Sunday suit, but we dress ourselves in careful corduroys and country shirts, like Boucher's shepherdesses in frills and ribbons. Like the eighteenth-century parks, our country clothes are "the utmost simplicity of cultivated order," and just as the parks were not laid out by countrymen but by the fashionable Mr. Brown, so we can never buy from a country tailor the consciously simple tweeds which fashion insists on for the Simple Life.

Rousseau, indeed, set his own style for the country. "I assumed Armenian costume," he says. "It was not a new idea but had occurred to me several times in the course of my life. . . . I had a little Armenian costume made . . . the jacket, the caftan, the fur cap and the belt . . . and I never wore any other dress." He is equally original in his version of the Simple Life. "I decided to learn to make laces, and took my cushion round with me on visits, or worked at my door, like the women, and gossiped with passers-by. . . . To find some use for my laces, I gave them as presents to my young friends on their marriages, on condition that they should suckle their children." No wonder the country people thought him odd (though he never understood why), for how could they know that such fancies, if indulged in less earnestly, were the height of fashion? Like Rousseau, high society idealized the Noble Savage none of them had ever met, and consigned all drawing-rooms to the devil. "I was so tired of reception rooms, fountains, shrubberies, and flower-beds, and of those most tiresome people who made a show of them; I was so weary of pamphlets, clavichords, wool-sorting, and making knots, of stupid witticisms and tedious affectations, of tellers of little tales and great suppers, that when I spied a poor simple thorn bush, a hedge, a barn, or a meadow . . . I consigned all rouge, flounces, and perfumes to the devil."

Paul et Virginie is a charming story which it is hard not to read as a satire on Rousseau's ideas, though we are certainly not meant to. A girl and a boy grow up innocently amid the remote nature of a remote island, fall innocently in love, and just as innocently part. It is not what we expect of tropical climates, but never mind. In the end the heroine returns from Europe in a storm, but she is now so hampered with clothes that she cannot swim, and so infected with false modesty that she will not take her clothes off, and in this most civilized and symbolical dilemma she is drowned within sight of the shore and her waiting lover.

Or so I remember, but it is a long time since I read it. What I do remember very well is what a delightful ballet it would make, danced to eighteenth-century music (Vivaldi perhaps), with Derain to design sophisticated-simple clothes and a decorative mock-primitive setting.

People who live in drawing-rooms have their own troubles. These are not troubles which would beset a cottage. Therefore a cottage is a humble Utopia where trouble is unknown. We can only suppose that that was the reasoning (for it is much the same logic which makes Rousseau's savage noble) which led the eighteenth century to set a cottage as a decoration in a park. "It shows us a dwelling where happiness may reside unsupported by wealth —as it shows us a resource where we may still continue to enjoy peace, though we should be deprived of all the favours of fortune." Not that one needs to be Marie Antoinette to enjoy the delusion, for every true Cockney believes the same—that they only need a country cottage to be happy ever after—or at least every Cockney who was not driven out to languish in a real-life cottage during the war. I dare say it is a common delusion of all town-dwellers.

The eighteenth century also had a fancy for ornamental farms, which are much like the Cockney's cottage. These were for "poor Patrons" who could not afford to give up the whole of their estate to pleasure, and Batty Langley, who mixed ideas of profit with pleasure, was known as the Poor Man's Brown. Flowers were to be planted in field corners, the hedges varied with different shrubs, vegetables instead of exotics grown in the greenhouses, and the ornamental waters stocked with fish. At every view-point there were seats, and urns with verses to departed friends; though you must be careful with the inscriptions, one adviser warns us, and allusions to pastoral Greece are not suitable for an English farm. "Even the clucking of poultry is not omitted; for a menagerie of a very simple design is placed near the Gothic building; a small serpentine river is provided for the water-fowl, while the others stray among the flowering shrubs on the banks, or straggle about the neighbouring lawn." Shenstone made an ornamental farm called the Leasowes, which Dr. Johnson considered "the envy of the great and the admiration of the skilful." Which is exactly what we should expect from a townsman, and the heart of Johnson's world was Charing Cross. But it would be hard to imagine anything more likely to infuriate a genuine countryman. It is a test of the true farmer that he has no time at all for gardens; even his wife's square of flowers in front of the house he would plough up if he dared. "I'd cart dung all day," said the old farmer I once knew well, "rather than do an hour's digging in the wife's border." But *he* was the real right thing and wore his oldest blue trousers for the carting.

The more simple-minded enthusiasts of the eighteenth-century Simple Life might pursue their fancies to bankruptcy—many did —but the more sophisticated knew very well that the whole thing was a fashionable game. "I am now, as I told you, returned to my plough. . . . We lead quite a rural life, have had a sheep-shearing, a hay-making, a syllabub under the cow, and a fishing of three gold-fish out of Poyang [Walpole's goldfish pond] for a present to Madam Clive." All at Strawberry Hill, a comfortable ride from his town house in Saint James's.

The eighteenth century is our Classical age, the age of reason and good sense and proportion. And because the intellectual foundation is so steady, it can support superficial fashions of quite astonishing absurdity. For the fashionable taste of the eighteenth century is often wonderfully silly, which is perhaps why the best writing is satirical, and why there is no great imaginative literature. So I had decided (refusing to consider Blake), for large-scale theorizing is one of the most satisfying occupations. But then one of the children came home from school with Gray's

"Elegy." He was to learn the first seven verses for homework, he said, so I read it again for the first time for years, astonished at its excellence.

> *Can storied urn or animated bust*
> *Back to its mansion call the fleeting breath?*
> *Can Honour's voice provoke the silent dust,*
> *Or Flatt'ry soothe the dull cold ear of death?*

There it is, one of the great English poems, making nonsense of all my neat categories.

But still every theory is useful if only to be disproved, for we can use it as a tool to turn over the unorganized mass of facts and arrange them in some kind of order. With a new subject we need lots of theories, one after the other, and as we pursue them and discard them we gradually get to know our material, like harrowing new ground first one way and then the other to break it up fine. It is only important to remember that our theories are only tools and not truths. In the end, when the ground is worked enough, we must leave them all behind in the tool-shed to go out by ourselves with an open mind, and look again as if for the first time.

But my eighteenth-century ground is still disconcertingly rough, and I am glad of any point of view which will help me to see a little further. So I try them all. The eighteenth century is the Classic Age. Yes, but that is no help with its romantic gardens. The Age of Reason. I dare say, but it plays at the Simple Life like a child playing at being sophisticated. The age of fashionable follies. Yes. And for the moment (and since it is my own theory) I can think of no buts. So Gray's "Elegy," I tell myself, belongs only incidentally to its period. Certainly it speaks English with a new eighteenth-century accent, but its subject is still man's ancient sorrow, that we all must die and nothing can save us. Its true tradition is the poetry of melancholy which goes right back through the Middle Ages to the first Old English lyric. It is Pope's "Rape of the Lock" which is essentially of the eighteenth century—as Pope was, too, playing the fashionable games, building a grotto in his garden at Twickenham. But Gray was ill at ease in sophisticated society, was "the worst company in the world," said Walpole, who went to Florence with him, "of a melancholy turn . . . living reclusely." (But, all the same, he writes an amusing post-script to one of Walpole's letters.)

"Enthusiasm always leads to the verge of ridicule, and seldom keeps totally within it," said Uvedale Price in his "Essay on the Picturesque," though he seems quite unconscious of how very far beyond the verge much of his own book lies. And if we want to understand the fashionable taste of the day we should read Mrs. Radcliffe's *Mysteries of Udolpho*, for, as Walpole says of someone else, she "collects the follies of the age for the information of posterity." That Mrs. Radcliffe was quite unconscious of the follies only makes them more convincing. I cannot remember ever reading a sillier book (certainly not in three volumes), and it was enormously popular. The heroine is a pale romantic miss whose excessive sensibility is only rivalled by her complete lack of common sense, and the story is divided almost equally between her melancholy musing in suitable gardens and scenery, and the wildly romantic and deliciously horrifying Italian adventures from which she escapes both unscathed and unsullied. And how people enjoyed it! It was the culmination of fashionable taste. Even Jane Austen, who kept so brilliantly within the boundary which concentrated her gifts, was tempted to mock its absurd popularity in *Northanger Abbey*.

The Picturesque style of gardening set out to produce the wild scenery of *Udolpho* beneath our own mild skies. Little English hills steepen to rude precipices with a cottage on the edge to raise our hair, dark caves are hollowed out of hillsides, and our gentle woods become wild forests to harbour banditti, those picturesque ruffians of Salvator Rosa's pictures who so enchanted an age which seems no longer to have had highwaymen enough of its own to satisfy its liking for violent adventure, even though citizens were still robbed between Kensington and London. Roads wind indefatigably—"Let it wind," says Gilpin with a fine heroic flourish, but still it must seem to wind naturally, as if only to avoid some obstacle. "Mr. Brown," he says, "was often very happy in creating these artificial obstructions," which, since Mr. Brown led the rival school, is a generous if extraordinary compliment. Streams, in the Picturesque park, are disguised as mighty rivers (there are hints on placing bridges to encourage the deception), rivers are pumped to hill-tops to make waterfalls ("springs that long to be cascades"), and if you are lucky enough to possess "a chasm between two high ranges of hill," you can deepen the gloom by "an iron forge, covered with a black cloud of smoak, and surrounded with half-burned ore, with coal, and with cinders."

So that there shall be no suspicion that this elaborately contrived wilderness is not the real thing, whole villages are moved beyond the park wall, the public road is diverted out of sight, and the mansion rises desolately from a sweep of rough grass. The kitchen garden (there is no other) is banished to the boundary, and in the most thorough Improvements the servants creep into the house by underground passages. It seems a very long way from our modern kitchen-diningrooms, but I daresay our food is hotter. However, there were other inconveniences besides having to smuggle in the servants. The deer, since this is wild nature, must roam freely round the house, as indeed they do in all the illustrations; but still it was inconvenient to have antlered stags peering in the ground-floor windows, and even worse if the entrance door were left open and they came into the house. So there were chains across fashionable doorways to keep out the cattle when the door was set open in the summer. And if one's house pretends to be a desolate castle, then everything else must be equally in fancy dress. A ruined abbey turns out to be a farm, and there are cottages disguised as hay-carts or hidden in wood-stacks. We cannot help wishing we could overhear the cottagers' comments.

None of the gardeners surpasses Dr. William Gilpin, who wrote *Remarks on Forest Scenery*, and who keeps up a steady level of high-flown absurdity. The New Forest, he says reprovingly, as if the trees should have known better, has tracts of open country "larger than picturesque beauty requires." And although undergrowth in a forest is "useful" because it connects the trees in dignified masses, it should never "straggle too far from the clumps and appear as spots in . . . the middle space between the different combinations." As for the bramble, that has no picturesque virtue of any kind "to recommend it." "It is a plant which one should almost wish to have totally exterminated from landscape."

Nor is the distant view exempt from his fault-finding. "Continuous woods stretching along the horizon without any break . . . is formal, heavy, and disgusting . . . a regular line at the base is almost as disgusting." It seems a strong word for a view not quite varied enough to suit his taste, but then Gilpin is an enthusiast, and even castles must be blown up in a picturesque style. During the "civil wars of the last century," he says, Farnham Castle was blown up, "though not with that *picturesque judgement* with which many castles in those times were demolished." They are his own italics.

We can see why Walpole felt that England was the true home of eccentrics. "The most remarkable thing I have observed since I came abroad," he writes from Florence, "is that there are no people so obviously mad as the English. The French, the Italians, have great follies, great faults; but then they are so national that they cease to be striking. In England, tempers vary so excessively, that almost every one's faults are peculiar to himself. I take this diversity to proceed partly from our climate, partly from our government: the first is changeable, and makes us queer; the latter permits our queernesses to operate as they please. If one could avoid contracting this queerness, it must certainly be the most entertaining to live in England, where such a variety of incidents continually amuse."

But the noble race of English eccentrics has sadly declined since Walpole's day, for besides a changeable climate and a tolerant government, it needs a considerable income, which he never mentions. They are an irreplaceable loss, these wonderful exotic creatures who wither in the chill winds of income tax and death duties, and Sir George Sitwell is probably the last gardener who will encourage us to put our statues under water so that they look like mermaids.

When one side of our nature is denied, it seldom grows great in solitude, as we might hopefully suppose, but rather degenerates. So the Elizabethan theatre, suppressed by the Puritans, reappeared as Restoration comedy; and however much we enjoy those witty, light-hearted, and technically brilliant plays, they are scarcely to be compared with Shakespeare's. Or if Shakespeare is too giant-size for any useful comparison, then with Marlowe or Webster or Ben Jonson. In the same way, the rational eighteenth century ignored that side of the English spirit which we may call poetic, or perhaps romantic; but whatever word we use, we know very well what we mean, for it built the mediæval churches and wrote the literature of the early seventeenth century. And since this inborn quality was discouraged by the climate of the Age of Reason from sharing the open daylight, it grew sickly in cellars, and appears in fashionable life as the Cult of Sensibility. Eighteenth-century sensibility has the same relation to real feeling as the hunger of a dieting beauty to the hunger of a starving man. One of Rousseau's amusements was to sit and weep into the Lake of Geneva—"I indulged my feelings. I sighed and cried like a child. How often I would stop to weep at my leisure and, sitting on a large stone, would be amused to see my tears fall into the water." We feel sure that he took great care to choose a comfortable stone before he started. The heroine of *Udolpho* (she is so unreal a puppet that it is impossible to remember her name) is never so happy as when she is sunk in melancholy musing. Most of her adventures, we come to suspect, are merely an excuse for page after page of mass-produced sensibility, which we soon learn to skip. For "Melancholy" was fashionable; it provided the shadowy background for the bright lights of the drawing-rooms and coffee-houses and public gardens, lights which cast no shadows of their own. It was the common thing, said Walpole, "to set aside a quarter of one's garden to be melancholy in." We must aim at "that pleasing melancholy," says another gardener, and the Gloomy Style was considered the height of good taste. Tombs were a choice ornament of fashionable gardens; Pope built one for his mother at the end of an avenue of funereal cypresses, and the Picturesque island where Rousseau was buried had the extra attraction of the grave of a young man crossed in love and inspired by Rousseau's writing to romantic suicide. A young lady was said to have visited it and composed appropriate verses, as the heroine of *Udolpho* does at every opportunity—they are astonishingly bad. "Magnificently triste," says Walpole, who is always witty, even at his most fashionably absurd.

The Style of Terror was also much admired, and was not to be confused, so they tell us, with the Melancholy, "for it must ever be remembered, that where terror prevails, melancholy is but a secondary consideration." This desirable sensation of delicious horror was suggested by rocks and torrents and gloomy thickets, which cannot have been easy to contrive in the cheerful landscape of the Home Counties. "The terrors of a scene in nature are like those of a dramatic representation; they give us alarm; but the sensations are agreeable, so long as they are kept to such as are allied only to terror, unmixed with any that are horrible and disgusting." Clearly no one must fall over the precipices, and the wildness, moreover, must only be such "as was consistent with ease of access." "Art may therefore be used to heighten these scenes," and Art included such fancies as skulls carved over doorways, "shabby firs and sometimes a withering or a dead tree." Kent even went so far as to *plant* dead trees in his gardens until he was laughed out of it.

But if the scene is naturally gloomy, "less extravagance is required to support it: strange shapes in extraordinary positions; enormous weights unaccountably sustained; trees rooted in the sides and torrents raging at the foot of the rocks, are at the best needless excesses." It strikes us now as a very odd idea of a garden of pleasure, but then we remember Rousseau enjoying himself feeling dizzy. "The road has been edged with a parapet to prevent accidents, and so I was able to gaze into the depths and make myself as giddy as I pleased. For the amusing thing about my taste for precipitous places is that they make my head spin; and I am very fond of this giddy feeling so long as I am in safety. Supporting myself firmly on the parapet, I craned forward and stayed there for hours on end." I too would prefer the eighteenth-century precipice to the no doubt exactly similar delights of a ride over the horrifying switch-backs of the Big Dipper. It is so much more elegant.

Once during the war I rode from Aylesbury to Oxford on the top of a bus. Chattering to each other in the seat in front of me sat two small boys, sent into the country from London (so I made out) because their home had been bombed. They looked idly out of the window from time to time, and suddenly their very half-hearted interest in the countryside was jerked wide awake by a ruined castle at the side of the road. "It was a bomb like ours," said one of them happily, feeling unexpectedly at home in the desert of winter fields. "No," said the other one gloomily after a careful inspection, "it's only an old ruin," and they discussed with enthusiasm, and quite horrifying knowledge, the contrasting effects of ancient time and new destruction.

But both of them were wrong, for Dinton Castle was *built* as a ruin, as an "eye-catcher" for the house below. The cracks were there from the start, and there never was a roof. Small wonder that it should puzzle children brought up to consider adults as sensible creatures. For the eighteenth century loved ruins, and if there were none in their parks, then they built them, for they were not only Picturesque but an unsurpassed aid to melancholy. "At the sight of a ruin, reflections on the change, the decay, and the desolation before us naturally occur; and they introduce a long succession of others, all tinctured with that melancholy which these have inspired." I wonder if the eighteenth century would have appreciated our unprecedented wealth of ruins, or whether such an *embarras de richesses* would have sent them back, even more thoughtful, to their well-built houses.

The Chinese put ruins in their autumn gardens to suit the

fading season, but the landscape gardeners put them everywhere. Walpole, of course, was a connoisseur, for were they not in his favourite Gothick style? His friend Selwyn, he says approvingly, "begged . . . a pretty old gateway" from a ruined priory "to erect on the top of his mountain, and it will have a charming effect." In another castle he admired, "the stairs are gone, but it is now a most beautiful Ivy-mantled tower. The last Lord added a ruined round tower that has a good effect." One German enthusiast even considered adding a derelict wing to his mansion, and so many new ruins were set up that Whately gives us rules for building them. "They are a class by themselves," he says, "beautiful as objects, expressive as characters, and peculiarly calculated to connect with their appendages into elegant groups." (Now I come to think of it, Dinton Castle is remarkably elegant.) The original plan of the building must be clear, he goes on; "straggling ruins have a bad effect," and a confused chaos of stones has not the necessary air of the genuine—it will "raise doubts about the existence of the ancient structure; whereas the mind must be hurried away from examining into the reality, by the exactness and the force of the resemblance." It would be hard to choose between Mr. Whately and Dr. Gilpin for sustained absurdity.

A new cottage built within an "old" ruin he recommends as a convincing trick, or a "ruined" stone bridge restored with a few planks "will take off the idea of a childish conceit." But we must be careful to suit our ruins to the scenery, he warns us. "Open and polished scenes will generally be given to the Arcadian shepherd; and those in a lower degree of cultivation will be thought more conformable to the manners of the ancient British yeomanry." A cross, or an ancient church, or even a Maypole would be fitting, he thinks, half hidden in the "British" woods. But why be limited to ruins? he asks, "a hackneyed device immediately detected, unless their style be singular, or their dimensions extraordinary." Why not set up a Stonehenge? It could be done "with little trouble, and great success; the materials might be brick or even timber plaistered over, if stone could not easily be procured." But we must be careful not to introduce any other buildings in the same scene—"no Grecian temples, no Turkish mosques, no Egyptian obelisks or pyramids."

Grottoes, too, were popular (fine places for toads, said Dr. Johnson), and every fashionable park must have its hermitage. "A hermitage must not be close to a road, but whether it be exposed to view on the side of a mountain, or concealed in the depth of a wood is almost a matter of indifference." The hermit no doubt was rather less indifferent, and as if this solitude were not depressing enough, the gloomy character of the place must be "retained in the utmost purity." "About the hermitage [the wood] is thickened with trees of the darkest greens; a narrow gloomy path, overhung with Scotch and spruce firs, under which the fern seems to have been killed, not cleared, and scarce a blade of grass can grow, leads to the cell; that is composed of logs and of roots . . . and the furniture within is old and uncouth." No wonder that hermits refused to live in such gloomy hovels, though the cell, it was realized, needed an inhabitant if it were to impress visitors as genuine. But even the destitute could not be bribed to be hermits for long; or if they put up with the life for a week or two in the summer, then there was either trouble with the neighbouring milkmaids, or neighbours with a social conscience insisted that the hermit must be replaced by a dummy.

This impressing of visitors was one of the recognized intentions of the landscape park. Many of the new country gentry were self-made men; they might even, alas, have made their money from trade. And they were dreadful snobs. "The Gentleman will always shine," Bradley reassured them, "let his Circumstances be never so narrow." But it was not enough. To feel their social standing was secure, they must have land like the older aristocracy. Luckily this was the perfect time to acquire an estate, for although the enclosure of the old open fields had been going on in a haphazard way since Tudor times, in the eighteenth century it became the national policy, and the remaining common lands were divided up among the peasants in small allotments. Since many of these poor people could not afford even to enclose their land, they sold it, and a rich man could very easily buy himself a "seat." These grounds were often laid out more for show than for pleasure, and the height of happiness was to dazzle one's neighbours. And not only neighbours, for streams of curious visitors travelled along the improved roads of the late eighteenth century—"Coaches full of travellers . . . troops of holiday neighbours. The Lord of the Place can never call it his during the finest part of the year." Clearly there is nothing new in grand parks being open to the public, and even when the Lord of the Place was not at home, callers like Walpole made their way in and inspected his Improvements. "A visitor is disappointed," says one gardener, criticizing a scene he finds too humble, and there is no more to be said.

The fine houses, too, were not built to be lived in in comfort, but to look magnificent, to be approached from an angle to make them seem larger. And indeed they are almost uninhabitable, so huge and inconvenient and cold. As Walpole says of Italy, they "have found out how hot their climate is, but not how cold; for there are scarce any chimneys, and most of the apartments painted in fresco; so that one has the additional horror of freezing with imaginary marble." Since the gardens are part of this keeping up with the neighbours, one of their chief aims is to look larger than they are, "to extend the appearance of domain and the idea of a seat." "Nothing gives a mansion so much dignity as these home demesnes, or contributes more to mark its consequence. . . . A noble park is the natural appendage of an ancient mansion." The boundary must never be seen, but sunk in a ditch, so that more impressionable visitors may imagine the whole countryside belongs to the mansion. At Chatsworth there was a painted *trompe-l'œil* perspective at the end of one of the vistas, as if Derbyshire were not already depressingly large enough.

It was a great advantage of the natural style of gardening that there was no obvious division between park and country. Though even this had its drawbacks, they found, for how were visitors to know they were on your own private drive and not simply the public road? But equally, on the other hand, how could they know that the public road was not your private drive? Whately has various suggestions for encouraging such a delusion in visitors. You could plant specimen trees along the verges of the highway, he says, and in the hedges here and there an exotic shrub not found wild in England, or you could grow clumps of trees in the neighbouring fields to make them look like private parkland.

A Riding was an even more ambitious hoax: a carefully arranged circuit track to take visitors on horseback as if all the land were yours—"to extend the idea of a seat and appropriate a whole country to the mansion." The track itself could be made to seem private by the same tricks as the public road, and the destination should be "a small spot . . . enclosed from the fields and converted into a shrubbery. . . . It may be kept by the labour of one man," the writer says encouragingly, "and nothing so effectively extends the idea of a seat to a distance." If your Riding must willy-nilly be along the road through a village, then the village must be made "romantic." You might build a farm like a castle, or set up a "pretty" wellhead on the village green, or little fancy bridges over the streams, and "by the help of a few trifling plantations . . . there are few villages which may not easily be rendered agreeable." But beware of shams, he warns us, and none too soon. It is very well to build a farm "in the semblance of an abbey," but to set up only "a bit of a turret or the tip of a spire" is merely "frivolous."

Were the bits of turrets and tips of spires set up on poles among the trees, I wonder? And was the eighteenth century even more extravagantly absurd than I suspected at the beginning? But they amused each other, too, for one of them tells the story of the old lady (of the same race as Mme du Deffand, though cruder in her methods) who, when passing a pretentious entrance gate whose twin lodges reminded her irresistibly of tea-caddies, stopped her carriage, climbed out, and on one lodge wrote GREEN in large letters, and on the other BOHEA.

· · ·

The real trouble about these "pompous solitudes" as Walpole calls the larger parks, is that they can only be laid out in remote districts where land is cheap, and therefore the proud owner can never expect enough visitors to make the expense worth while. "Men tire of expense," he admits disarmingly, "that is obvious to few spectators." For it is no use pretending that this new style of gardening was for private pleasure, and even Whately, who gave us such unguarded advice on Ridings, regrets "the pride of making a lavish display to a visitor, without any regard to the owner's enjoyments." Walpole even relents enough to recommend a garden as we mean it, for "the total banishment of all particular neatness immediately about a house, which is frequently left gazing by itself in the middle of a park, is a defect." The English weather is not always suitable for such open spaces, and "whenever a family can purloin a warm and even something of an old-fashioned garden from the landscape designed for them by the undertaker in fashion, without interfering with the picture, they will find satisfactions on those days that do not invite strangers to come and see their improvements."

Walpole will only allow a garden if it does not interfere with the picture, for "flowerbeds hurt the eye by their littleness," and Knowle, he says, is spoilt by "trumpery fragments of gardens." But there were plenty of old-fashioned people who went on happily growing flowers as they had always done, caring nothing at all for the garden as a work of art, but only that it should be an "out-of-door dwelling-place for plants and people." They regretted the seventeenth-century gardens which the Improvers had destroyed: "whole woods of venerable plants have been swept away to make room for a little grass. Our virtuosi have scarcely left an acre of shade, nor three trees growing in a line, from Land's-end to the Tweed," and Cowper gives half a page of the *Task* to reviling Capability Brown.

Nor were all the eighteenth-century gardens in the landscape style. In Canaletto's pictures we can still see the gardens Pepys admired, with trees in rows and open grass for walking. There are bills in the royal accounts for looking after the avenues and

putting new gravel on the paths. Ranelagh, too, was more beloved than any "pompous solitude," and, like Vauxhall, it was in
the old fashion of formal avenues, regular canals, and straight
hedges "which are cut with the utmost exactness and look extremely neat." Even fashionable writers like Gilpin and Repton
recommend a garden near the house, and there are plenty of gardening books on growing fruit and flowers. Miller's *Gardeners
Dictionary* was reprinted several times, and is probably the most
famous gardening book since Parkinson. Bradley published a
steady stream of horticultural advice, and even Cowper tells us
in heroic verse how to make a hot-bed.

> *The stable yields a stercoraceous heap,*
> *Impregnated with quick fermenting salts.*

I should think there has never been a more dignified dung-hill.
Switzer, too, despite his tiresomely fulsome style, was a true gardener with a proper gardener's enthusiasm for his soil, and he tells
us how to make a wide selection of different dung- and compost-
heaps; "Magazines" he calls them, and gives each one a number,
so that afterwards, telling us how to plant seeds or strike cuttings,
he can refer us most efficiently to the right number and even the
exact page. "Having committed the Seed to the Ground and covered it with a proper Thickness of Earth No. 1 page 105 . . .
spread it with an inch of fine clean rotten Dung, from Magazine
No. 4 page 106."

The flowers and trees popular in the eighteenth century have
changed little, though there is more interest in exotics like the
Great American Aloe, which was a wonderful attraction to the
Curious when it flowered in Mr. Cowell's greenhouse at Hoxton.
The books still offer the same advice on layering and grafting,
and give lists of the points to look for in fine flowers like tulips
and auriculas, perhaps to help the judges at flower shows. The
eighteenth-century gardeners, although they still valued striped
tulips, already suspected that the flaming was caused by "some
Weakness or Distemper," and John Cowell tells us how to make
them break. "Take the Plaister of old Walls, mix this with Drift-

Sand and to this add the Water that runs from a Dunghill or Jakes, and put it over the Surface of the Bed . . . and 'twill make them break into fine Stripes to a wonder, as it was related to me by a Gentleman of great Honour."

But Mr. Cowell's greatest contribution to our pleasure is a suggestion he offers for naming flowers so that we shall know their colour from a catalogue. First we must have a list of great Personages, Castles, Cities, etc., and also a table of colours: W for

Tulipa Jacobi Bommi lutei Coloris coccineis flammis diuisa et ornata

A flamed tulip. Drawing by Crispin de Passe.

White, Y for Yellow, and so on. The flowers are then given names whose initials correspond to their colours. "A Flower perhaps with White abounding, and marked with Crimson, may be called William the Conqueror; the W in William expressing the White abounding, and the C the Crimson: or the same flower might be named the Wonder of Constantinople. A Flower striped with Crimson and Purple may be called the Charming Phyllis, or the Curious Ptolemy" (though this is surely a rather perverse P, like saying G for gnome on the telephone). Even flowers already named may have epithets added to show their colour, "as for Example the fine Carnation which is called the Princess Amelia, whose Principal is White, and mark'd with Violet: To this might be added, the Worthy Virgin." Carnation Princess Amelia, the Worthy Virgin. But what happens when Amelia marries? It seems never to have occurred to him that it might be inconvenient to name flowers after the more ephemeral attributes of human beings.

"I have made great progress," says Walpole, "and talk very learnedly with the nurserymen, except that now and then a lettuce run to seed overturns all my botany, as I have more than once taken it for a curious West-Indian flowering shrub." But flowers have even less place in the landscape gardens than in Le Nôtre's. "A Serpentine River and a Wood are become the absolute Necessities of Life" (it is Walpole again), and trees are the true inhabitants of the new parks. "It is no exaggerated praise," says Gilpin, who always exaggerates, "to call a tree the grandest and most beautiful of all the productions of the earth." The new gardening books are full of advice not only for growing trees, but also for grouping and spacing them: a very much more difficult art than we might suppose from the seemingly accidental perfection of the finished landscape gardens.

Rivers, as Walpole said, must always wind (the eighteenth century even made a new verb, to serpentize), and all water had to follow Hogarth's Line of Beauty, an irregular curve where no part repeated any other. "Clever," said one Improver when he saw the serpentine meanderings of the River Thame across the landscape, and though they told him it was simply the natural course of the river, he still insisted. "Clever," he said in admiration of a river which had learnt so thoroughly the lessons of Capability Brown. But I know what he meant, for I felt the same about the trees in Bramham Park.

Much of the eighteenth-century advice on gardens is no longer of everyday use. We are never likely to need to know how to dig out a lake and pile up the earth to make a hill, nor how to make artificial waterfalls look natural, nor how to break up the offensively regular "grazing-line" which the deer make under trees by eating the lower branches, nor whether a temple or a cottage is better to enliven the view. Nor is Uvedale Price really useful—"I conceive that in most situations it may be quite possible, with some sacrifice of expense, to introduce here and there broken rocky precipices, of more or less magnitude, that might serve to give the happiest variety to the aquatic scene which the improver is forming . . . before admitting the water into the valley to be flooded, to open up a large irregular quarry in the sloping side of the hill; and to secure the essential point that the rocks may rise naturally out of a certain depth of the future water, the operation of quarrying may be made to commence at any given depth below the line of its intended level. Very picturesque little irregular rocky bays may thus be formed."

By the eighteenth century, science had spread far beyond the garden wall, but the gardeners are still amateurs, and in the introduction to his *Dictionary* Miller gives an explanation of wind by differences in the "Spring of the Air" which only needs to write *pressure* for *Spring* to be quite up-to-date still. Besides the Circulation of Sap, which has already occupied gardeners for a century, they are beginning to understand "the Generation of Plants by coupling with one another," and Linnæus's system of classifying brought scientific order to the chaos of muddled plant names. They are indefatigable experimenters, and one result which they tell with amazement in book after book is that the bud of a variegated jasmine, when grafted on an ordinary green jasmine, caused the whole of the host plant to become variegated.

But there is still plenty of very curious science for the credulous. Silkworms are destroyed by thunder, and "it would be well to try whether the firing of Guns near such Trees as are infected with Caterpillars would not destroy those Insects." Blights of caterpillars are carried by the east wind, and if we light fires to windward of orchards, the smoke will suffocate the grubs, which can then be swept up in heaps. The plague, so Bradley thought, and not so very wrongly, was carried by tiny insects: "In Turkey Egypt and Barbary, when the Plague rages, the Franks, the English etc. are seldom infected with it" because the Insects "having their certain natural Nourishments respectively appointed them" (the Turks and Egyptians, I suppose), "do not in those Places infect Strangers." Among the experiments Bradley wants to try is whether snails would acquire medicinal value by feeding on medicinal herbs, but Walpole can think of better experiments: "The deliberation with which trees grow, is extremely inconvenient to my natural impatience," and he would like an invention for moving ancient oaks as easily as tulip bulbs. This will be simple to future ages, he prophesies, and "I have even begun a treatise or panygeric on the great discoveries made by posterity in all the arts and sciences. . . . The delightfulness of having whole groves of humming-birds, tame tigers taught to fetch and carry, pocket spying glasses to see all that is doing in China, with a thousand other toys, which we now look upon as impracticable, and which pert posterity would laugh in one's face for staring at, while they are offering rewards for perfecting discoveries, of the principles of which we have not the least conception!"

Well, we have our tigers now, though they are only half tame, and I doubt whether Walpole would like them any more than we do ourselves. We much prefer his eighteenth-century gardens, and it is interesting to consider why they are so satisfying. For they are not gardens at all by ordinary standards, they are views. "You must send for a landscape painter," said Vanbrugh when they asked him who should lay out the gardens at Blenheim, and that is what they are: real-life models of landscape pictures. They are there to be looked at, not to explore or to live in or to grow flowers in or to love for their intimate pleasures, for they have none, but to be looked at, from a distance and from a particular point of view. They are the backgrounds for Watteau's pictures, a kind of photographer's backcloth raised to the height of poetry.

For Watteau, too, was a Romantic in a Classical age. His "costly perfumed people" are quiet with some strange unhappiness. Even in the music and dancing they are sad, a graceful and poetic brokenheartedness which is perhaps what the Melancholy style of gardens was meant for. And through the mind of a great painter the cult of sensibility becomes deep feeling, so that Watteau's indefinable melancholy is a true experience and leaves us richer, like reading elegiac poetry. Besides, there is always the pleasure of seeking through the sad groups of merry-makers for that figure he loved both to draw and to paint: a young woman seen from behind, her head bent forward and a little to one side, her hair brushed up smoothly to show her quite enchanting neck.

But Watteau brings us no nearer to understanding why we like the landscape parks today. One reason, indeed, is quite simple: they are *here* and we *can* like them, for, needing very little labour to keep them, they have survived when other gardens have vanished. Then we, too—like the eighteenth century, though for different reasons—feel ourselves hemmed in by order. Theirs was an order of the mind, ours is the mechanical pattern of industrial life, but, none the less, the deliberate naturalness of landscape gardening suits us both. Nature abhors a straight line,

and so do we after a day in a city. So that as city parks these contrived landscapes are happier than they ever are in the country.
The billowing masses of trees, the long curving sweeps of grass
and water are a perfect contrast to the neat regular detail of the
architecture which surrounds them. The buildings which enclose
Saint James's Park are changed to palaces from fairy-tale, the
Regent's Park terraces are bewilderingly beautiful, pale and remote on winter mornings through the dark network of the trees,
beyond the misty levels of the lake.

This "natural" scenery is as exotic in a city as flowers in the
wrong climate: it has the same fascination as lilac at Christmas,
or orchids kept by glass from the frost outside. And it is curiously
elegant, for the artificiality which seems sterile in the country is
changed by its city context to elegance and grace. Perhaps if we
lived in these empty parks we might find them as disappointing
as I did as a child, but we never do live in them, we are only visitors, and that, quite exactly, is what they are meant for. The first
view is overwhelming, and we are never there long enough to
grow tired of it.

Beneath the froth of fashionable follies, the eighteenth century
was blessed with a fundamental good taste and sense of proportion which are often at their best in its humbler creations. We
live in London in an ordinary terrace house, put up about the
middle of the eighteenth century by a working builder whose
name no one remembers. London is full of similar dignified but
unpretentious houses built for ordinary middle-class families, and
they are most satisfying to live in. There are no affectations, no
exaggerations; the proportions are simple, discreet, and gracious,
both inside and out. They are probably the best town houses ever
built. In the same way, the underlying proportions of the eighteenth-century parks are excellent and unobstrusive. It is a proof
of their rightness that we can accept them as natural, that this
man-made landscape can seem to us as convincing as the scenery
moulded by thousands of years of weather, that our first thought
is how fortunate the gardener was to find his piece of ground.
And now that the more inappropriate follies have vanished, we

are left only with this perfectly proportioned landscape of grass and trees and water.

The grass of England is unrivalled, the trees are unsurpassed, and the water is here in abundance; the landscape parks are created of materials beautiful in themselves, as clipped hedges and gravel paths never were in the formal gardens. And for us, two centuries after they were planted, these magnificent forest trees have reached their perfect maturity. We are seeing the gardens as their creators must have imagined, but never saw them. For trees grow slowly and must be planted small, and the dark masses of woods which sweep up Brown's hillsides were only for him a nursery of saplings. He must have known when he planted them how perfectly the arrowy tall poplars on the island in Blenheim lake would enhance the level water and the curving shores, but still it seems a pity that he can never have seen them. Though perhaps, as his enemies feared, Brown is busy improving heaven, and surely there his plantations would shoot up full-size overnight, for what could be a more suitable heavenly reward for a good gardener?

Horace Walpole's Tailpiece.

CHAPTER NINE

WHAT DO
WE
WANT NOW?

ONCE DURING THE WAR WE WENT TO LIVE
in a sixteenth century farmhouse which had no garden.
Perhaps there once had been one, for there was a moat round the
house at just the distance one would choose as a boundary for a
garden. Perhaps there once were Tudor plots and fancies, knots
perhaps and gillyflowers, for the old house had certain elegancies
of carved oak and wide stairs, was more than a mere work-a-day
shelter for the farmer and his family. A most lovable house—but
it has been the hero of one book already, and must not come tres-
passing in this one. In any case, it was a house without a garden,
for until we came no one had lived there for fifteen years, and
any garden there might once have been had vanished with no
trace left to guess by, no paths or hedges, no flowers struggling
to survive among the weeds, no grass smooth enough even to be
imagined as a lawn. The farm came up to the house on one side,
the orchard on the other. Through one lot of windows we looked
into a bower of apple blossom, through the others we watched
the heavy cows lurch by from the meadows to be milked. For
the first week it was an idyllic setting, and I wondered why anyone should labour to make a garden when simply by doing nothing at all the little wild flowers of the orchard came up to the
very doorstep.

But I soon found out. Even on the lowest and most practical level, untouched nature will not do. The space round a house is used too much to be left to look after itself; at the end of a week it is not flowers we find on our doorstep, but mud. There is too much traffic in and out of a house for anything to serve but surfaces of stone or brick or gravel. There must be hard paths, and if there are paths, the animals must be kept off them, the cows must be shut out with walls or hedges. And if the animals are shut out, then something must be done with the grass and weeds which grow up uncontrolled by grazing.

All this I found despite my first conviction, which I have never changed, that the English countryside is far more beautiful than any garden I shall ever make. Yet there already was my garden, an enclosed space where the vegetation was controlled by my arbitrary choice and by my constant labour. And since I must needs have a garden, what sort should it be to suit our twentieth-century life? What had happened since the landscape parks? How had gardens changed with the Industrial Revolution of the nineteenth century?

Mostly they had shrunk, and ours certainly was small enough, well under an acre. But as for new ideas, the nineteenth century seems to have produced no valid new styles in gardening any more than in architecture. There was still some landscape gardening more or less in the authentic tradition; there were still a few follies put up, but with less conviction. Shrubberies became smaller and gloomier and too full of laurels, and carpet-bedding was a popular degeneration of the formal parterre. There was also a revival of the wild garden, the "wilderness" of the Tudors and the seventeenth century, and of the natural gardens of the Chinese, who "painted their way very artfully along the skirts of the plantation" with flowers.

The contribution which the late nineteenth-century gardeners have liked to consider particularly their own is the herbaceous border, but it is difficult to see why they claim it as new. A border where all kinds of flowers are grown together has always from the beginning been the chief delight of ordinary gardeners, though certainly for a time it had no place in the fine designs of the formal and landscape styles. But the gardener who loved flowers still kept his mixed border, even though he might hide it from the Improvers within the walls of the kitchen garden. Besides, even in the formal gardens of the seventeenth century there were lawns surrounded by simple beds of flowers which the French called English Parterres, and Bradley in the eighteenth century gives us advice for planting our herbaceous borders which would do perfectly well for today. "In planting a Border or Bed of Flowers, we may judiciously mix the several sorts . . . that they may be so disposed as to appear gradually one above the other, and add Beauty to each other by their Variety of Colours." He then gives us a plan of a border with "the tallest Blowers" at the back, the "Middle siz'd" next, and the "Lowest kinds" in front. His lists of flowers are very little different from the flowers we still grow in our twentieth-century borders; it is only that we have added new discoveries from the East, and used our new knowledge of genetics to improve the old favourites—or sometimes, alas, only to coarsen the elegant distinction of the original species to a gross display of formless colour.

"The practice of horticulture," says the preface to a mid-Victorian gardening book, "has been regarded as the most healthy employment and most delightful recreation in which human beings can be engaged. This remark holds good of all its branches, unless it be the forcing of flowers and fruits under glass, which is adverse to physical well-being. It is true that in the departments of culinary vegetables and fruits the element of utility is of first importance; but even they are not without their pleasures of a satisfactory nature. It is pleasing to enjoy the consciousness of skill applied, of diligence and power exercised and of cherished expectation gratified at length." (Oh, dear. There is nothing new, it seems, and the seventeenth century has said it all so very much better.) "Flower-gardening has less of material utility than the departments just referred to. It does not contribute to the substantials of the table, but it does to its elegancies, and has numerous other and more refining attractions, which have always made it a favourite pursuit."

He does not tell us what the more refining attractions are, but of course he quotes Keats on a joy for ever, as everyone has done ever since he wrote the Urn ode. We also know that Victorian flower beds had to be raised for ladies well above the paths, because the crinoline was such an embarrassingly unsuitable garment for stooping.

Perhaps, after all, our best inheritance from the Industrial Revolution is the lawn-mower; and perhaps it is symbolic that it should be a machine it gave us. But, in any case, it made little difference to garden design, for there had been lawns ever since the seventeenth century; it was only that they needed more labour to keep them smooth.

"*Un Français met des figures de Géométrie dans son jardin, un Anglais pose sa maison dans un pré, un Chinois fait devant sa fenêtre des cataractes épouvantables.*" But most people, if we ask them the simple question "What is a garden?" will answer quite simply, as unpretentious gardeners have always answered: "A garden is a place for growing flowers." For the true gardener "is inclined, even from the strength of his blood, to this love and labour." The flowery-bowery garden is one of the unthinking and immediate pleasures. It has a kind of artless generosity, a lush and lavish sweet-tooth atmosphere of fragrance and colour and silken petals. The love of flowers is the first delightful step towards appreciating a garden, and if we cannot have a large plot to grow them, then we make do with a small one; if we cannot have any garden at all, then we grow flowers in tubs and window-boxes, we fill our house with flower vases and "bough-pots" and plants in pots. We may even, as the seventeenth-century Londoners did, paint *trompe-l'œil* garden scenes and hang them outside our windows—"Those painted projections of our cockney glades," so Evelyn scornfully describes them, "which appeare like gardens of paste-board and march-payne, and smell more of paynt than of flowers." But Evelyn is seldom sympathetic, and we have more fellow-feeling for the gardenless Cockney than for Evelyn and all his ruined holly-hedges at Deptford.

Our delight in growing flowers is a complicated pleasure— partly an appreciation of their beauty and partly an affection for pets. For growing flowers is very much like keeping animals or looking after small children; to their keeper they become individual creatures whose health and happiness are his loving concern. We water our flowers even when we are tired, just as we feed our dog or listen to our children's troubles. We feel ourselves responsible for our dependents. The real gardener is paternal about his flowers, they are his pets; and his enemy is the housewife who regards them as so much material for filling vases for the house. Anyone who comes into the garden questingly with scissors is an inhuman despoiler, and never for a moment to be trusted out of sight.

A place to grow flowers. Yes. But that does not describe a garden so much as a floral allotment. A designer of gardens "ought to have a general Idea of everything that is Noble and Stately in the Productions of Art, for this lies open a Man's Thoughts and enlarges his Imagination." But we are not designers, we are flower-growers; we are occupied with the material of gardens, not the garden itself, the bricks in the wall and not the design of the house. Yet there is this great difference: that a brick has no value out of its context, but the living material of a garden is satisfying in its own right. A plant is not merely a unit in a design, but a complicated work of art more complete and beautiful than anything we shall ever make ourselves. It belongs to a different, a vegetable world which we cannot realize, it is governed by laws which we can only remotely understand, and it is adapted to this mysterious life in patterns of astonishing beauty. However minutely we consider them, the patterns of organic structure are always beautiful. It is not only the flowers we set admiringly in vases, nor the leaves we grow as plants in pots for decoration; if we pull a flower to pieces to examine the inside, or cut across an ovary to see the arrangements of seeds; if we look at tiny florets through a lens, at sections through a microscope, at viruses through an electron microscope, always at every level of the plant's construction we are astonished at its beauty, at what Sir Thomas Browne calls "the elegant co-ordination of vegetables." We can examine a flower by infra-red radiation, by ultra-violet light, by X-rays, and the one thing we can be certain of finding is new æsthetic pleasure: we are never disappointed. "All Nature is but Art unknown to thee," as a poet said whose name I cannot remember, but he must surely have been of the age of capital letters.

For a long time now I have lived with a background of doctors and hospitals. I have grown used to considering people as patients, I am no longer surprised at the peculiar rôle of priest and confessor which the public has thrust on the modern doctor; but one thing I have never got used to is the astonishing beauty of X-ray photographs. An ugly body of indiscriminate fat melts in the X-rays to a mysterious shadowy background of tissues, miraculously revealing the clear pattern of the bones drawn firm and delicate in dark-edged shapes, a skeleton of austere and significant curves. Even now, passing people in the street, I realize with sudden wonder that embedded in the formless flabby shapes of our urban bodies there lies an elegant construction of bones most perfectly shaped and articulated.

"But to return from this beautiful Digression," as Switzer says. For most people, flowers are the essential: it is why most gardens are ugly for half the year. Yet in the great gardens, flowers, for all their individual beauty, have been of little importance; they are incidental decoration and the finest taste has rejected them. But if flowers are not the essential of a garden any more than trimming is the essential of a dress, if a garden is not simply a place for growing flowers, then what is it?

"A Garden is a work of Art using the materials of Nature." It is a lucid definition which includes all fine gardens whatever their style, large or small, formal or wild. It explains why a garden composed only of the common plants of the country, as Versailles was, is so immensely more than the sum of its parts. It explains why gardens have been an expression of the ages they belonged to, and why there can be many styles of gardens, each equally satisfying to different people. But it is not a definition which includes our own much-loved vegetable hotch-potches of flowers and shrubs, nor does it explain the wide appeal of gardens among people who are not at all interested in the arts. I dare say the number of gardeners who consider their garden for its structural qualities is no greater than the number who look at paintings or read poetry. Cobbett had no doubt about it. "The far greater part of persons who possess gardens really know very little about the matter. They possess no 'principles' relating to the art."

But, luckily, we can enjoy our gardens very well without any principles at all, for unlike the materials of poetry and painting, the actual stuff of gardens is already significant in itself. Abstract poetry is Jabberwocky, abstract painting is decoration, but abstract flower-growing, although it may not be gardening at all, is a most satisfying occupation, and gives us gardens we delight in, however bad they may be as designs. We really do not *care* what Le Nôtre or Capability Brown would think of them, but all the same we should realize humbly that we are no longer the creators of the work of art, but only more or less ignorant patrons who by our protection encourage the plants to produce their own individual beauties.

"The Precepts of the Cultivating part of Gardening depend on observation and experience," so Switzer says, and he would consider us all now merely as Cultivators, "but this of Designing, on a noble and correct Judgement and Taste of Things . . . but everyone makes what Judgement he pleases, and thereby leaves Design in Confusion."

Since Switzer's day we have grown so used to being surrounded by Design in Confusion that we scarcely notice it in our gardens. Besides, plants, being all of the same vegetable race, group themselves together quite wonderfully well without any help from us. But it is no use supposing we are artists and can lay out our odd acre or so of land as a kind of vegetable poetry, as Le Nôtre did and Capability Brown. Nor have we any garden

Designers of noble and correct Judgement to help us, but only Cultivators, with here and there perhaps an eye for foliage or for putting colours together more or less happily. So we must please ourselves and lay out our plot "according to our best fantasie," as the Tudors did.

Yet still we must ask ourselves, what is it we want besides the mere presence of flowers and shrubs and trees? "A Garden is Nature disciplined by Art." Yes. But so is a racehorse or a beautiful woman or the English countryside. Indeed, all good farmers might be considered as artists *manqués*, or better still, as gardeners who have spread beyond the garden fence. It is probably why they have no interest in the patch round the house, for since the farm absorbs all their gardening enthusiasm, they leave the farm garden to their wives.

Every tree in a hedge cost the farmer fifty pounds, so my old farmer friend once told me. Fifty pounds for the harm it did shading the crops, starving the grass, and flattening the ripe corn with the swirling eddies it caused in the wind. And when he came to sell the tree for timber, he was lucky, he said, if it fetched enough to pay for the felling and carting away. So he told me one sunny morning as we stood in the front meadow and looked sadly at a huge tree blown down in the night like a fallen giant, spoiling the setting of his home, which had stood like a neat doll's-house between its pair of towering elms. Then why did he keep them? I asked, looking round his farm, where spreading trees stood nobly between every field, and why did he carefully spare a sapling here and there when he cut and laid his hedges? For I had often watched him hedge-laying on mild winter days, the work he best enjoyed of all the farm year. Oh, he liked to see them about, he said, half embarrassed. The place would look bare without a few trees here and there. Like them scientific farms, he said, like a factory. Yes, he liked to see them about, it looked more natural, it made the place more home-like.

So now I never see the sparse grass under a hedge-row elm, nor the heavy-headed corn tangled and beaten down in the lee of a spreading beech, without being grateful to all farmers for their artist's eye, and remembering with affection his half-apologetic embarrassment.

But a farmer does not lay out his farm by æsthetic considerations: his very embarrassment shows that he considers them frivolous; and since we can scarcely hope to make a garden as satisfactory as a well-run farm, we should perhaps do well to follow the farmer and keep to practical reasons. Then what do we want of our gardens besides flowers and fruit and vegetables? Well, we want a hobby. "Hobby . . . Gardening." Hobby is an unfortunate word with its associations of fretwork and stamp-collecting, and certainly it is not the attitude of the great designers, but there are plenty of entries in *Who's Who* to support it as a point of view. We want an out-of-door occupation which gives us mild exercise and more interest than the hitting or kicking of balls.

The labour of a garden is strenuous but healthy, says Miller in his introduction. "It is true, since the Fall of our Progenitors, the work is not so easy as before it was, the Curse having covered the Ground with Thorns and Briars, so that the Ground which before, without Cultivation, would have been spontaneously Obedient to vegetative Nature, must now, by the Sweat of the Brow, and no little Labour, be brought under Subjection: But then at the same time, to make Amends, this very Labour is salutiferous: The Exercise of the Body prevents the Blood and Juices from stagnating and growing corrupt; and the Labourer is every Moment drawing in with his Breath a wholesome and enlivening Stream from the Earth, which causes the Blood and spirits to circulate briskly; and together with the Motion of the Body, forces out and expels the morbid Parts through the Pores, which exhaling, leaves what remains more pure and uncontaminated. Besides, Labour sets an Edge to the Appetite, gives a more grateful and delicious Relish to the Products of the Earth, and at Night disposes the whole bodily Frame into a Capacity for the full Enjoyment of those refreshing Slumbers, that balmy Sleep, which generally forsakes the Downy Couches of the inactive indolent Great."

We feel we have only to take up a spade and dig and we shall never be ill again, though we are almost as far removed now from the inactive indolent Great as we are from the dinosaurs. I dare say it is why some people garden, or at least why they begin, for I think no one could potter for long in a garden without becoming at least a flower-fancier. "The Gardiner," says Evelyn in his instructions for his own gardener at Sayes Court, "should walke aboute the whole Gardens every Monday-morning duely, not omitting the least corner." Certainly we will, not omitting even the least flower, and not only on Mondays, for the chief pleasure of a garden is simply to walk round and watch things grow.

But as a hobby, gardening has more to offer than healthy exercise and prizes at the flower show; or even than catalogues and fireside garden books and exotic afternoons at Chelsea. "If you would know a man," said Confucius, "find out in what he is at peace." And peace surely is among the many things we seek from our gardens.

"For more than thirty years," says Repton, whose own garden was small and cottage, "I have anxiously retreated from the pomp of palaces, the elegances of fashion and the allurements of dissipation." For most of us it is not quite like that. We have never been offered the pomp of palaces, and the allurements of dissipation are mostly confined, alas, to the imaginations of Puritans. But after the "various bustle of resort," after the noise and clocks and telephone bells, the trains and traffic and too many people, most especially after the people, we need somewhere to go away in quiet and restore ourselves. It is no use to sit in a chair and say to ourselves: "Be still, stop fidgetting, be peaceful and recover." We are only more restless with nothing to do. We need some tranquil occupation to smooth the fidgetting to a steady rhythm. "I have need to busy my mind with quietness," and gardening does very well: taking cuttings of our choicest shrubs, tying back the winter jasmine, staking the fragrant top-heavy lilies, or only lazily deciding that in the autumn we will move the winter cherry to a sheltered corner where its January pink and white will escape the east winds.

For a garden, as the seventeenth-century writers will prove for us, can soothe all our senses. "If a man be wearied with over-much study (for study is a wearinesse to the Flesh as Solomon by experience can tell you,) there is no better place in the world to recreate himselfe than a Garden, there being no sence but may be delighted therein. If his sight be obfuscated and dull, as it may easily be, with continually poring, there is no better way to relieve it, than to view the pleasant greennesse of Herbes, which is the way that Painters use, when they have almost spent their sight by their most earnest contemplation of brighter objects: neither doe they only feed the Eyes, but comfort the wearied Braine with fragrant smells which yield a certaine Kinde of nourishment.

"The Eares also (which are called the Daughters of Musick, because they delight therein) have their recreation by the pleasant noise of warbling notes, which the chaunting birds accent forth from amongst the murmuring leaves. As for the Taste, they serve it so exceedingly, that whether it be affected with sweet, sower or bitter things, they even prostitute themselves. And for the feeling likewise, they entertain it with as great variety as can be imagined, there being some Plants as soft as silke, and some as prickly as a Hedgehogge: so that there is no outward sense which can want satisfaction in this Cornucopia."

I dare say many other occupations would do as well to bring us back to quiet, but if we are gardeners, it is our gardens we use to "sway our spirits to peace." Our very conception of a garden is of a place serene. We think of noisy cities, pounding seas, wind-tossed woods, but whenever we think of a garden it is serene, peaceful and calm, and above all, kind. For a garden is one of the very few expressions of man's nature which is altogether benign, and I think no one would be frightened of his fellows in a garden. We understand very well what the writer meant who said: "The chief flower in his Garden is heartsease, because 'tis very scarce in the world."

. . .

L. Viola tricolor Ded.
G. Pensees
A. Hartes eafe
Ge. Freyfam kraut.

Drawing by Crispin de Passe.

Since human beings are gregarious creatures, there are many things we share quite happily with our neighbours. But gardens are not one of them. Our garden must be private, must be our own individual kingdom, however small. "Many men must be content with any plot of ground of what forme or quantity soever it bee, more or lesse, for their Garden, because a more large or convenient cannot bee had for their habitation." Never mind, we will be well content so long as it is our own.

It is not really dog-in-a-mangerness which shuts out our neighbours, though Repton thinks it is, and is half ashamed of "that charm which only belongs to ownership, the exclusive right of enjoyment, with the power of refusing that others should share our pleasure." But it is not the power of refusing others which draws us, it is the need to have some little corner of land which is our own personal territory to do as we like with. Certainly public parks will not do. They may be very fine, we may admire them prodigiously, but we feel no affection for them; they are other people's children, not our own. Montaigne could never see that the peas he grew himself were better than anyone else's, which only proves that he was no gardener. For of course our own peas are best—best for us, which is all that matters. The palest primrose which grows inside our own garden wall is for that very reason more precious than all the fine flowers in the park. We may have no illusions about our own children, but still our affection is not changed because they are not top of the class: it does not depend on their merits, but on our attachment. Which is just as well, or who would love the dull ones?

In *Binsey Poplars* Hopkins mourns the destruction of a scene he loved, a "sweet especial scene . . . Sweet especial rural scene" now lost forever with the felling of the trees. "After-comers cannot guess the beauty been."

It was not that this corner was lovelier than a hundred others, but that for him it had grown familiar and dear. "My aspens dear," he begins, and they were his because he loved them, as Traherne had felt the whole world to be his personal treasure bought with the wealth of his love. "The streets were mine, the people were mine, their clothes and gold and silver were mine, as much as their sparkling eyes, fair skins, and ruddy faces. The skies were mine, and so were the sun and moon and stars, and all the world was mine, and I the only spectator and enjoyer of it."

We are neither mystics nor prose poets, but we are gardeners, and for us our garden is our own sweet especial scene more precious than any other; our affection makes it more valuable than acres of fine flowers.

What do you want of your garden? It is a most revealing question. Flowers, says one. A hobby. A retreat. We could learn to assess a man, I suppose, by what he wanted of his garden as easily as by anything else. A garden, says another, reaches its highest

perfection when it is planned as a room for out-door living. And
that, as we might guess, was the opinion of the editor of a paper
on houses and gardens. But it is a reasonable intention for a small
garden, especially in northern countries and in cities where we
all of us live too much indoors. It does us good to be outside,
without a roof and walls to enclose our neurotic preoccupations
in shelter where they can flourish. (At least it does us good as
human beings; as artists no doubt it might well be disastrous, as
few but the greatest would have any subject matter left.) But as
people we grow moody living too much indoors, introspective,
and over-sensitive of personal trifles. We watch the face, and not
the whole man as the Classic races did. But in the open we feel
our worries and annoyances, our obsessions and pettinesses evap-
orating like mist in the sunshine; "out of the complicated house"
we recover a proper sense of proportion.

Besides, there is our particular English compulsion to eat out-
of-doors, and what place more fitting than our own garden? Of
course there are ants; sweet-tooth wasps arrive from nowhere,
suicidal flies drown in our tea, the cake dries to sawdust, the
chocolate biscuits melt to lava, the edges of sandwiches curl up
like toast. And certainly we spend quite twice as long carrying
everything in and out of the house as we should to eat indoors
and be done with it. But never mind. Nothing is so delightful as
tea in the garden, everyone is agreed about it.

Then there are the "meridian naps," as Switzer absurdly calls
them. It is one of the tranquil pleasures to fall asleep in a garden
and wake up only because the sun has slanted behind the trees
and we are chilly lying in the shadow. There is sitting out-of-
doors in the pale sunshine of a still winter day, for with careful
shelter a south wall is warm enough for sitting as soon as there
is sun enough to open the aconites and snowdrops, the early
crocuses and winter irises. There is the view from the house windows, a mental extension of the house into the garden which enlarges the smallest room and lets us live half out-of-doors even
though we may never leave the house all day. It is a very particular pleasure in winter to see frozen snow and warm carpet

separated only by an invisible wall of glass—like the scene at the beginning of *Jane Eyre* where a girl sits in a window watching a violent storm beyond the frail glass. I dare say it is no more than a line or two of description, perhaps only a single sentence, but it is the only passage from all the Brontë books which I remembered vividly as a child.

The life we live in a city is one we have created for ourselves within its walls. In streets and shops and offices, in theatres and libraries and houses we are shut away from the rhythm of the natural year which dominates life in the open. In London the changing seasons are little more than changing weather on the window-pane, changing clothes hanging in our wardrobe. Our lives are much the same all the year round, whether we wear cotton frocks or overcoats, and whether the window is open to the sun or shut against the rain. Yet the seasons are as satisfactory a way for dividing up the year as waking and sleeping are for the day and night. Summer and winter impose on our life in the country a significant pattern which banishes monotony; they keep us in touch with a rhythm of living as satisfying as the swaying of a swing when we are children. Living in cities, we have lost this fundamental variety of the natural year, but in gardens we still feel it faintly—the strong beat of seed-time and harvest muted to the frailty of cherry blossom and the changing colours of autumn leaves; as paddlers on the edge of the sea feel faintly in the little waves which wash their ankles, the strong surge of the ocean tides.

"A garden should be" (and it is better this time not to consider the speaker too closely) "should be a place private enough to make love wherever one fancies." Certainly Chaucer's young lady in the pear tree would have agreed, and so I dare say would the Chinese princes. But I am not sure. It is a very exact degree of privacy: less secret than murder, more secluded than tea on the lawn. Of course it would be very pleasant and convenient, but unless one were quite unusually indifferent to an audience I think it would make a garden too shut in, too cramped and shadowed and gloomy. Private enough for sun-bathing—that surely is a better qualification. Besides, what about aeroplanes? Are we never to see the sky in our amorous gardens? Or do we simply ignore pilots as part of their machines?

What do you want? I asked the children, who were equally decided. We want somewhere to have bonfires. We want a garden with lots of good places for hide-and-seek. We want somewhere to play cricket without losing the ball, and we want enough grass to do tricks with our bikes on so that it doesn't hurt when we fall off. Poor long-suffering garden. For now it must be a recreation ground as well as everything else.

I had my own garden games as a child, but girls, it seems, are less destructively active than boys. Certainly I picked the buds of poppies, but then poppies grow so many more, and undoing their buds was one of the most engrossing of pleasures for a summer morning. First you squeezed them till they burst open with a faint pop, like shelling peas. Then you peeled off the hairy green sepals to find the crumpled petals screwed up inside, a ball of delicate silken paper. Very gently you coaxed them to unfold, smoothing them out carefully to an open flower. The result was a quite astonishing amount to unpack from so small a bud—not only the four wide petals, but also the urn-shaped head in the middle, and the fringe of stamens as soft and uncertain in this abortive appearance as the legs of a moth newly struggled from its chrysalis.

Even from wild scarlet poppies the petals varied through all colours from the red of those which would have opened tomorrow, through the pink of buds not ready to unfold for several days, to the white embryos which had not even dreamed yet of the sun. It was my favourite game to make a carefully shaded range of colours from white to scarlet, better even than finding the man in the pansy who went out and caught a cold, and sits now as the fat ovary in every fading flower, wrapped in a blanket of stamens up to his chin, with his feet in a mustard bath— the spur, which will pull off gently and leave two long spindly legs quite shiveringly exposed.

There were other games, too—snapdragon heads, and fox-glove thimbles, and nibbling the bottoms of larkspurs for the honey. And other tricks (most of them nasty) which the boys prefer—ear-splitting squeaks with leaves of grass and privet, catapults with plantain heads, and pulling a twist of hair with a denuded fox-tail grass, which they call Chinese Tortures.

And children have other, more private games, day-dreams and fantasies for secret hiding-places safe from interruption. A French admirer said of the gardens of Versailles that they were an equally happy setting for courtly ceremony or the sighing of a melancholy lover. Our own hurried generation scarcely spends time enough on love-sickness for it to be worth making a garden as a suitable background, but even in a modern garden there should be corners secluded enough to indulge our private fancies without disturbance.

One early summer day when I was a child I lay under a sycamore tree and gazed up into the green tiers of branches. The new leaves made an over-lapping mosaic of brilliant yellow-green, each bough on its own plane, the different levels shuffled loosely together like a sheaf of papers, and each layer held easily as it grew on the firm but delicate scaffolding of the black twigs. Beneath the leaves swung the loose tassels of yellow flowers humming with bees, and through the spaces between, the sky shone an intense and bottomless blue.

I was a city child unused to such beauty, and to senses un-dimmed by custom it was almost unbearably vivid: the colours and shapes, the warm light, the eager generous life, the summer hum, and the scent of honey. I gazed until the blue and green smudged together in sudden uncontrollable tears, then rolled over in the grass and wept for pleasure.

But as the first disturbing delight faded, I realized piercingly that this same tree which seemed to me mine because I loved it, had flowered a score of times before I was born, would rouse to equal beauty every spring when I was dead. And I suffered a great stab of sorrow, of unrequited love, felt I had received an inmost wound that never could be healed, because the things I loved more than all else in the world were utterly indifferent to my existence.

The sorrows of children are profound and unsuspected, and through all my growing-up I was preoccupied with the question of whether, when it came to dying, it would be an anguish or a consolation that the too-much-loved earth went on without me. No doubt all children puzzle over questions equally unlikely, but we shall never know, for they will never tell us, fearing not so much our lack of understanding, which they are used to, but rather our understanding, our intrusion into the fiercely guarded privacy of their intimate world.

Although I thought about it for years, with other metaphysical questions equally impractical, I never did make up my mind whether I should die sad or happy to leave a world which went on unchanged. The poets, I found, had thought about it too, but they were little help, being of almost equally divided opinion, though with perhaps a slight leaning to the dying anguish.

In any case, a garden should be a place where children can feel a favourite tree belongs to them, where they can weep without embarrassment and be ridiculous without an audience, where they can pursue (unlike Wordsworth) their Intimations of Mortality in Early Childhood.

But gardens are for the old even more than the young, and ever since Tudor times, and probably earlier if there had been gardening books to tell us so, a garden has been considered an ideal place for men to grow old in. "A retreat for toil-worn millionaires" a more recent writer expresses it, but there is really no need for such a spectacular bank-balance, and a setting for their retirement seems always to have been one of the things ordinary men have wanted of their gardens. After all, there are few places where we can so successfully be busy and peaceful both together, nor win so much satisfaction with so little labour. In a garden carefully planned and planted at the start, we can spend the rest of our time in the most delightful pottering, watching Nature flourish with only a secateured hand to Guide her Extravagancies. And there is always some new business to keep us happy—trying a fresh grouping of shrubs, opening out a shut-in view, mowing a new grass walk through the orchard tangle, coaxing an ambitious lily to feel at home in some carefully prepared corner. "For the Pleasure of Gardening is not in Finishing them in too great Haste; but after a general Scheme is laid, to make Annual Advances 'till the Whole is compleated."

Repton, perhaps because he lived to be an old man himself, considered carefully how a garden should be planned for the comfort of old age. The paths, he says, should not be of gravel but of grass or brick, for gravel, he warns us, is so excessively noisy beneath the wheels of a bath-chair. The beds, too, should be built up high enough for the master to reach them from his

Gathering strawberries from a bath-chair.

bath-chair without stooping. There is a picture of the aged gardener gathering strawberries from a raised bed while his chair-attendant waits modestly behind. They are both wearing top hats.

But I think when I reach my own bath-chair stage I will sit in the sun on the veranda, and leave what one writer calls "the insulting Weeds" to live their own life, only admiring in short-sighted contentment the general prospect of thriving green.

Other gardeners make less depressing suggestions for our old-age comfort: that the greenhouse should have a door leading into the dwelling-house so that we can reach it without going out into the bad weather, and that the whole garden should be reached by "little walks" where we can go "cleanly and decently," so that "the Owner may walk round it and across it in his Night Gown and Slippers; and visit all his Affairs, either late at Night or early in the Morning, without either Dirt or Dew. Seeing those are the chief times, either for Business or Pleasure, in the whole Day." I have never walked round the garden in my Night Gown and Slippers, but certainly I will on the next warm evening.

Lulled by the song of a nightingale, Keats fell half in love with easeful Death, and reading the gardening books, we too fall half in love with our far-off gardening retirement. We have no need of Fairchild to persuade us that we must garden while we are still in cities to train ourselves for the pleasures of gardening in our old age. We are only impatient that our retirement will not be long enough for all we plan to do. But Gervaze Markham, who is my favourite of all my new garden friends, is comfortably reassuring. We "may live near a hundred years," he says, if we follow his counsel. "For your health eat meats that are hot and nourishing, drink good wine that is neat, sprightly and lusty, keep thy body well clad, and thy house warm, forsake whatever is flegmatick, and banish all care from thy heart, for nothing is more unwholesome than a troubled spirit."

If you would be happy all your life, plant a garden.

But as to what kind of gardens we should plant in our modern age, that, if we thought about it, which we seldom do, is very much more difficult to decide.

A garden, since it is the setting for a house, should be in harmony with its architecture, and the best modern building is surprisingly like the simpler architecture of the eighteenth century, more essentially like it than any other English style before or since.

The Victorians, feeling that they continued the Classical tradition, loaded their heavy erections with Classical-style decoration. The twentieth-century architect no longer cares for pillared façades and acanthus leaves (for our so-called neo-Georgian is a pastiche in the nineteenth-century manner), but modern building is nearer, I think, to the eighteenth century than anything the Victorians built. For styles of architecture do not resemble each other by applying similar decoration to a finished construction, but by working with the same essentials and leaving the decoration to look after itself. Our best modern architects compose with the same fundamentals as the eighteenth century: simple rectangular shapes, an orderly repetition of forms, and a most sparing use of applied decoration. The effect of the building depends not on decoration at all, but on the shape of the whole structure, the spacing of windows and doors, the areas of the walls between, the contrast and interrelation of the different planes. So our modern blocks of flats, our factories and schools and houses are close in spirit to the eighteenth century. Indeed, if both are stripped of their respective layers of new paint and old dirt, a terrace of houses in one of the new towns is surprisingly like the eighteenth-century terraces of quiet town houses all over London. Our buildings are less symmetrical, less formal than the eighteenth century's because our lives are less formal, more diverse because the activities they shelter are more diverse (for the eighteenth century built no factories or flats, no schools except as modelled on houses). But the beauty of our buildings, when they do achieve beauty, is the same austere elegance as the eighteenth century's, the same material impression of lightness and space, the same intellectual quality of order and repose.

As in modern building, the effects of eighteenth-century architecture depend scarcely at all on the natural texture of the materials used. We are not conscious of the bricks, as we are in Tudor buildings, nor of the stone as we are in mediæval churches and Cotswold villages. The eighteenth century made no use of wood except for construction; they preferred it covered with featureless paint, and it was later taste which stripped the panelling to the bare grain. We, too, use our materials discreetly, and do not allow the charm of incidentals to distract us from the whole. In a modern building we are conscious of the proportion, the elegance, the serenity, and it is only the architect who notices the materials, for they are used not for their own sake, but for their structural capabilities. So that modern synthetic materials and methods of construction might well have suited the eighteenth-century architects even better than the traditional materials they had to use. The wide expanses of windows, the narrow supporting walls between, the unbroken stretches of floor—these surely they would have achieved more easily with steel and concrete than with bricks and wood. Our shallow modern roofs would have suited them excellently, for the eighteenth century hid the necessary pitch of their slates and tiles behind horizontal screening parapets. And if they had had concrete to build with, they need not have plastered their brick walls with stucco, its indistinguishable but inefficient relation.

For, living in an eighteenth-century house, I know only too well that the stucco cracks and falls from the walls, that the snow piles up behind the parapet, and unless it is cleared away, leaks through the slate roof as it melts. Shovelling it off after a snowfall is a winter-morning game for the boys, who are old enough now not to fall over the parapet, still agile enough to climb through the attic window, and not yet bored with the exhilarating experience of flinging snow triumphantly into space, of the new view of their familiar world spread out as a map below.

In summer, too, I am reminded every day of the architect's difficulty with his great floor-to-ceiling windows; how perilously heavy they are to hang on sash-cords. And struggling to open them and water the window-boxes, wondering whether the cord will break as I lean out to pick the dead heads off the petunias, I sigh for the modern steel frames and reliable metal hinges which the eighteenth century so badly needed.

If modern building has much in common with the eighteenth-century spirit, so too perhaps the next style of gardening will be a modern adaptation of the landscape park. It is easy to see how suitable it would be as a setting for blocks of flats and public buildings, but even in our little private gardens we are perhaps moving towards a natural way of trees and shrubs and flowers which is an unconscious echo of the eighteenth-century style.

"A garden is an expression of Man in a state of Society." It is a definition with many meanings, and we might think of Man as a single human being growing up through various stages to become an adult social creature. When we are children we can neither understand nor control the world around us; we shut ourselves in a self-contained universe of our own, an enclosed garden which has very little contact with the world outside except in the sun and rain, which come down willy-nilly from a sky we cannot change. But inside our sheltering walls we gradually develop. We grow older and stronger, grow curious, we peep over the garden fence as the Tudors did, we begin to realize the possibilities of the world outside and to feel confident we can take our place there. Then comes the fine flowering of energy and enthusiasm in a creature who has reached adult strength but not yet an adult's need to compromise. For we are all perfectionists at this hopeful age; we see quite clearly that there is an ideal order which the world must be moulded to for its own good, whether it likes it or not. We are undaunted by the obvious difficulties, we do not see the subtler ones, we have energy and to spare, and we never for a moment doubt that our way is the best. We make the gardens of Versailles.

It is a very proper way of behaving for the young and confident and enthusiastic, but unless we outgrow our simple ideals as we outgrow our youth, we shall certainly be disappointed, for we shall certainly outgrow our confidence. Reforming the world, so reformers are disillusioned to find, is rather like rolling a stone up a hill: as soon as they stop pushing, it rolls down again. And because it is natural for idealists to push their stone as high as their utmost energies can reach, it must always begin to slip down again as soon as they begin to grow old or tired or doubtful of their own wisdom. The world does not stay reformed any more than houses stay clean or gardens stay weeded, and adults must come to some workable compromise. It is no use deciding

that the world must conform to our way as the only way—
which is what the formal gardeners did, so that as soon as the
armies of labourers ceased working, the flower beds were lost in
weeds, the regular clipped hedges sprouted untidily to trees, the
formal pools were choked with slime, and the stone had rolled
back again to the bottom of the hill. For a straight line must stay
straight, not wobble, and if the effort to keep it straight needs
more energy than we have to spare, then we do better to choose
an irregular curve at the beginning. Which is what the eighteenth-century gardeners did. They did not rule out a pattern on
paper ("Paper Engineers" one critic calls such gardeners) and
then impose it on a stretch of land, on trees and hedges with their
own different patterns of growing; instead, they considered the
scene of their future garden with no preconceived plan except a
desire for the "natural." They then designed parks which accepted the English landscape as their material, and heightened
its effects by using grass and trees and water in as natural a manner as possible. It is the adult's compromise expressed in gardens,
and we should do well to consider them carefully.

In the landscape park the eighteenth century found a perfect
labour-saving compromise. But the landscape style needs space:
it is easy to keep because it works with large effects of grass and
trees: woodland where weeds do not matter, and sweeps of grass
wide enough to give the effect of smooth lawn without being
neatly mown. But if we have less than an acre for our planning,
and if growing flowers is our greatest pleasure, we shall have to
transform the landscape style as thoroughly as our seventeenth-
century gardeners transformed Versailles. "This first setting out
is generally the Rock that all Mankind split upon," and in our
first plan for a garden we should consider exactly how much
work our designs will need, not so much to lay them out, but to
keep them in order year after year. It is no use listening to siren
voices which assure us that "a man for a shilling a day will weed
an acre of land in three days." If there is weeding to do, we shall
have to do it ourselves. If there are hedges to cut and lawns to
mow and edges to trim, it is we who shall have to get up and do

them on summer afternoons when all we want is to lie in the shade and look at the sky through the branches of our favourite tree.

To judge a good housewife, it is no use going to see her clean new house the month she moves in. We are all of us idealists in a new house. The true test is to see what compromise she has reached after ten years or so of constant war with dirt and untidiness. If her house is no better than a slum, then quite clearly the dirt has triumphed, though it is possible that no one minds. If her house is still as clean as the first week, then she is spending all her energies in a war which can never end except by her defeat; and her success is almost certainly a Pyrrhic victory won at the cost of making her family wretched by nagging, and turning herself into a dismal domestic drudge.

Most of us now put away the silver, keep our rooms clear of dusty oddments, and dress our children in clothes which need no ironing. But we also, after ten years of learning to compromise between living in a house and keeping it in order, clear up the children's rooms only once a week, do not look too closely into cupboards we turn out only once a year, nor worry ourselves in the tidy drawing-room because we know the attic looks like a jumble sale.

It is wisdom which gardeners seem to arrive at more slowly. Beds and edges, paths and hedges—gardeners have not yet learnt to mistrust them as instinctively as a housewife mistrusts a dress which must be ironed every time it is worn. They do not accept the hard fact that if they are to have any leisure, they must plan their garden with plants sturdy enough to thrive with an undergrowth of weeds. They do not decide from the start that far corners of the garden can be left to grow what tangle they please without in the least spoiling the view from the veranda. But they should. It is the landscape style we must adapt for our new needs and not the formal fashion of beds and hedges, not unless we are to spend every summer week-end as labourers in gardens which were meant to be places of pleasure. What a wise gardener (or perhaps only a lazy one) plans for is "Nature a little guided in her Extravagancies by the Artist's Hand." If, like the eighteenth century, we avoid paper planning and arbitrary designs, we shall find that our gardens will achieve random happy effects almost without our interference, and, "being of a much more natural Aspect than Set Gardens, the less Keeping will suffice."

But as Walafred Strabo would have said, I have written too long already to begin now wondering what our new gardens may be like, and that must wait for another volume. And I doubt whether the new kind of garden I found last summer could be considered either as a setting for architecture or an expression of Man in Society.

When we first went to our week-end house in the country we found a nineteenth-century garden run to wilderness, and at the bottom an old croquet lawn, a lush tangle of grass and meadow flowers springing with green frogs as you walked, as plentiful as grasshoppers. They still hop about in wet summers among the shrubs and weeds and lilies, and visiting children collect them delightedly, carrying them home in treacle-tins of wet moss with holes punched in the lid. And we still sometimes for convenience call it the Croquet Lawn, as the children always have done from the start; but because twentieth-century children know nothing of croquet, but only of frogs, the lawn they talk of is the Croaky Lawn. "Dear Dardy" (I found out in a thank-you letter from a small boy visitor who had spent the week-end busy and happy down in the tangle, only coming up to the house when we rang the bell for meals) "Dear Dardy, Thankyou for having me. I had a lovely time. I like all your garden, but I like the Croaky Lawn best, there's such a lovely lot of Frogs. Please will you give them some water if they need some." So I went down to look, and found under the willows a square of trampled grass fenced in with old boards, and inside, a pile of grass-cuttings, some bread-crumbs, and a jam-jar brimful of water. But not a sign, alas, of even the smallest frog. Only on the highest board was written in white chalk capitals: "GARDEN FOR FROGS."

Though who was meant to read it I never have decided.

SHORT
BIBLIOGRAPHY

This is a list of most of the books quoted in the text. They are grouped in chapters as they occur, since this seemed the simplest way to arrange them. The date is generally that of the book's first appearance, but when this is unknown, or long after the author's death, then of the approximate time when it was written.

CHAPTER TWO

Celtic Myth and Legend—C. Squire, 1910.
England Before the Norman Conquest—R. W. Chambers, 1926.
Ecclesiastical History of the English Nation—Bede, ninth century.
Anglo-Saxon Poetry—edited R. K. Gordon, 1926.
Life of Alfred—Asser, ninth century.
"Navigation of the Norsemen"—G. J. Marcus in the *Mariner's Mirror*, May 1953.
Gudrun—Anon., thirteenth century.
English Lyrics of the Thirteenth Century—edited Carleton Brown, 1932.
Hali Meidenhad—Anon., thirteenth century.
Ancren Riwle—Anon., thirteenth century.
Hortulus or the Little Garden—Walafridus Strabo, ninth century.

CHAPTER THREE

Lays—Marie de France, twelfth century.
Aucassin and Nicolette—Anon., thirteenth century.
Floris and Blancheflour—Anon., thirteenth century.
Religious Lyrics of the Fourteenth Century—edited Carleton Brown, 1924.
Oxford Book of Carols—edited P. Dearmer, etc., 1928.

CHAPTER FOUR

English Social History—G. M. Trevelyan, 1942.
A Survey of London—John Stow, 1598.
Brief Lives—John Aubrey (1626–1697).
Musæum Tradescantianum—John Tradescant, 1656.
The Gardeners Labyrinth—Didymus Mountain (Thomas Hill), 1577.

Paradisi in Sole, Paradisus Terrestris—John Parkinson, 1629.
"On Gardens"—Francis Bacon, 1625.
Sylva Sylvarum or a Naturall Historie—Francis Bacon, 1627.
Five Hundreth Pointes of Good Husbandrie—Thomas Tusser, 1573.
Adam in Eden or Natures Paradise—William Coles, 1657.
The Spirituall Uses of an Orchard—Ralph Austen, 1653.
"A Survey of the Manor of Wymbledon in 1649"—*Archæologia*, Vol. 10, 1792.

CHAPTER FIVE

Maison Rustique or the Countrie Farme—trans. Richard Surflet, 1600.
A New Orchard and Garden—William Lawson, 1618.
Country Contentments—Gervaze Markham, 1640.
Letters—Sir Thomas Browne (1605–1682).
Religio Medici—Sir Thomas Browne, 1643.
The Garden of Cyrus—Sir Thomas Browne, 1653.
Directions for the Gardiner at Says-Court—John Evelyn, 1687.
Centuries of Meditations—Thomas Traherne (1634–1704).
Oxford Book of Seventeenth Century Verse—edited H. J. C. Grierson and G. Bullough, 1934.
A Perfect Boke for Keping of Sparhawkes or Goshawkes—Anon., c. 1575.
An Approved Treatise of Hawkes and Hawking—Edmund Bert, 1619.
Hawking or Faulconry—Richard Blome, 1686.

CHAPTER SIX

Studies in the History of the Renaissance—Walter Pater, 1873.
The Theory and Practice of Gardening—Le Blond, trans. John James, 1703.
Letters—John Evelyn (1620–1706).

CHAPTER SEVEN

The Voyage of the Beagle—Charles Darwin, 1839.
Charles Darwin and the Voyage of the Beagle—Nora Barlow, 1933.
Through England on a Side-Saddle in the Time of William and Mary—Celia Fiennes, 1685–1703.
The English Gardener—Leonard Meager, 1670.
Flora Ceres et Pomona—John Rea, 1676.
The Gentlemans Recreation—John Laurence, 1716.
Diaries—Samuel Pepys, 1660–9.

Short Bibliography

Sylva, or a Discourse of Forest-Trees—John Evelyn, 1664.
Terra, a Philosophical Discourse of Earth—John Evelyn, 1676.
The Story of My Life—Augustus Hare, 1896–1900.
Essays in *The Spectator*—Joseph Addison, 1711–12.
The Dutch Gardener, or the Complete Florist—Van Oosten, 1711.
Upon the Gardens of Epicurus, or of Gardening in the Year 1685—
Sir William Temple.
The City Gardener—Thomas Fairchild, 1722.
Systema Horticulturæ, or the Art of Gardening—John Woolridge,
1677.

Chapter Eight

Letters—Horace Walpole (1717–1797).
An Essay on Modern Gardening—Horace Walpole, 1770.
Journals of Visits to Country Seats—Horace Walpole. 16th annual
volume of the Walpole Society.
Travels—Marco Polo (1254–1324).
Unconnected Thoughts on Gardening—William Shenstone, 1764.
*Ichnographia Rustica—the Nobleman Gentleman and Gardeners
Recreation*—Stephen Switzer, 1718.
New Improvements of Planting and Gardening—Richard Bradley,
1717.
The Gardeners Dictionary—Philip Miller, 1731.
A Dissertation on Oriental Gardening—Sir William Chambers, 1772.
Confessions—Jean-Jacques Rousseau, 1781–8.
Paul et Virginie—Bernardin de Saint-Pierre, 1787.
A Sure Method of Improving Estates—Batty Langley, 1728.
An Essay on the Picturesque—Sir Uvedale Price, 1794.
The Mysteries of Udolpho—Mrs. Radcliffe, 1794.
Remarks on Forest Scenery—William Gilpin, 1791.
On the Making of Gardens—Sir George Sitwell, 1909.
Observations on Modern Gardening—Thomas Whately, 1770.
The Curious and Profitable Gardener—John Cowell, 1730.
*Observations on the Theory and Practice of Landscape Gardening
etc.*—Humphrey Repton, 1803.

A NOTE ON THE TYPE
IN WHICH THIS BOOK IS SET

This book was set on the Linotype in Janson, a recutting made direct from the type cast from matrices (now in possession of the Stempel foundry, Frankfurt am Main) made by Anton Janson some time between 1660 and 1687. This type is an excellent example of the influential and singularly sturdy Dutch types that prevailed in England prior to Caslon. It was from the Dutch types that Caslon developed his own designs.

Of Janson's origin nothing is known. He may have been a relative of Justus Janson, a printer of Danish birth who practised in Leipzig from 1614 to 1635. Some time between 1657 and 1668 Anton Janson, a punch-cutter and type-founder, bought from the Leipzig printer Johann Erich Hahn the type-foundry which had formerly been a part of the printing house of M. Friedrich Lankisch. Janson's types were first shown in a specimen sheet issued at Leipzig about 1675. Janson's successor, and perhaps his son-in-law, Johann Karl Edling, issued a specimen sheet of Janson types in 1689.

The book was composed, printed, and bound by KINGSPORT PRESS, INC., *Kingsport, Tennessee. Paper manufactured by* P. H. GLATFELTER CO., *Spring Grove, Pa. Designed by* HARRY FORD.